Taming Java Threads

ALLEN HOLUB

Taming Java Threads
Copyright ©2000 by Allen I. Holub

ISBN (pbk): 1-893115-10-0

Printed and bound in the United States of America   345678910

Copy Editor: Tom Robinson, TSI Graphics

Artist: Warren Fischbach, TSI Graphics

Compositor and Pretty Good Vorpal Player: Susan Glinert

Indexer: Nancy Guenther

Project Manager: Grace Wong

Cover and Interior Design: Derek Yee Design

Distributed to the book trade in the United States by Springer-Verlag New York, Inc., 175 Fifth Avenue, New York, New York, 10010

and outside the United States by Springer-Verlag GmbH & Co. KG, Tiergartenstr. 17, 69112 Heidelberg, Germany

In the United States, phone 1-800-SPRINGER; orders@springer-ny.com; http://www.springer-ny.com

Outside the United States, contact orders@springer.de; http://www.springer.de; fax +49 6221 345229

For information on translations, please contact Apress directly: Apress, 901 Grayson Street, Suite 204, Berkeley, CA 94710

Phone: 510-549-5930, Fax: 510-549-5939, info@apress.com, www.apress.com

Contents at a Glance

To Deirdre, Philip, and Amanda

Contents

Preface

PROGRAMMING JAVA THREADS is not nearly as easy (or as platform-independent) as most books would have you believe. Threading also happens to be an essential part of Java programming. All Java programs that use a graphical user interface must be multithreaded, for example. Threading, though, is tricky to do right, and it usually has to be built into your code from Day 1. This book discusses the things you need to know to program threads effectively in the real world, focusing on the legion of problems that arise when you try to use Java's built-in threading support.

The first couple chapters look at threading-related problems that are created by the underlying operating environments, and then at threading problems—such as *deadlock*—that are inherent to all multithreaded systems.

The middle chapters present a host of classes that implement threading primitives—various semaphores, timers, and so forth—that you can use to solve the problems created by Java's less-than-ideal threading architecture.

Chapters 8 and 9 focus on threading in object-oriented systems, and present architectural solutions to threading problems that tend to work better in some situations than the more atomic solutions presented in earlier chapters.

The final chapter proposes a few modifications to the Java language to clean up the problems discussed in the rest of the book.

When you're done, you'll have a complete toolkit of thread-management classes and architectures that you can apply to most of the threading issues that will arise in your programs. You'll also understand the Java threading model thoroughly.

This book is based on a series of nine articles that originally appeared in my "Java Toolbox" column from the on-line magazine *Javaworld* (*http://www.javaworld.com*). The code has been reworked considerably, and I've also added quite a bit of material, so you should consider this book to be ver. 2 of the original series.

Prerequisites

This is not a book for "dummies" or "idiots." This book is for intermediate-to-advanced Java programmers—people who know the basics of the language and want to program at an expert level. I'm assuming that you've already read and assimilated a reasonable introduction-to-Java book. In particular, I assume that you:

- know the syntax of the Java programming language, including inner classes (anonymous and otherwise).

- know how to create threads using `Thread` and `Runnable`.

- know how `synchronized`, `wait()`, and `notify()` work in a general way.

- have a reading-level familiarity with the methods of the `Thread` class.

- know the basics of the AWT/Swing "listener" event model.

If that's not the case, you should put this book down and read a good intro-to-Java book. (If you know C++, David Flanagan's *Java in a Nutshell* presents the differences between Java and C++ in a very condensed format that I happen to like. Non-C++ programmers, and those of you who want to take things more slowly, will be better served by Peter van der Linden's *Just Java 2, 4th Edition*).

Getting and Using the Code

The code presented in this book is available on line at *http://www.holub.com*. The version on the Web site is kept up to date and incorporates fixes for the inevitable bugs. (If you find any bugs, by the way, please report them to me at *bugs@holub.com*.)

The code in this book is not in the public domain. Nonetheless, you may use it in your programs if you put the following notice in your about box or sign-on screen (or in your documentation if you don't have an about box or sign-on screen).

> This program includes code from Allen Holub's book *Taming Java Threads*.
> © 2000 Allen I. Holub. All rights reserved.
> *http://www.holub.com*

Since I don't want hacked up versions floating around on the Net bearing my name, you may not redistribute the source code.

If you've read my original series of articles in *Javaworld*, the code in the current volume differs a bit from that published in the original series. I'm sorry if these changes cause any problems for those of you who are using the earlier implementation, but the current version is simply better than the old one. It is probably worth your while to upgrade. I don't plan any harmful changes to the interfaces in the current implementation. (I might add methods here and there, but I won't modify the signatures of [or remove] existing methods.) It should be safe to use this code as it evolves without having to change your own programs.

—Allen Holub

CHAPTER 1

The Architecture
of Threads

PROGRAMMING JAVA THREADS is not nearly as easy (or platform independent) as most books would have you believe, and all Java programs that display a graphical user interface must be multithreaded. This chapter shows you why these statements are true by discussing the architectures of various threading systems and by discussing how those architectures influence how you program threads in Java. Along the way, I'll introduce several key terms and concepts that are not described very well in most intro-to-Java books. Understanding these concepts is essential if you expect to understand the code in the remainder of the book.

The Problems with Threads

Burying your head in the sand and pretending that you don't have to worry about threading issues is a tempting strategy when writing a Java program, but you can't usually get away with it in real production code. Unfortunately, virtually none of the books on Java address threading issues in sufficient depth. If anything, the books go to the opposite extreme, presenting examples that are guaranteed to cause problems in a multithreaded environment as if the code is flawless.

In fact, multithreading is a problem that infuses all your Java code, because you have no way of predicting in exactly what context a particular object or method will be used. Going back after the fact and trying to make non-thread-safe code work in a multithreaded environment is an immensely difficult task. It's best to start out thinking "threads," even if you don't plan to use the code you're writing in a multithreaded way in the future. Unfortunately, there is often a performance penalty to be paid for thread safety, so I can't recommend that *all* code should be thread safe, because paying the penalty can just be too high in some situations. Nonetheless, you should always consider the threading issues when designing the code, even if you end up consciously rejecting thread safety in the implementation.

All Nontrivial Java Programs Are Multithreaded

All Java programs other than simple console-based applications are multithreaded, whether you like it or not. The problem is in Java's Abstract Windowing Toolkit (AWT). (Throughout this book, I'll use "AWT" to mean both the 1.1 AWT library and and the *Swing* extensions to AWT as well.) AWT processes operating-system events on a special thread, created by AWT when a program "realizes" (makes visible) its first window. As a consequence, most programs have at least two threads running: the "main" thread, on which main() executes, and the AWT thread, which processes events that come in from the operating system and calls any registered listeners in response to those events. It's important to note that all your listener methods run on the AWT thread, not on the main thread (where the listener object is typically created).

There are two main difficulties to this architecture. First, although the listeners run on the AWT thread, they are typically inner-class objects that access an outer-class object that was, in turn, created by (and is accessed by) the main thread. Put another way, listener methods running on AWT thread often access an object that is also manipulated from the main thread—the outer-class object. This is a worst-case synchronization problem, when two threads compete for access to the same object. Proper use of synchronized is essential to force the two threads to take turns accessing the object, rather than trying to access it simultaneously.

To make matters worse, the AWT thread that handles the listeners also handles events coming in from the operating system. This means that if your listener methods spend a long time doing whatever they do, OS-level events (such as mouse clicks and key presses) will not be serviced by your program. These events are queued up waiting for service, but they are effectively ignored until the listener method returns. The result is an unresponsive user interface: one that appears to hang. It's immensely frustrating to a user when a program ignores clicks on a Cancel button because the AWT thread has called a listener method that takes forever to execute. (The mouse clicks are ignored until the listener method finishes executing.) Listing 1.1 demonstrates the unresponsive-UI problem. This program creates a frame that holds two buttons labeled "Sleep" and "Hello." The handler for the Sleep button puts the current thread (which will be the Swing event-handler thread) to sleep for five seconds. The Hello button just prints "Hello world" on the console. During the five seconds that elapse after you press the Sleep button, pressing the Hello button has no effect. If you click the Hello button five times, "Hello world" is printed five times as soon as the sleep finishes. The button-press events are queued up while the Swing thread is sleeping, and they are serviced when the Swing thread wakes up.

Listing 1.1: /text/books/threads/ch1/Hang.java

```
01: import javax.swing.*;
02: import java.awt.*;
03: import java.awt.event.*;
04:
05: class Hang extends JFrame
06: {
07:     public Hang()
08:     {   JButton b1 = new JButton( "Sleep" );
09:         JButton b2 = new JButton( "Hello" );
10:
11:         b1.addActionListener
12:         (   new ActionListener()
13:             {   public void actionPerformed( ActionEvent event )
14:                 {   try
15:                     {   Thread.currentThread().sleep(5000);
16:                     }
17:                     catch(Exception e){}
18:                 }
19:             }
20:         );
21:
22:         b2.addActionListener
23:         (   new ActionListener()
24:             {   public void actionPerformed( ActionEvent event )
25:                 {   System.out.println("Hello world");
26:                 }
27:             }
28:         );
29:
30:         getContentPane().setLayout( new FlowLayout() );
31:         getContentPane().add( b1 );
32:         getContentPane().add( b2 );
33:         pack();
34:         show();
35:     }
36:
37:     public static void main( String[] args )
38:     {   new Hang();
39:     }
40: }
```

Many books that discuss java GUI building gloss over both the synchronization and the unresponsive-UI problems. They can get away with ignoring synchronization issues because the trivial examples in those books are often single threaded. That is, 100% of the code in the program is defined inside one or more listeners, all of which are executed serially on the single (AWT) thread. Moreover, the listeners perform trivial tasks that complete so quickly that you don't notice that the UI isn't responding.

In any event, in the real world, this single-threaded approach (doing everything on the AWT thread) just doesn't work. All successful UIs have a few behaviors in common:

- The UI must give you some feedback as an operation progresses. Simply throwing up a box that says "doing such-and-such" is not sufficient. You need to tell the user that progress is being made (a "percent complete" progress bar is an example of this sort of behavior).

- It must be possible to update a window without redrawing the whole thing when the state of the underlying system changes.

- You must provide a way to cancel an in-progress operation.

- It must be possible to switch windows and otherwise manipulate the user interface when a long operation is in progress.

These three rules can be summed up with one rule: **It's not okay to have an unresponsive UI.** It's not okay to ignore mouse clicks, key presses, and so forth when the program is executing a listener method, and it's not okay to do lots of time-consuming work in listeners. The only way to get the reasonable behavior I just described is to use threads. Time-consuming operations must be performed on background threads, for example. Real programs will have many more than two threads running at any given moment.

Java's Thread Support Is Not Platform Independent

Unfortunately, though it's essential to design with threading issues in mind, threads are one of the main places where Java's promise of platform independence falls flat on its face. This fact complicates the implementation of platform-independent multithreaded systems considerably. You have to know something about the possible run-time environments to make the program work correctly in all of them. It is possible to write a platform-independent multithreaded Java program, but you have to do it with your eyes open. This lamentable situation is not really Java's fault; it's almost impossible to write a truly platform-independent threading system. (Doug Schmidt's "Ace" Framework is a good, though complex, attempt. You can get more information at http://www.cs.wustl.edu/~schmidt/ACE.html.) So, before I can talk about hardcore Java programming issues in subsequent chapters, I have to discuss the difficulties introduced by the platforms on which the Java virtual machine (JVM) might run.

Threads and Processes

The first OS-level concept that's important is that of the thread itself (as compared to a *process*). What exactly is a thread (or process), really? It's a data structure deep in the bowels of the operating system, and knowing what's in that data structure can help us answer the earlier question.

The process data structure keeps track of all things memory-related: the global address space, the file-handle table, and so forth. When you swap a process to disk in order to allow another process to execute, all the things in that data structure might have to be staged to disk, including (perhaps) large chunks of the system's core memory. When you think "process," think "memory." Swapping a process is expensive because a lot of memory typically has to be moved around. You measure the context-swap time in seconds. In Java, the process and the virtual machine are rough analogs. All heap data (stuff that comes from new) is part of the process, not the thread.

Think of a thread as a thread of execution—a sequence of byte-code instructions executed by the JVM. There's no notion of objects, or even of methods, here. Sequences of instructions can overlap, and they can execute simultaneously. It's commonplace for the same code to be executing simultaneously on multiple threads, for example. I'll discuss all this in more detail later, but think "sequence," not "method."

The *thread* data structure, in contrast to the process, contains the things that it needs to keep track of this sequence. It stores the current machine context: the contents of the registers, the position of the execution engine in the instruction stream, the run-time stack used by methods for local variables and arguments. The OS typically swaps threads simply by pushing the register set on the thread's local stack (inside the thread data structure), putting the thread data structure into some list somewhere, pulling a different thread's data structure off the list, and popping that thread's local stack into the register set. Swapping a thread is relatively efficient, with time measured in milliseconds. In Java, the thread is really a virtual-machine state.

The run-time stack (on which local variables and arguments are stored) is part of the thread data structure. Because multiple threads each have their own run-time stack, the local variables and arguments of a given method are always thread safe. There's simply no way that code running on one thread can access the fields of another thread's OS-level data structure. A method that doesn't access any heap data (any fields in any objects—including static ones) can execute simultaneously on multiple threads without any need for explicit synchronization.

Thread Safety and Synchronization

The phrase *thread safe* is used to describe a method that can run safely in a multi-threaded environment, accessing process-level data (shared by other threads) in a safe and efficient way. The self-contained method described in the previous paragraph is certainly thread safe, but it is really a degenerate case. Thread safety is usually a difficult goal to achieve.

At the center of the thread-safety issue is the notion of *synchronization*— any mechanism that assures that multiple threads:

- start execution at the same time and run concurrently, or

- do not run simultaneously when accessing the same *object*, or

- do not run simultaneously when accessing the same *code*.

I'll discuss ways to do all three of these things in subsequent chapters, but for now, synchronization is achieved by using various objects known collectively as semaphores. A *semaphore* is any object that two threads can use to communicate with one another in order to synchronize their operation. In English, a semaphore is a way to send messages using signalling flags:

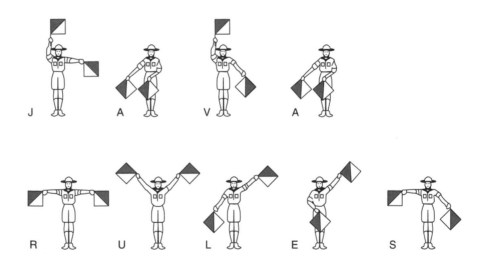

Some of you may have learned the semaphore alphabet in the Boy Scouts. Napoleon used the vanes of windmills to send semaphore messages across vast distances; a Java thread uses a semaphore to communicate with another thread. It's not an accident that you are said to *signal* a semaphore (or put it into the *signalled* state)—it's the same metaphor.

Don't be confused by Microsoft documentation that incorrectly applies the word "semaphore" only to a Dijkstra counting semaphore. A semaphore is any of what Microsoft calls "synchronization objects."

Without Java's `synchronized` keyword, you couldn't implement a semaphore in Java, but the `synchronized` keyword alone is not enough. That's not to say that you should throw platform independence out the window and use JNI to call OS-specific synchronization objects; rather, you should build these objects in Java, using the building blocks provided by the language, such as `synchronized`. I'll do just that in subsequent chapters.

Synchronization Is Expensive

One of the main problems with synchronization, whether you use a semaphore or the `synchronized` keyword directly, is overhead. Consider the code in Listing 1.2, which is a simple benchmark meant to demonstrate just how expensive synchronization is. The `test(...)` method (Listing 1.2, line 13) calls two methods 1,000,000 times. One of the methods is synchronized, the other isn't. Results can vary from run to run, but here's a typical output (on a 200MHz P5, NT4/SP3, using JDK ver. 1.2.1 and HotSpot 1.0fcs, build E):

```
% java -verbose:gc Synch
Pass 0: Time lost: 234 ms. 121.39% increase
Pass 1: Time lost: 139 ms. 149.29% increase
Pass 2: Time lost: 156 ms. 155.52% increase
Pass 3: Time lost: 157 ms. 155.87% increase
Pass 4: Time lost: 157 ms. 155.87% increase
Pass 5: Time lost: 155 ms. 154.96% increase
Pass 6: Time lost: 156 ms. 155.52% increase
Pass 7: Time lost: 3,891 ms. 1,484.7% increase
Pass 8: Time lost: 4,407 ms. 1,668.33% increase
```

The `test()` method has to be called several times in order to get the HotSpot JVM to fully optimize the code. That's why the "Pass 0" results seem confusing. This pass takes the most overall time, but the ratio of synchronized to nonsynchronized call time is relatively small because neither method is particularly efficient. Once things settle down (in pass 6), you see that a synchronized call takes about half again as much time to execute as the nonsynchronized variant.

This 1.5-times penalty is significant, but is nothing when compared to passes 7 and 8. The difference is that the earlier passes were all running on a single thread. In the final two passes, two threads are both trying to call the same synchronized method simultaneously, so there is contention. The numbers here are much more significant, with the call to the synchronized method on the order of 150 times less efficient than the nonsynchronized variant. This is a *big* deal. You don't want to synchronize unnecessarily.

A Digression

It's worthwhile explaining what's going on here. The Hotspot JVM typically uses one of two methods for synchronization, depending on whether or not multiple threads are contending for a lock. When there's no contention, an assembly-language atomic-bit-test-and-set instruction is used. This instruction is not interruptible; it tests a bit, sets various flags to indicate the result of the test, then if the bit was not set, it sets it. This instruction is a crude sort of semaphore because when two threads try to set the bit simultaneously, only one will actually do it. Both threads can then check to see if they were the one that set the bit.

If the bit is set (i.e., there is contention), the JVM has to go out to the operating system to wait for the bit to clear. Crossing the interprocess boundary into the operating system is expensive. In NT, it takes on the order of 600 machine cycles just to enter the OS kernel, and this count doesn't include the cycles spent doing whatever you entered the kernel to do. That's why passes 7 and 8 take so much more time, because the JVM must interact with the operating system. Alexander Garthwaite from Sun Labs brought up a few other interesting issues in a recent email to me:

- Synchronized blocks are often different from synchronized methods in that the generated byte code need not properly nest these. As a result, these are often slightly more expensive (particularly in lock-release).

- Some locking strategies use caches of monitors. So, the number and order in which objects are locked can affect performance. More generally, the locking subsystem may use growable structures for various purposes, and these will become more cumbersome to manage as the number of locked objects increases.

- Some locking strategies use a thin-lock/fat-lock strategy. In the thin lock, only simple synchronization is supported and locking depth is often limited to a small number (often somewhere between 16 and 64). Lock inflation occurs when this count is exceeded, when there is contention on the lock, or when a wait or notify operation is performed. Lock deflation can also add costs if it is supported at all.

- For space efficiency in object headers, other information is often either stored in the same word as locking state or it forces lock inflation. A common example is the object's `hashcode()` method. This means that accessing this information in locked objects is often more expensive, and objects with hash codes may be more expensive to lock than ones without.

One other thing that I'll add, if you can reduce the odds of contention, then the locking process is more efficient. This reasoning implies that you should make the synchronization blocks as small as possible so that a given lock will be unlocked most of the time.

Listing 1.2: /text/books/threads/ch1/Synch.java

```
01: import java.util.*;
02: import java.text.NumberFormat;
03:

    /**

        A benchmark to test the overhead of synchronization on a simple
        method invocation. Benchmarking java, particularly when Hot-
        Spot is in the equation, is tricky. There's a good tech note on this
        subject at http://java.sun.com/products/hotspot/Q+A.html.
     */
04: class Synch
05: {
06:     private static long[]      locking_time     = new long[100];
07:     private static long[]      not_locking_time = new long[100];
08:     private static final int   ITERATIONS       = 1000000;
09:
10:     synchronized long locking    (long a, long b){return a + b;}
11:     long              not_locking (long a, long b){return a + b;}
12:
13:     private void test( int id )
14:     {
15:         long start = System.currentTimeMillis();
16:
17:         for(long i = ITERATIONS; --i >= 0 ;)
18:         {   locking(i,i);
19:         }
20:
21:         locking_time[id] = System.currentTimeMillis() - start;
22:         start            = System.currentTimeMillis();
23:
24:         for(long i = ITERATIONS; --i >= 0 ;)
25:         {   not_locking(i,i);
26:         }
27:
28:         not_locking_time[id] = System.currentTimeMillis() - start;
```

```
29:     }
30:
31:     static void print_results( int id )
32:     {
33:
34:         NumberFormat compositor = NumberFormat.getInstance();
35:         compositor.setMaximumFractionDigits( 2 );
36:
37:         double time_in_synchronization = locking_time[id] - not_locking_time[id];
38:
39:         System.out.println( "Pass " + id + ": Time lost: "
40:                 + compositor.format( time_in_synchronization                    )
41:                 + " ms. "
42:                 + compositor.format( ((double)locking_time[id]/
43:                                             not_locking_time[id])*100.0)
43:                 + "% increase"
44:                 );
45:     }
46:
47:     static public void main(String[] args) throws InterruptedException
48:     {
49:         // First, with no contention:
50:
51:         final Synch tester = new Synch();
52:         tester.test(0); print_results(0);
53:         tester.test(1); print_results(1);
54:         tester.test(2); print_results(2);
55:         tester.test(3); print_results(3);
56:         tester.test(4); print_results(4);
57:         tester.test(5); print_results(5);
58:         tester.test(6); print_results(6);
59:
60:         // Now let's do it again with contention. I'm assuming that
61:         // hotspot has optimized the test method by now, so am only
62:         // calling it once.
63:
64:         final Object start_gate = new Object();
65:
66:         Thread t1 = new Thread()
67:         {   public void run()
68:             {   try{ synchronized(start_gate) { start_gate.wait(); } }
69:                 catch( InterruptedException e ){}
70:
71:                 tester.test(7);
72:             }
73:         };
74:         Thread t2 = new Thread()
```

```
75:            {   public void run()
76:                {   try{ synchronized(start_gate) { start_gate.wait(); } }
77:                    catch( InterruptedException e ){}
78:
79:                    tester.test(8);
80:                }
81:            };
82:
83:            Thread.currentThread().setPriority( Thread.MIN_PRIORITY );
84:
85:            t1.start();
86:            t2.start();
87:
88:            synchronized(start_gate){ start_gate.notifyAll(); }
89:
90:            t1.join();
91:            t2.join();
92:
93:            print_results( 7 );
94:            print_results( 8 );
95:        }
96: }
```

Avoiding Synchronization

Fortunately, explicit synchronization is often avoidable. Methods that don't use any of the state information (such as fields) of the class to which they belong don't need to be synchronized, for example. (That is, they use only local variables and arguments—no class-level fields—and they don't modify external objects by means of references that are passed in as arguments.) There are also various class-based solutions, which I discuss in subsequent chapters (such as the synchronization wrappers used by the Java collection classes).

You can sometimes eliminate synchronization simply by using the language properly, however. The next few sections show you how.

Atomic Energy: Do Not Synchronize Atomic Operations

The essential concept vis-a-vis synchronization is *atomicity.* An "atomic" operation cannot be interrupted by another thread, and naturally atomic operations do not need to be synchronized.

Java defines a few atomic operations. In particular, assignment to variables of any type except long and double is atomic. To understand ramifications of this statement, consider the following (hideously non-object-oriented) code:

```
class Unreliable
{   private long x;

    public long get_x(             ){ return x;   }
    public void set_x(long value ){ x = value;  }
}
```

Thread one calls:

```
obj.set_x( 0 );
```

A second thread calls:

```
obj.set_x( 0x123456789abcdef );
```

The problem is the innocuous statement:

```
x = value;
```

which is effectively treated by the JVM as two separate 32-bit assignments, not a single 64-bit assignment:

```
x.high_word = value.high_word;
x.low_word  = value.low_word;
```

Either thread can be interrupted by the other halfway through the assignment operation—after modifying the high word, but before modifying the low word. Depending on when the interruption occurs (or if it occurs), the possible values of x are 0x0123456789abcdef, 0x0123456700000000, 0x0000000089abcdef, or 0x0000000000000000. There's no telling which one you'll get. The only way to fix this problem is to redefine both set_x() and get_x() as synchronized or wrap the assignment in a synchronized block.

The volatile **Keyword**

Another keyword of occasional interest is volatile. The issue here is not one of synchronization, but rather of optimization. If one method sets a flag, and another tests it, the optimizer might think that the value of the flag never changes and optimize the test out of existence. Declaring the variable as volatile effectively tells the optimizer not to make any assumptions about the variable's state. In general, you'll need to use volatile only when two threads both access a public flag, something that shouldn't happen in well-crafted OO systems. In any event, for reasons that I don't want to go into here, volatile can behave in unpredictable ways on multiprocessor machines. Until the Java language specification is fixed, it's best to use explicit synchronization to avoid these problems.

Fortunately, this problem doesn't arise with 32-bit (or smaller) variables. That is, if all that a method does is set or return a value, and that value is *not* a long or double, then that method doesn't have to be synchronized. Were the earlier x redefined as an int, no synchronization would be required.

Bear in mind that only assignment is guaranteed to be atomic. A statement like x=++y (or x+=y) is *never* thread safe, no matter what size x and y are. You could be preempted after the increment but before the assignment. You must use the synchronized keyword to get atomicity in this situation.

Race Conditions

Formally, the sort of bug I just described—when two threads simultaneously contend for the same object and, as a consequence, leave the object in an undefined state—is called a *race condition*. Race conditions can occur anywhere that any sequence of operations must be atomic (not preemptable), and you forget to make them atomic by using the synchronized keyword. That is, think of synchronized as a way of making complex sequences of operations atomic, in the same way that assignment to a boolean is atomic. The synchronized operation can't be preempted by another thread that's operating on the same data.

Immutability

An effective language-level means of avoiding synchronization is immutability. An *immutable* object is one whose state doesn't change after it's created. A Java String is a good example—there's no way to modify the String once it's created. (The expression string1 += string2 is actually treated like string1 = string1 + string2; a third string is created by concatenating the two operands, then the target is overwritten to reference this third string. As usual, this operation is not atomic.)

Since the value of an immutable object never changes, multiple threads can safely access the object simultaneously, so no synchronization is required.

Create an immutable object by making *all* of the fields of a class `final`. The fields don't all have to be initialized when they are declared, but if they aren't they *must* be explicitly initialized in every constructor. For example:

```
class I_am_immutable
{   private final int MAX_VALUE = 10;
    private final int blank_final;

    public I_am_immutable( int initial_value )
    {   blank_final = initial_value;
    }
}
```

A `final` field that's initialized by the constructor in this way is called a *blank final*.

In general, if you are accessing an object a lot, but not modifying it much, making it immutable is a good idea since none of the methods of the object's class need to be synchronized. If you modify the object a lot, however, the overhead of copying the object will be much higher than the overhead of synchronization, so an immutable-object approach doesn't make sense. Of course, there is a vast gray area where neither approach is obviously better.

Synchronization Wrappers

Often it's the case that you need synchronization sometimes, but not all the time. A good example is the Java 2 `Collection` classes. Typically, collections will be accessed from within synchronized methods, so it would be contraindicated for the methods of the collection to be synchronized, since you'd be unnecessarily acquiring two locks (the one on the object that used the collection and the other on the collection itself). Java's solution to this problem is generally applicable: use a synchronization wrapper. The basic notion of the Gang-of-Four *Decorator* design pattern is that a Decorator both implements some interface and also contains an object that implements the same interface. (The "Gang-of-Four" referenced in the previous sentence are Erich Gamma, Richard Helm, Ralph Johnson, and John Vlissides, the authors of the excellent book *Design Patterns: Elements of Reusable Object-Oriented Software* [Reading: Addison Wesley, 1995].) The container implements the same methods as the contained object, but modifies the behavior of the method as it passed the request through to the contained object. The classes in the java.io package are all Decorators: A `BufferedInputStream` both implements `InputStream` and contains an instance of some `InputStream`—you talk to the contained object through the container, which modifies the behavior of the contained object. (The `read()` method buffers characters in the `BufferedInputStream` decorator and doesn't buffer in the contained `FileInputStream`. The `BufferedInputStream` container gets its characters from the contained `FileInputStream` object.)

You can put this technique to use to provide synchronization on an as-needed basis. For example:

```java
interface Some_interface
{   Object message();
}

class Not_thread_safe implements Some_interface
{
    public Object message()
    {   // ... Implementation goes here
        return null;
    }
}

class Thread_safe_wrapper implements Some_interface
{
    Some_interface not_thread_safe;

    public Thread_safe_wrapper( Some_interface not_thread_safe )
    {   this.not_thread_safe = not_thread_safe;
    }

    public Some_interface extract()
    {   return not_thread_safe;
    }

    public synchronized Object message()
    {   return not_thread_safe.message();
    }
}
```

When thread safety isn't an issue, you can just declare and use objects of class `Not_thread_safe` without difficulty. When you need a thread-safe version, just wrap it:

```java
Some_interface object = new Not_thread_safe();
//...

object = new Thread_safe_wrapper(object); // object is now thread safe
```

when you don't need thread-safe access any more, unwrap it:

```java
object = ((Thread_safe_Wrapper)object).extract();
```

Concurrency, or How Can You Be Two Places at Once (When You're Really Nowhere at All)

The next OS-related issue (and the main problem when it comes to writing platform-independent Java) has to do with the notions of *concurrency* and *parallelism*. Concurrent multithreading systems give the appearance of several tasks executing at once, but these tasks are actually split up into chunks that share the processor with chunks from other tasks. Figure 1.1 illustrates the issues. In parallel systems, two tasks are actually performed simultaneously. Parallelism requires a multiple-CPU system.

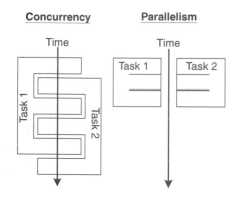

Figure 1.1. Concurrency vs. Parallelism

Multiple threads don't necessarily make your program faster. Unless you're spending a lot of time blocked, waiting for I/O operations to complete, a program that uses multiple concurrent threads will often run slower than an equivalent single-threaded program (although it will often be better organized than the equivalent single-thread version). A program that uses multiple threads running in parallel on multiple processors will run much faster, of course. If speed is important, a multithreaded program should have no more threads running at any given moment than there are processors in the system. More threads can exist in this program, but they should be suspended, waiting for some event to occur.

The main reason that Java's threading system isn't platform independent is that parallelism is impossible unless you use the underlying operating system's threading model. Java, at least in theory, permits threading to be simulated entirely by the JVM, thereby avoiding the time penalty for entering the OS kernel that I discussed earlier. This approach precludes any parallelism in your application, however: If no operating-system-level threads are used, the OS looks at the JVM instance as a single-threaded application, which will be scheduled to a single processor. The net result would be that no two Java threads running under the same JVM instance would ever run in parallel, even if you had multiple CPUs and your JVM was the only process that was active. Two instances of the JVM running separate applications could run in parallel, of course, but I want to do better than that. To get parallelism, the JVM *must* map Java threads through to operating-system threads. Unfortunately, different operating systems implement threads in different ways; so, you can't afford to ignore the differences between the various threading models if platform independence is important.

Get Your Priorities Straight

I'll demonstrate the ways that all the issues I just discussed can impact your programs by comparing two operating systems: Solaris and Windows NT.

Java, in theory at least, provides ten priority levels for threads. (If two or more threads are both waiting to run, the one with the highest priority level will execute.) In Solaris, which supports 2^{31} priority levels, having ten levels is no problem. You give up a lot of fine control over priority by restricting yourself to one of these ten levels, but everything will work the way that you expect.

NT, on the other hand, has at most seven priority levels available, which have to be mapped into Java's ten. This mapping is undefined, so lots of possibilities present themselves. (Java priority levels 1 and 2 might both map to NT priority-level 1, and Java priority levels 8, 9, and 10 might all map to NT level 7, for example. Other combinations, such as using only five of the available levels and mapping pairs of Java levels to a single NT level, are also possible). NT's paucity of priority levels is a problem if you want to use priority to control scheduling.

Things are made even more complicated by the fact that NT priority levels are not fixed. NT provides a mechanism called "priority boosting," which you can turn off with a C system call, but not from Java. When priority boosting is enabled, NT boosts a thread's priority by an indeterminate amount for an indeterminate amount of time every time it executes certain I/O-related system calls. In practice, this means that a thread's priority level could be higher than you think because that thread happened to perform an I/O operation at an awkward time. The point of the priority boosting is to prevent threads that are doing background processing from impacting the apparent responsiveness of UI-heavy tasks. Other operating systems have more-sophisticated algorithms that typically lower the priority of background processes. The down side of this scheme, particularly when implemented on a per-thread rather than per-process level, is that it's very difficult to use priority to determine when a particular thread will run.

It gets worse.

In Solaris—as is the case in all Unix systems and every contemporary operating system that I know of *except* the Microsoft operating systems—processes have priority as well as threads. The threads of high-priority processes can't be interrupted by the threads of low-priority processes. Moreover, the priority level of a given process can be limited by a system administrator so that a user process won't interrupt critical OS processes or services. NT supports none of this. An NT process is just an address space. It has no priority per se and is not scheduled. The system schedules threads; then, if that thread is running under a process that is not in memory, the process is swapped in. NT thread priorities fall into various "priority classes," that are distributed across a continuum of actual priorities. The system is shown in Figure 1.2.

The columns are actual priority levels, only twenty-two of which must be shared by all applications. (The others are used by NT itself.) The rows are priority classes.

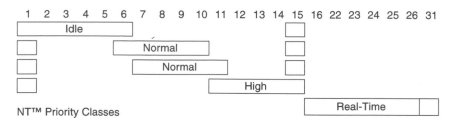

Figure 1-2. Windows NT's Priority Achitecture

The threads running in a process pegged at the "Idle" priority class are running at levels 1–6 and 15, depending on their assigned logical priority level. The threads of a process pegged as "Normal" priority class will run at levels 1, 6–10, or 15 if the process doesn't have the input focus. If it does have the input focus, the threads run at levels 1, 7–11, or 15. This means that a high-priority thread of an idle-priority-class process can preempt a low-priority thread of a normal-priority-class process, but only if that process is running in the background. Notice that a process running in the "High" priority class only has six priority levels available to it. The other classes have seven.

NT provides no way to limit the priority class of a process. Any thread on any process on the machine can take over control of the box at any time by boosting its own priority class, and there's no defense. Solaris, on the other hand, does support the notion of process priority precisely because you need to prevent screen savers from interfering with system-critical tasks. A high-priority process simply shouldn't be preempted by a low-priority process, particularly in a server. I guess the good people at Microsoft didn't think that anyone would *really* be using NT as a server operating system. Anyway, the technical term I use to describe NT's priority is "unholy mess." In practice, priority is virtually worthless under NT.

So what's a programmer to do? Between NT's limited number of priority levels and its uncontrollable priority boosting, there's no absolutely safe way for a Java program to use priority levels for scheduling. One workable compromise is to restrict yourself to `Thread.MAX_PRIORITY`, `Thread.MIN_PRIORITY`, and `Thread.NORM_PRIORITY` when you call `setPriority()`. This restriction at least avoids the ten-mapped-to-seven-levels problem. I suppose you could use the `os.name` system property to detect NT, and then call a native method to turn off priority boosting, but that won't work if your app is running under Internet Explorer unless you also use Sun's JVM plug-in. (Microsoft's JVM uses a nonstandard native-method implementation.) In any event, I hate to use native methods. I usually avoid the problem as much as possible by putting most threads at `NORM_PRIORITY` and using scheduling mechanisms other than priority. (I'll discuss some of these in subsequent chapters.)

Cooperate!

There are typically two threading models supported by operating systems: cooperative and preemptive.

The Cooperative Multithreading Model

In a *cooperative* system, a thread retains control of its processor until it decides to give it up (which might be never). The various threads have to cooperate with each other or all but one of the threads will be *starved* (never given a chance to run). Scheduling in most cooperative systems is done strictly by priority level. When the current thread gives up control, the highest-priority waiting thread gets control. (An exception to this rule is Windows 3.x, which uses a cooperative model but doesn't have much of a scheduler. The window that has the focus gets control.)

The main advantage of cooperative multithreading is that it's very fast and has a very low overhead when compared to preemptive systems. For example, a *context swap*—a transfer of control from one thread to another—can be performed entirely by a user-mode subroutine library without entering the OS kernel (which costs 600 machine cycles in NT). A user-mode context swap in a cooperative system does little more than a C setjump/longjump call would do. You can have thousands of cooperative threads in your applications without significantly impacting performance. Because you don't lose control involuntarily in cooperative systems, you don't have to worry about synchronization either. Just don't give up control until it's safe to do so. You never have to worry about an atomic operation being interrupted. The two main disadvantages of the cooperative model are:

1. It's very difficult to program cooperative systems. Lengthy operations have to be manually divided into smaller chunks, which often must interact in complex ways.

2. The cooperative threads can never run in parallel.

The Preemptive Multithreading Model

The alternative to a cooperative model is a *preemptive* one, where some sort of timer is used by the operating system itself to cause a context swap. That is, when the timer "ticks" the OS can abruptly take control away from the running thread and give control to another thread. The interval between timer ticks is called a *time slice*.

Preemptive systems are less efficient than cooperative ones because the thread management must be done by the operating-system kernel, but they're easier to program (with the exception of synchronization issues) and tend to be more reliable because starvation is less of a problem. The most important advantage to preemptive systems is parallelism. Because cooperative threads are scheduled by a user-level subroutine library, not by the OS, the best you can get with a cooperative model is concurrency. To get parallelism, the OS must do the scheduling. Four threads running in parallel on four processors will run more than four times faster than the same four threads running concurrently (because there is no context-swap overhead).

Some operating systems, like Windows 3.1, only support cooperative multi-threading. Others, like NT, support only preemptive threading. (You can simulate cooperative threading in NT with a user-mode library. NT has such a library called the "fiber" library, but fibers are buggy, and aren't fully integrated into the operating system.) Solaris provides the best (or worst) of all worlds by supporting both cooperative and preemptive models in the same program. (I'll explain this in a moment.)

Mapping Kernel Threads to User Processes

The final OS issue has to do with the way in which kernel-level threads are mapped into user-mode processes. NT uses a one-to-one model, illustrated in Figure 1.3.

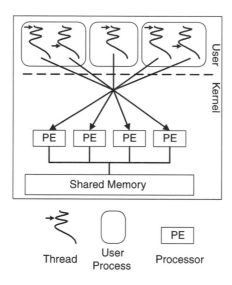

Figure 1.3. The NT Threading Model

NT user-mode threads effectively *are* kernel threads. They are mapped by the OS directly onto a processor and they are always preemptive. All thread manipulation and synchronization are done via kernel calls (with a 600-machine–cycle overhead for every call). This is a straightforward model, but is neither flexible nor efficient.

The Solaris model in Figure 1.4 is more interesting. Solaris adds *lightweight process* (LWP) to the notion of a thread. The LWP is a schedulable unit on which one or more threads can run. Parallel processing is done on the LWP level. Normally, LWPs reside in a pool, and they are assigned to particular processors as necessary. An LWP can be *bound* to a specific processor if it's doing something particularly time critical, however, thereby preventing other LWPs from using that processor.

Up at the user level, you have a system of cooperative, or *green* threads. In a simple situation, a process will have one LWP shared by all of the green threads. The threads must yield control to each other voluntarily, but the single LWP that the threads share can be preempted by an LWP in another process. This way the processes are preemptive with respect to each other (and can execute in parallel), but the threads within the process are cooperative (and execute concurrently).

A process is not limited to a single LWP, however. The green threads can share a pool of LWPs in a single process. The green threads can be attached (or bound) to an LWP in two ways:

1. The programmer explicitly "binds" one or more threads to a specific LWP. In this case, the threads sharing a LWP must cooperate with each other, but they can preempt (or be preempted by) threads bound to a different LWP. If every green thread was bound to a single LWP, you'd have an NT-style preemptive system.

2. The threads are bound to green threads by the user-mode scheduler. This is something of a worst case from a programming point of view because you can't assume a cooperative or a preemptive environment. You may have to yield to other threads if there's only one LWP in the pool, but you might also be preempted.

The Solaris threading model gives you an enormous amount of flexibility. You can choose between an extremely fast (but strictly concurrent) cooperative system, a slower (but parallel) preemptive system, or any combination of the two. But (and this is a *big* "but") none of this flexibility is available to you, the hapless Java programmer, because you have no control over the threading model used by the JVM. For example, early versions of the Solaris JVM were strictly cooperative. Java threads were all green threads sharing a single LWP. The current version of the Solaris JVM uses multiple LWPs and no green threads at all.

So why do you care? You care precisely because you have no control—you have to program as if all the possibilities might be used by the JVM. In order to write platform-independent code, you must make two seemingly contradictory assumptions:

1. You can be preempted by another thread at any time. You must use the `synchronized` keyword carefully to assure that nonatomic operations work correctly.

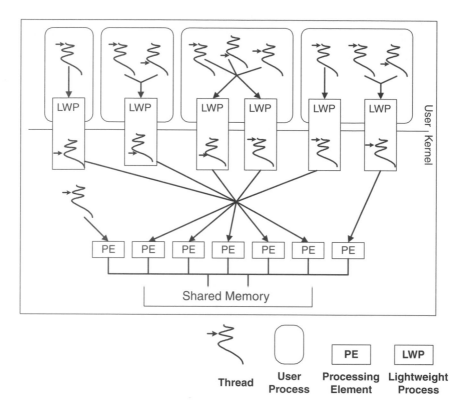

Figure 1.4. The Solaris Threading Model

2. You will never be preempted unless you give up control. You must occasionally perform some operation that will give control to other threads so that they can have a chance to run. Use `yield()` and `sleep()` in appropriate places (or make blocking I/O calls). For example, you might want to consider calling `yield()` every 100 iterations or so of a long loop, or voluntarily going to sleep for a few milliseconds every so often to give lower-priority threads a chance to run. (The `yield()` method will yield control only to threads running at your priority level or higher).

Wrapping Up

So those are the main OS-level issues that you have to consider when you're writing a Java program. Since you can make no assumptions about your operating environment, you have to program for the worst case. For example, you have to assume that you can be preempted at any time, so you must use `synchronized` appropriately, but you must also assume that you will never be preempted, so you must also occasionally use `yield()`, `sleep()`, or blocking I/O calls to permit other threads to run. Any use of priority is problematic: You can't assume that two adjacent priority levels are different. They might not be after NT has mapped Java's ten levels into its seven levels. Similarly, you can't assume that a priority-level-two thread will always be higher priority than one that runs at level 1—it might not be if NT has "boosted" the priority level of the lower-priority thread.

CHAPTER 2

The Perils
of Multithreaded
Programming

THIS CHAPTER DISCUSSES the perils that await the unwary programmer once threads come on the scene. The bugs I'm discussing can be nasty ones to find because they're often timing related. They tend to manifest once a month (or once a year), not every time the program executes, and they can be almost impossible to duplicate when they do occur. (The actions that caused the program to hang once might not cause it to hang all the time, and in fact, might have been working fine for the last year.) This unpredictability makes it all the more important to recognize and stamp out these bugs early in the design process.

Monitors and Exclusion Semaphores (Mutex)

Just to make sure that we're all starting from the same place, a little review of terms is in order. The central concept for synchronization in the Java model is a *monitor*, developed 20 or so years ago by C.A.R. Hoare. A *monitor* is a body of code (not necessarily contiguous), access to which is guarded by a mutual-exclusion semaphore (or *mutex*) that's associated with an *object*. The central notion of a mutex is ownership. Only one thread can own the mutex at a time. If a second thread tries to *acquire* ownership, it will *block* (be suspended) until the owning thread *releases* the mutex.

If several threads are simultaneously waiting to acquire the same mutex, only one will actually get it when it's released. (The others will continue to block.) Unfortunately, Java does not guarantee that any particular thread will actually acquire the lock—it depends on the platform. Typically, priority order, FIFO (first in, first out) order, or some combination of these is used to determine who gets control. You *guard* a block of code by acquiring a mutex at the top of the block and releasing it at the bottom. That is effectively what the synchronized statement does in Java. If you imagine that a Mutex class exists (I'll develop one in Chapter 3), then the following code:

```
synchronized( obj )
{
    // guarded code
}
```

is effectively the same as this code:

```
obj.my_mutex.acquire();
try
{    // guarded code
}
finally
{    obj.my_mutex.release();
}
```

The guarded code (within the monitor) does not have to be contiguous: Several noncontiguous code blocks could all acquire and release the same mutex, and all of this code is considered to be in the same monitor since it's locked by a common mutex. It's the mutex that defines the monitor, not the code.

The best analogy that I know for a monitor is an airplane bathroom. Only one person (we hope) can be in the bathroom at a time. Everybody else is queued up in a rather narrow aisle waiting to use it. As long as the door is locked, the waiting passengers can't access the bathroom. The object is the airplane. The passengers are the threads. The bathroom is the monitor (assuming that there's only one bathroom). The lock on the door is the mutex.

In Java, every *object* has one and only one monitor (and mutex) associated with it. However, the single monitor has several doors into it, each indicated by the synchronized keyword. When a thread passes over the synchronized keyword, it effectively locks all the doors. Of course, if a thread doesn't pass across the synchronized keyword, it hasn't locked the door, and some other thread can barge in at any time. In the following code, one thread can be in thelma(), in the middle of modifying x, when it's preempted by a second thread that calls louise().

```
class Ooops
{
    double x;

    public void synchronized thelma()
    {    x = 0;
    }

    public void louise()      // WRONG! doesn't acquire mutex
    {    x = -1;               // before modifying (non-atomic)
    }                          // field.
}
```

The louise() method is effectively a door without a lock on it.

Bear in mind that the monitor is associated with the *object*, not the class. Several threads can all be executing the same method in parallel, but the receiving objects (as identified by the this references) have to be different. For example, several instances of a thread-safe queue could be in use by several threads. These threads could simultaneously enqueue objects to different queues, but they could not enqueue to the same queue at the same time. Only one thread at a time can be in the monitor for a given queue.

To refine the earlier analogy, the airplane is still the object, but the monitor is really all of the bathrooms combined (each synchronized chunk of code is a bathroom). When a thread enters any bathroom, the doors on all the bathrooms are locked. Different instances of a class are different airplanes, however, and if the bathroom doors in your airplane are unlocked, you don't really care about the state of the doors in the other airplanes.

Race Conditions and Spin Locks

A *race condition* occurs when two threads try to access the same object at the same time, and the behavior of the code changes depending on who wins. Figure 2.1 shows a single (unsynchronized) object accessed simultaneously by multiple threads. A thread can be preempted in fred() after modifying one field but before modifying the other. If another thread comes along at that point and calls any of the methods shown, the object will be left in an unstable state, because the initial thread will eventually wake up and modify the other field.

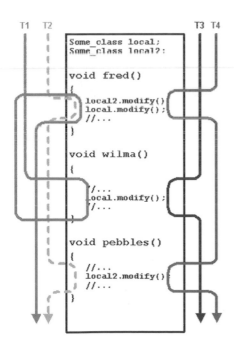

Figure 2.1. Four Threads Simultaneously Accessing a Single Object

Usually, you think of objects sending messages to other objects. In multi-threaded environments, you must think about message handlers running on threads. Think: "This thread causes this object to send a message to that object." A race condition can occur when two threads cause messages to be sent to the same object at the same time.

I'll show you how to cure a race condition with the Simple_notifying_queue class, which demonstrates a blocking queue used by one thread to notify another when some event occurs. (We'll see a more realistic version of this class in Chapter 8, but for now I want to keep things simple.) The basic notion is that a thread that tries to dequeue from an empty queue will block until some other thread puts something in the queue. The queue is implemented as a *ring buffer*, in which the first element effectively follows the last element. The circular behavior is implemented by MODing the index by the array size every time it's incremented (on lines 10 and 42 of Listing 2.1). The queue is empty when the head and tail indexes match, so one slot in the queue is always wasted.

Listing 2.1: /text/books/threads/ch2/Simple_notifying_queue.java

```
01: public class Simple_notifying_queue
02: {
03:     private static final int QUEUE_SIZE = 10;
04:     private Object[]        queue      = new Object[ QUEUE_SIZE ];
05:     private int             head       = 0;
06:     private int             tail       = 0;
07:
08:     public synchronized void enqueue( Object item )
09:     {
10:         tail         = ++tail % QUEUE_SIZE;
11:         queue[ tail ] = item;
12:         this.notify();                      // The "this" is there only to
13:     }                                       // improve readability.
14:
15:     public synchronized Object dequeue( )
16:     {
17:         try
18:         {   // If the queue is empty, wait for some other thread to
19:             // enqueue something. The following test MUST be a while,
20:             // not an if, statement.
21:
22:             while( head == tail )
```

```
23:            this.wait();
24:        }
25:        catch( InterruptedException e )
26:        {
27:            // If we get here, we were not actually notified.
28:            // returning null doesn't indicate that the
29:            // queue is empty, only that the waiting was
30:            // abandoned.
31:
32:            return null;
33:        }
34:
35:        // Remove the object from the queue. Note that the assignment
36:        // of null to the vacated slot is essential. If I didn't do
37:        // it, the reference to the dequeued object could stay alive
38:        // until the queue is garbage collected, even though the object
39:        // has been "removed" from the queue. Who says there's no such
40:        // thing as a memory leak in Java?
41:
42:        head                  = ++head % QUEUE_SIZE;
43:        Object dequeued_object = queue[ head ];
44:        queue[head]            = null;
45:        return dequeued_object;
46:    }
47: }
```

Starting with an empty queue, let's follow the sequence of operations when one thread does a dequeue and then another (at some later time) enqueues an item:

1. The dequeueing thread calls dequeue() (Listing 2.1, line 15), entering the monitor (and locking out other threads until the monitor is released). The thread tests for an empty queue (head==tail) and then calls wait(). (I'll explain why this test must be implemented as a loop in a moment.)

2. The wait() call releases the lock. (The current thread *temporarily* leaves the monitor.) It then blocks on a second synchronization object called a *condition variable*. [The basic notion of a condition variable is that a thread blocks until some condition becomes true. In the case of Java's built-in condition variable, the thread will wait until the notified condition is set (to true) by some other thread calling notify().] It's important to realize that the waiting thread has released the monitor when it's waiting for the condition variable to change state. The wait() method is effectively implemented as follows:

```
this.mutex.release();
this.condition.wait_for_true(); // we are now blocked in this call
this.mutex.acquire();
```

3. A second thread now comes along and enqueues an object, eventually calling notify(), thereby releasing the waiting (dequeueing) thread.

4. The dequeueing thread now has to wait to reacquire the monitor before wait() can return, so it blocks again, this time on the lock associated with the monitor. It can't acquire the monitor because the second thread hasn't returned from enqueue() yet.

5. The enqueueing thread now returns from the enqueue() method releasing the monitor.

6. The dequeueing thread acquires the monitor, wait() returns, an object is dequeued, and dequeue() returns, releasing the monitor.

That innocuous while loop (Listing 2.1, line 22) is pretty important. First, consider what would happen if you replaced the notify() call with a call to notifyAll() Imagine that several threads were simultaneously trying to dequeue something from the same empty queue. All of these threads are blocked on a single condition variable, waiting for an enqueue operation to be executed. When enqueue() sets the condition to true by calling notifyAll(), the threads are all released from the wait (moved from a suspended to a runnable state). The released threads all try to acquire the monitor at once, but only one wins and gets the mutex, dequeueing the (one-and-only) object.

The other threads, have been released from their wait, however, so they will each return from wait(), one at a time, and dequeue an element from an empty queue. Because these other threads don't retest for an empty queue, they will dequeue garbage. That's one of the reasons why we need that while statement—the other threads will all loop back up, notice that the queue is empty, and go back to waiting. This sort of loop is called a *spin lock*.

The spin lock solves another less obvious problem. What if we leave the notify() statement in place and don't use notifyAll()? Because notify() releases only one waiting thread, couldn't we get rid of the loop and replace it with an if statement? Well, no. Here's what can happen.

1. The dequeueing thread is blocking in the wait(), decomposed as follows:

```
this.mutex.release();
this.condition.wait_for_true(); //<-- we are now blocked in this call
this.mutex.acquire();
```

2. The enqueueing thread calls notify(), releasing the condition variable, effectively moving the enqueueing thread to here:

    ```
    this.mutex.release();
    this.condition.wait_for_true();
    this.mutex.acquire();           //<-- we are now blocked in this call
    ```

3. The dequeueing thread is preempted, just after calling notify(). The enqueue() method hasn't returned, so the enqueueing thread is still holding the lock.

4. A third thread now comes on the scene and calls dequeue(). There are now two threads both trying to acquire the same monitor at the same time: the dequeueing thread and the third thread I just introduced into the mix.

5. Because both dequeueing threads are blocked, the enqueueing thread is allowed to run. It returns successfully, releasing the mutex associated with the monitor.

6. There's no way to determine exactly what will happen next. One of the two dequeueing threads will actually acquire the mutex, but we have no way of predicting which one. For the sake of argument, let's assume that the third thread gets it. This thread successfully dequeues the object; wait() is never called since the queue isn't empty.

7. Now the original dequeueing thread wakes up. Because we cleverly used a while statement instead of an if, the original dequeueing thread will notice that the queue is empty, even though it has been notified, and go back to waiting. If I had used an if instead of a spin lock, the code would have failed at this juncture and garbage would have been dequeued from an empty queue.

The real issue here is that the Java specification does not require that wait() be implemented as an atomic operation (one that can't be preempted while moving from the condition variable to the monitor's lock). This means that using an if instead of a while might work in some Java implementations, but the behavior is really undefined. Using a spin lock instead of a simple if statement is cheap insurance against implementations that don't treat wait() as atomic.

While we're on the subject of wait(), there's one additional point to consider. Many programmers believe (incorrectly) that wait() returns as soon as the notify is issued, but that's simply not the case. **The wait() call doesn't return until the method that calls notify() releases the monitor.** Remember, you must be in the monitor to call either method. In the following code, wait() won't return until the read() operation completes:

```
class Dysfunctional
{
    public synchronized void reader()
    {   notify();
        f.read();
    }
    public synchronized void wait_for_read()
    {    wait();
    }
}
```

The **Spin_lock** Class

There's one final problem that needs to be solved for the spin lock discussed in the previous section to be production quality. The timeout passed to wait() should be the maximum time required to acquire the lock. In the example I just covered, it's possible for another thread to come in and steal the thing we're waiting for just before the timeout expires. In this case, the simple spin lock will just go back to waiting, so you can wait much longer than expected.

The problem is solved by the Spin_lock class (Listing 2.2) by using the system time. (The relevant code is on lines 16 to 21.) An expiration time is computed by adding the timeout to the current system time. Then, in each iteration of the spin lock, the time remaining until the expiration time is determined and an exception is thrown if the time has expired, otherwise the method waits for the time remaining until expiration (not for the original timeout interval).

The condition itself is specified with a Gang-of-Four *Strategy* object. You pass in an object that implements Condition in such a way that the satisfied() method returns true when the condition for which you're waiting is satisfied. The while loop in Listing 2.1, line 22 can be replaced with:

```
Spin_lock lock = new Spin_lock();

public synchronized Object dequeue( )
{   //...
    lock.acquire(   new Spin_lock.condition()
                    {   public boolean satisfied()
                        {   return head != tail;
                        }
                    },
                    1000 // wait at most 1 second
                );
    //...
}

public synchroinzed void enqueue( Object item )
```

```
{   //...
    lock.release();
    //...
}
```

There's another example in the Test class on Listing 2.2, line 29.

Implemenation note: I often embed a unit test within a static *inner class [called* Test*] of the class that I'm testing. This inner class is written to a separate class file than the class being tested, so the binary version of the test code is easily discarded when you ship the product simply by not including it in the shipped version. Execute the test with:*

```
java Spln_lock\$Test
```

(Leave out the backslash if you're running under Windows rather than UNIX.)

Whether it's worth using a Spin_lock depends on whether the inherent inefficiency of repetitive calls to condition() is worth your while—you always lose some efficiency when you introduce a generic mechanism to a program. You can always use the wait-for-a-specific-time strategy directly, however.

Listing 2.2: /src/com/holub/asynch/Spin_lock.java

```
01: package com.holub.asynch;
02: import    java.util.*;         // just for testing
03:
04: import com.holub.asynch.Semaphore; // contains definition of timeout exception
05:

    /**
          A simple generic spin lock. Use it to wait for some
          condition to be true when a notify is received. For
          example, this code:

              boolean some_condition = false; // set true by another thread

                  Spin_lock lock = new Spin_lock();
                  lock.acquire(   new Spin_lock.Condition()
                              {   public boolean satisfied()
                                  {   return some_condition == false;
                                  }
                              },
```

```
                                  1000      // wait at most one second
                    );
        //...
        lock.release();
```

has roughly the same effect as:

```
        Object lock;

        while( some_condition == false )
            lock.wait(1000);
        //...
        lock.notify();
```

The timeout will be reliable if you use the `Spin_lock`; it may not be reliable if you use `wait()`.

@author *Allen I. Holub*
```
    */
```

```
06: public final class Spin_lock
07: {
```

```
        /**
```
A Gang-of-Four Strategy object that tells the spin lock the condition for which we're waiting. Override `satisfied()` to return true when the condition for which we're waiting becomes true.
```
        */
08:     public interface Condition
09:     {   boolean satisfied();
10:     }
11:
```

```
        /**
                Block until the condition specified by condition
                becomes true and the current Spin_lock is passed a
                release() message after the condition becomes true.
                @throws Semaphore.Timed_out if the timeout expires
                @throws  InterruptedException if another thread
                interrupts the timeout
         */
12:     public synchronized void acquire( Condition condition, long timeout )
13:                                             throws   Semaphore.Timed_out,
14:                                                      InterruptedException
15:     {
16:         long expiration = System.currentTimeMillis() + timeout;
17:         while( !condition.satisfied() )
18:         {   timeout = expiration - System.currentTimeMillis();
19:             if( timeout <= 0 )
20:                 throw new Semaphore.Timed_out("Spin lock timed out.");
21:             wait( timeout );
22:         }
23:     }
24:
25:     public synchronized void release()
26:     {   notify();
27:     }
28:


        /******************************************************************
                Test class, prints "hello world" when executed.
         */

29:     public static final class Test
30:     {   public static void main( String[] args ) throws Exception
31:         {
32:             final Stack stack    =  new Stack();
33:             final Spin_lock lock =  new Spin_lock();
34:             new Thread()
35:             {   public void run()
36:                 {   try
37:                     {   lock.acquire(   new Spin_lock.Condition()
38:                                     {   public boolean satisfied()
39:                                         {   return !stack.isEmpty();
40:                                         }
41:                                     },
42:                                     4000
```

```
43:                                              );
44:
45:                      System.out.println( stack.pop().toString() );
46:                  }
47:              catch(Exception e){}
48:          }
49:      }.start();
50:
51:      Thread.currentThread().sleep(500); // give the thread a
52:                                         // chance to get started.
53:      stack.push("hello world");
54:      lock.release();
55:      }
56:  }
57: }
```

Threads Are Not Objects

Now let's move on to harder-to-find problems. The first difficulty is the common-place confusion of threads and objects: *Methods run on threads, objects do not.* Put another way: **the only way to get a method to run on a given thread is to call it (either directly or indirectly) from that thread's** run() **method**. Simply putting a method into the Thread derivative is not enough. For example, look at the following simple thread (which just prints its fields every so often):

```
class My_thread extends Thread
{
    private int field_1 = 0;
    private int field_2 = 0;

    public void run()
    {
        setDaemon(true);  // this thread will not keep the app alive

        while( true )
        {   System.out.println(   " field_1=" + field_1
                             + " field_2=" + field_2 );
            sleep(100);
        }
    }

    synchronized public void modify( int new_value )
```

```
    {   field_1 = new_value;
        field_2 = new_value;
    }
}
```

You could start up the thread and send it a message like this:

```
public static void main( String[] args )

{
    My_thread test = new My_thread();

    test.start();
    //...
    test.modify(1);
    //...
}
```

The only functions that run on the new thread are run() itself and println()
[which run() calls]. The modify() method *never* runs on the same thread as the
println() call; rather, it runs on whatever thread was running when the call was
made. (In this case, it runs on whatever thread main() is running on.) Depending
on timing, the earlier fragment could print:

```
field_1=0, field2=0
```

But it could just as easily print:

```
field_1=0, field2=1
```

or

```
field_1=1, field2=1
```

There's no telling. (In the first and last cases, the thread would have been outside the println() statement when modify() was called. In the second example, the
thread would have been halfway through evaluating the arguments to println(),
having fetched field_1, but not field_2. It prints the unmodified field_1 and the
modified field_2.

There's no simple solution to this problem. The modify() method is indeed
synchronized in this earlier example, but run() can't be. Were it synchronized, you'd
enter the monitor (and lock the object) when you started up the thread. Thereafter, any other thread that called any synchronized method on the object, such as
modify(), would block (be suspended) until the monitor was released. Because
run() doesn't return (as is often the case), the release will never happen, and the
thread will act like a black hole, sucking up any other thread that calls any of its
synchronized methods. In the current example, the main thread would be

suspended, and the program would hang. So just using the synchronized keyword in a naive way gets us nowhere.

One possible solution is to synchronize only while the fields are accessed, like this:

```java
public void run()
{   setDaemon(true);   // this thread will not keep the app alive

    while( true )
    {   int copy_1;
        int copy_2;

        synchronized(this)
        {   copy_1 = field_1;
            copy_2 = field_2;
        }

        System.out.println(   " field_1=" + copy_1
                            + " field_2=" + copy_2 );
        sleep(100);
    }
}
```

This solution won't work in all situations, however.

Deadlock

Synchronizing run() is a good example of a simple *deadlock* scenario, where a thread is blocked forever, waiting for something that can't happen. Let's look at a few examples that are more realistic than the previous example.

The most common deadlock scenario occurs when two threads are both waiting for each other to do something. The following (admittedly contrived) code snippet makes what's going on painfully obvious:

```java
class Flintstone
{
    int field_1;    private Object lock_1 = new Object();
    int field_2;    private Object lock_2 = new Object();
```

```
public void fred( int value )
{   synchronized( lock_1 )
    {   synchronized( lock_2 )
        {
            field_1 = 0;
            field_2 = 0;
        }
    }
}

public void barney( int value )
{   synchronized( lock_2 )
    {   synchronized( lock_1 )
        {
            field_1 = 0;
            field_2 = 0;
        }
    }
}
}
```

Now, imagine a scenario whereby one thread (call it "Wilma") calls fred(), passes through the synchronization of lock_1, and is then preempted, allowing another thread (call it "Betty") to execute. Betty calls barney(), acquires lock_2, tries to acquire lock_1, but can't because Wilma's got it. Betty is now blocked, waiting for lock_1 to become available. So Wilma wakes up and tries to acquire lock_2 but can't because Betty has it. Wilma and Betty are now deadlocked. Neither thread can ever execute.

Note that lock_1 and lock_2 are raw Object objects. The Object class isn't abstract, precisely so that you can use it as a roll-your-own lock. Of course, any Object will do as the argument to a synchronized statement; even an array will work. You can't use a primitive (like an int or boolean) for this purpose, however.

Wilma and Betty are a contrived example, but the multiple-lock situation comes up frequently. I'll give a more detailed example in the Chapter 3. Deadlock can occur any time that multiple threads each attempt to acquire several locks, but in a different order.

Get out the Magnifying Glass

If all deadlock scenarios were as easy to recognize as Wilma and Betty, deadlock wouldn't be a problem. Consider the code in Listing 2.3, when the following sequence of operations occurs:

1. One thread (call it "Alfred") issues a to_the_bat_cave() request to the batman object passed to it from main().

2. The batman object starts to process the method, but is preempted just before it calls robin.get_in_the_car(). At this juncture, Alfred has acquired the lock for the batman object.

3. Now along comes a second thread (call it "Joker"), which issues a sock_bam_pow() message to the robin object that it got from main().

4. The robin object (whose sock_bam_pow() method is running on the Joker thread) tries to send a hold_on() message to batman, but can't because Alfred owns the lock on batman. So the Joker thread is now blocked, waiting for Alfred to release the lock on batman.

5. Now Alfred gets a chance to run, and it tries to send a get_in_the_car() message to the robin object, but it can't because the Joker thread owns the lock on robin. Both threads are now deadlocked (sound familiar?).

Listing 2.3: Batman.java

```
01: class Boss
02: {
03:     private Side_kick robin;
04:
05:     public synchronized void set_side_kick( Side_kick kid_in_tights )
06:     {   robin = kid_in_tights;
07:     };
08:
09:     public synchronized void to_the_bat_cave()
10:     {   robin.get_in_the_car();
11:     }
12:
13:     public synchronized void okay()        // sent to us by robin
14:     {   //...
15:     }
16:
17:     public synchronized void hold_on()    // sent to us by robin
18:     {   //...
19:     }
20: }
21: //------------------------------------------------------------------
22: class Side_kick
23: {
24:     private Boss batman;
25:
```

```
26:      public synchronized void set_boss( Boss guy_in_cape )
27:      {    batman = guy_in_cape;
28:      }
29:
30:      public synchronized void get_in_the_car()  // sent by batman
31:      {    batman.okay();
32:      }
33:
34:      public synchronized void sock_bam_pow()     // sent from outside
35:      {    batman.hold_on();
36:      }
37: }
38: //-------------------------------------------------------------------
39: class Gotham_city
40: {    static Boss       batman = new Boss();
41:      static Side_kick robin  = new Side_kick();
42:
43:      public static void main( String[] args )
44:      {
45:          batman.set_side_kick( robin );
46:          robin.set_boss( batman );
47:
48:          // spawn off a bunch of threads that use batman and robin...
49:      }
50: }
```

This situation is, of course, much harder to see than the Wilma/Betty problem because the locks in the batman/robin example are the natural locks associated with individual objects. There are no stand-alone synchronized statements in the batman/robin code, and the locks are associated with two completely distinct objects. Nonetheless, it's really the same problem as Wilma/Betty: two threads each attempt to acquire the same two locks, but in a different order.

Multithreaded programmers tear their hair out looking for the causes of these sorts of problems, and there are only two solutions. The first is to thoroughly design the code before implementing it, to really study the design before you even think about implementing it, and to implement the code exactly as designed. When I do multithreaded programs, I spend much more time doing code and design reviews than I spend coding.

The other solution is to use an architecture that tends to minimize these sorts of problems. (Various threading architectures will be the subject of subsequent chapters.)

There is no magic bullet there. I've seen ads for a couple of products that instrument a JVM in a way that, in theory, will detect deadlock and race conditions.

The problem, though, is a classic Heisenberg-uncertainty dilemma: There is no way to observe the process without impacting it. If the problem is timing-related, adding a print statement or changing to a debugging version of the JVM will change the timing, perhaps eliminating the problem.

Nested-Monitor Lockout

Another important form of deadlock is not discussed much in the Java-language books: *nested-monitor lockout*. This problem usually occurs when you call a blocking function from within a synchronized method, and the only way to release the block is to call another synchronized method. The following code demonstrates the issues:

```
class Black_hole
{
    // The Simple_notifying_queue (Listing 2.1)
    // blocks on an attempt to dequeue from an empty queue:
    private Simple_notifying_queue queue = new Simple_notifying_queue(5);

    public synchronized void put( Object thing )
    {   queue.enqueue( thing );
    }


    public synchronized Object get( )
    {   return queue.dequeue();
    }
}
```

Consider what happens when you try to dequeue something from an empty queue:

1. You call get() to get the item from the queue.

2. get() is synchronized, so the Black_hole is now locked.

3. get() calls dequeue(), which blocks, waiting for some other thread to enqueue something. get() does not return.

4. Another thread tries to enqueue something, but the only way to enqueue something is by calling put(), which you can't do because the Black_hole is locked. That is, any thread that tries to put() will block because the first thread has not returned from get() yet.

The Black_hole now sucks up all threads that try to put() or get() anything. They all block forever. Depending on where this occurs, the black hole could suck up every thread in your program.

Also bear in mind that this problem can occur anytime you have a blocking call (such as a socket or file read) inside a synchronized method. Consider the following example (I've removed exception handling):

```
class Black_hole
{   private InputStream input;
    public Black_hole()
    {   input = new Socket("www.holub.com",80)
                            .getInputStream();
    }
    public synchronized int read()
    {   return input.read();
    }
    public synchronized void close()
    {   input.close();
    }
}
```

A thread tries to read from the socket and blocks because no data is available. Any threads that come along and try to call close() will block because the first thread is in the monitor (blocked). The close can't occur until some data is read, but you probably wanted to call close() because you didn't expect any more data.

The only cures to nested-monitor lockout are:

1. Don't make blocking calls in synchronized methods.

2. Make sure there is a way to talk to the blocking object via another class or a non-synchronized method.

In the current examples, you could just not synchronize put() or close(), but that wouldn't work in a more realistic situation where put() accessed class fields that were accessed by other methods, or you didn't want to close the socket while a thread was in the middle of a read operation.

Synchronization Wrappers

The synchronization decorator discussed in Chapter 1 is also helpful in avoiding nested-monitor lockout. You can work with an non-synchronized object when within a synchronized method. When you're in a method that isn't synchronized, you can temporarily wrap the non-`synchronized` object in a synchronization wrapper to provide thread-safe access.

Time Out!

Nested-monitor lockout isn't the only problem caused by Java's implementation of `wait()`. Though you can pass `wait()` a timeout—a maximum time to wait before returning—for mysterious reasons, there is no way to determine whether `wait()` has returned because the time-out has expired or because the associated object was sent a `notify()` message or equivalent. This odd omission can cause problems when two threads are working together to perform a single task. Imagine that you need to look up some information that's distributed between two databases, and your server fires up two threads to process incoming requests. Thread A reads from Database A, puts the result of the query into some predetermined place, then sends Thread B a `notify()`. Meanwhile, Thread B reads from Database B, waits for Thread A to notify it, concatenates the information from database B to the information gleaned by Thread A, and then returns the result to the original requester. If Thread B's `wait()` operation returned because of a timeout, then the information in the shared memory is invalid. It's not acceptable for Thread B to wait forever, however, because Thread A might never send the notification, and we want to detect this bug gracefully.

The `wait()` method *could* solve the problem by returning a `boolean` value that indicated whether it timed out, but it doesn't.

The other timeout-related problem in Java is that there is no way at all to specify a timeout when acquiring a mutex using `synchronized`. When you call a `synchronized` method, you must agree to wait forever.

I'll look at a solution to the problem with `synchronized` in Chapter 3, but you can address the wait-not-returning-a-value problem using the kludge in Listing 2.4. This class is a specialized implementation of a timer. (I discuss timers further in Chapter 5.) The basic idea is that the `Terminator` object waits for a predetermined interval, and then terminates a `victim` thread by sending it an `interrupt()` message. (Both the timeout and the victim are passed in as constructor arguments.)

The `Test` class (Listing 2.4, line 23) demonstrates how to use the `Terminator`. Here is the important code:

```
try
{   new Terminator( this, 1000 );
    synchronized(this){  wait();  }
    System.out.println("Notified");
}
catch( InterruptedException e )
{   System.out.println("Timed out");
}
```

If the wait is satisfied by somebody sending the current object a notify() message, wait() just returns normally and the string "Notified" is printed. If the Terminator object wakes up before a notification is received, it interrupts the waiting thread, wait() returns with an exception toss, and the message "Timed out" is printed. It's ugly, but it works.

Note that you do not need to preserve the references to the Terminator object, because a Terminator is a thread, and the system keeps a list of references to all active threads. Threads aren't garbage collected until they stop running. The Terminator thread is started in the Terminator class's constructor (Listing 2.4, line 7), so the system-level reference is created as a side effect of creating the Terminator object itself. Also note that the Terminator runs at very high priority in the hope that the timing will be reasonably accurate.

Listing 2.4: /src/com/holub/asynch/Terminator.java

```
01: package com.holub.asynch;
02:

    /**
        Objects of the Terminator class terminate a thread
        by sending it an interrupt() message. One use is
        to terminate a wait() operation in such a way that
        you can detect whether the wait() timed out:

        new Thread()
        {   public void run()
            {   try
                {   new Terminator( this, 1000 );
                    synchronized(this){ wait(); }
                    System.out.println("Notified");
                }
                catch( InterruptedException e )
                {   System.out.println("Timed out");
                }
            }
        }.start();

        Note that all you have to do is create a new
        Terminator. You do not have to keep a reference
        to it.
```

@author *Allen I. Holub*

```
    */
03: public final class Terminator extends Thread
04: {   private final Thread     victim;
05:     private final long       timeout;
06:

    /**
        Creates an object that terminates the victim
        thread by sending it an interrupt message after
        timeout milliseconds have elapsed.
    */

07:     public Terminator( Thread victim, long timeout )
08:     {   this.victim = victim;
09:         this.timeout = timeout;
10:         setDaemon(true);
11:         setPriority( getThreadGroup().getMaxPriority() );
12:         start();
13:     }
14:

    /**
        Do not call.
    */

15:     public void run()
16:     {   try
17:         {   sleep( timeout );
18:             victim.interrupt();
19:         }
```

```
20:            catch( InterruptedException e ){/*ignore*/}
21:        }
22:
23:        private static final class Test
24:        {
25:            public static void main( String[] args )
26:            {
27:                new Thread()
28:                {   public void run()
29:                    {   try
30:                        {   new Terminator( this, 1000 );
31:                            synchronized(this){ wait(); }
32:                            System.out.println("Notified");
33:                        }
34:                        catch( InterruptedException e )
35:                        {   System.out.println("Timed out");
36:                        }
37:                    }
38:                }.start();
39:            }
40:        }
41:    }
```

A Digression on Style

The listings in the current chapter are among many that comprise the
com.holub.asynch package, which I'll be presenting throughout the rest of the
book. It seems, then, that a few notes on style are in order.

Names

I strongly believe that the best way to make your code self documenting is to carefully choose names that accurately reflect the purpose of the named thing. My
names are *always* real English words or short phrases. I run my code through a spell
checker to keep myself honest. (This practice has the added benefit of checking the
spelling in my comments as well.) For the most part, I do not abbreviate words.
(The only exceptions are commonplace abbreviations like i for a counter and str
for a string.) This way a non-English speaker (and most programmers—even the
ones who were born in the U.S. and educated in an American public school—fall into
that category) can look up the word in a dictionary if they don't know what it means.

In order to facilitate the spell-check process, I use underscores to separate
words. (All the spelling checkers I use treat underscores as punctuation.) I never

use the PascalStyleMungingTogetherOfWords that's mandated by the Java Language Specification (JLS). Not only does this style mess up my spelling checker, `itsVeryHardToReadAsWell`. Frankly, I think that a language specification has no business mandating formatting conventions; it should restrict itself to defining the grammar and syntax of the language. If the Java specification really requires the use of munged-together names, it should not permit an underscore in an identifier. As an added advantage to using underscores, you can tell at a glance which methods are yours and which ones are part of some *java.* * package (all of which used MungedTogetherNames).

I, of course, do use the standard conventions of upper-class initial letters in class names and lower case initial letters in method and variable names, and so forth.

Test Classes

Most of my classes contain a static inner class called `Test`, which contains a `main()` that runs a unit test on the class. To test the `Terminator`, for example, you'd execute the following line:

```
java com.holub.tools.Terminator\$Test
```

(Omit the backslash if you're using Windows.) Since the class file for the test class (*Terminator$Test.class*) is distinct from the one for the `Terminator` itself (*Terminator.class*), you can reduce the size of the final program simply by not putting the test class into the .jar file that you ship.

Inner Classes

I use inner classes heavily throughout the book. A program is simply easier to read and maintain if you define all symbols in the most restrictive scope possible. The same thinking that precludes you from moving your local variables out to class scope, should be applied to classes as well. They have no business being at package scope unless they're used by more than one class. That is, if some "helper" class is used only by one other class, the helper class should be defined as an inner class of the class that uses it. This way the package-level name space isn't cluttered with irrelevant class names. Function-scope and anonymous inner classes are better still, since the class-level namespace is also simplified.

Bear in mind that the `new` operator evaluates to a reference to the newly created object, so code like:

```
new Thread()
{
    public void run(){ /*...*/ }

}.start();
```

is both legal and reasonable (if you don't need to store the object reference). I'm both defining and creating a new instance of some anonymous class that extends Thread, and then sending the newly created object of that class a start() message.

Why Is suspend() Deprecated?

The implementation of wait() isn't an unmitigated disaster; at least it *does* release the monitor before waiting on the condition variable. You can see why this behavior is useful by considering the (now deprecated) suspend() method. The main problem with suspend() is that you can call it from within the monitor, but unlike wait(), it doesn't release the lock before it suspends the current thread. Consider the following code:

```
class Wrong extends Tread
{   //...
    public synchronized void take_a_nap()
    {   suspend();
    }

    public synchronized void wake_up()
    {   resume();
    }
}
```

Once a thread has entered take_a_nap(), all other threads will block on a call to wake_up() because they can't acquire the monitor—the first thread has gone into the bathroom, locked the door, and fallen into a drug-induced coma. This code provides another example of a nested-monitor lockout deadlock: Thread 1 is suspended waiting for another thread to resume it. Thread 2 is suspended waiting to acquire the mutex and enter the wake_up() method. The only way for Thread 1 to be reactivated is for Thread 2 to enter wake_up(). The only way for Thread 2 to enter wake_up() is for Thread 1 to exit take_a_nap(). Both threads are effectively suspended forever.

Solve the problem by using a different strategy for suspension:

```
class Right extends Thread
{   public synchronized void take_a_nap()
    {   try
        {   wait();
        }
        catch(InterruptedException e)
        {
            /*do something reasonable*/}
        }
```

```
        }
        public synchronized void wake_up()
        {    notify();
        }
    }
```

The lock is released by wait() before the thread is suspended, and the lock is reacquired before the wait() returns, so a second thread can now get into wake_up() to call notify(). Note, however, that releasing the lock may not be a good thing. If the object is in an unstable state—if it's been partially modified—then another thread *can* access the object while the first thread is waiting. That is, a wait()/notify() strategy doesn't behave identically to suspend()/resume(), so simply replacing one with the other in existing code might give you surprising results. Be careful.

A related issue is sleep() and yield(), neither of which give up locks while the thread is suspended. If you want to give up a lock while you're sleeping, use

```
Object lock = new Object;
lock.wait( 1000 );            // sleep for 1000 milliseconds
```

instead of sleep(1000) since a notify() is never sent to the lock object, the wait() effectively suspends the current thread until the timeout expires. You can use the same strategy (but with a shorter timeout) for a lock-releasing yield operation.

Deadlock on a Blocking I/O Operation

In the case of wait(), it's at least *possible* to detect a timeout or terminate the wait with an interrupt() call. Unfortunately, the interrupt() call doesn't work with any of the blocking I/O operations, which are after all, waiting as well. This means that you can't use the Terminator strategy to abort a blocking I/O operation. In fact, there's no way to break out of any blocking I/O call short of a pathological abort. This flaw in Java compounds the problems of nested-monitor lockout because it becomes very difficult to break out of the nested monitor using a simple timeout strategy.

Consider the code in Listing 2.5. The code on lines 12 to 25 creates a thread that fires up a server-side socket and then sits on it: A client connection is established, but no data is ever sent to the client. Down on line 35, a client-side socket is created and connected to the server-side socket. A second thread is then created to read from that client-side socket (on line 42). This thread blocks on the read, since the server never writes anything.

The interesting code is line 59, which does absolutely nothing. The reading thread continues to block on the read even though the thread has, in theory, been interrupted. The only way to break out of the read() (other than dumping some data down the socket) is to close the input stream (which I do on line 61). Closing the stream, however, causes read() to throw an IOException rather than returning normally. You could also close the Socket object directly rather than the associated stream.

Admittedly, this particular example could be reimplemented, passing the Socket object a setSoTimeout() message that would cause the read() to time out if no data is retrieved within a predetermined interval, but that reworking wouldn't solve the problem of a read operation blocked on standard input or a UNIX named pipe—it's not a general solution.

Listing 2.5: /text/books/threads/ch2/Io_block.java

```
01: import java.net.*;
02: import java.io.*;
03: import com.holub.tools.Std;
04:
05: public class Io_block
06: {
07:     public Io_block()
08:     {
09:         // Create a Server thread that opens a server-side
10:         // socket and just sits on it.
11:
12:         Thread server = new Thread()
13:         {   public void run( )
14:             {   try
15:                 {   ServerSocket server = new ServerSocket(9999);
16:                     Socket client = server.accept();
17:                     synchronized(this){ wait(); }
18:                 }
19:                 catch(Exception e)
20:                 {   Std.out().println( e.getMessage() );
21:                     return;
22:                 }
23:             }
24.         };
25:         server.start();
26:
27:         // Create a Client-side socket that reads from the
28:         // Server-side socket. Then create a thread that
29:         // attempts to read from the client-side socket.
30:         // I expect this thread to block since the server
31:         // never writes anything.
32:
```

```
33:          try
34:          {   Thread.currentThread().sleep( 5 );
35:              Socket socket = new Socket("localhost", 9999);
36:              final InputStream in = socket.getInputStream();
37:
38:              Thread client = new Thread()
39:              {   public void run()
40:                  {
41:                      try
42:                      {   in.read();
43:                      }
44:                      catch(Exception e)
45:                      {   Std.out().println("-------------------");
46:                          Std.out().println("  READ  EXCEPTION ");
47:                          Std.out().println("-------------------");
48:                          e.printStackTrace();
49:                      }   Std.out().println("-------------------");
50:
51:                  }
52:              };
53:              client.start();
54:
55:
56:              // The client is now blocked, waiting for the server
57:              // thread to write something (which it never does).
58:
59:              client.interrupt(); // This operation blocks forever
60:
61:              in.close();         // This operation causes read() to
62:                                  // return with an I/O exception.
63:          }
64:          catch(Exception e)
65:          {   Std.out().println( e.getMessage() );
66:              return;
67:          }
68:      }
69:
70:      public static void main( String[] args )
71:      {   new Io_block();
72:      }
73: }
```

Stopping Threads

Stopping a thread in an orderly way also turns out to be a procedure fraught with difficulty. Java used to define a stop() message that could be sent to a Thread object, but stop() has been deprecated for a couple of reasons:

NT leaves dynamic-link libraries (DLLs), including some system DLLs, in an unstable state when threads are stopped externally. (The DLL's equivalent to main() isn't called, and it should be). This behavior has always been mysterious to me since it seems to be by design; I can't for the life of me figure out why you'd want to render the OS inoperative by shutting down a thread.

In all operating systems, not just NT, the thread is stopped rather abruptly— in the middle of doing whatever it does—and *all* the monitors held by the stopped thread are released. For example, a thread could call a synchronized method which, in turn, calls a synchronized method on a second object, thereby holding two monitors at once—one for each object—and both of these monitors are released by stop(). (Somebody can be in several bathrooms at the same time, in this model.) These objects might be in an "unstable" (partially modified) state when stop() is executed; the thread might be halfway done modifying the state of an object. The modification process is simply abandoned at that point, not completed in an orderly way. The object itself is not destroyed by the stop() request, though, so it might now be both accessible and in an invalid state. Consequently, other threads can access the partially modified (and now unlocked) object, with disastrous results.

The only solution to this problem is to explicitly code a stop mechanism into your thread. Instead of this:

```
class Wrong
{
    private Thread t = new Thread()
                        {   public void run()
                            {   while( true )
                                {   //...
                                    blocking_call();
                                }
                            }
                        };

    public stop(){ t.stop(); }
}
```

do this:

```
class Right
{   private Thread t =  new Thread()
                    {   public void run()
                        {   try
                            {   while( !isInterrupted() )
                                { //...
                                    blocking_call();
                                }
                            }catch(InterruptedException e)
                            {/*ignore*/}
                        }
                    };

  public stop(){ t. interrupt() ;}
}
```

I'll discuss these issues in greater depth in Chapter 5.

Of course, an object of the Terminator class discussed earlier can interrupt the thread as easily the stop() method.

Starvation and Synchronizing run()

The final commonplace threading problem that I need to mention is *starvation*— the situation where a schedulable thread never gets a chance to execute.

The most common form of starvation occurs when a low-priority thread never runs because there is always some higher-priority thread waiting in the wings when the scheduler wakes up. This behavior is often deliberate, however (as in a screen saver).

A more insidious example (read: bug) of starvation occurs when a thread can't acquire a lock, even though another thread releases it. Consider the following code:

```
public class Gourmand extends Thread
{
    private static Object lock = new Object();

    public void run()
    {   while(true)
        {   synchronized( lock )
            {   //do stuff
            }
```

```
            }
        }
}

public class Test
{   public static void main( String[] args )
    {   new Gourmand().start();
        new Gourmand().start();
    }
}
```

Threads are typically rescheduled in preemptive systems only when the system timer ticks or an I/O operation completes. In the foregoing code, the timer can tick at any time, but for the running Gourmand thread to be preempted by the second Gourmand thread, the preempting thread has to acquire the mutex associated with lock. The mutex is only released by the Gourmand for a few microseconds, though—for the time required to execute the single goto instruction that jumps us back up to the top of the loop. If the timer tick doesn't happen during the execution of that goto instruction, the second instance of the Gourmand thread can't run because it can't acquire the lock, so it's effectively starved.

The general solution is to insert an occasional yield() call (or execute a blocking operation like wait() or read()) into your loops:

```
for( int i = 1000000; --i >= 0; )
{   // do stuff

    if( i % 1000 == 0 )                  // yield every 1000 iterations
        Thread.currentThread().yield();
}
```

Any locks that you hold should probably be released before yielding. I could fix the earlier code as follows:

```
public void run()
{   while(true)
    {   synchronized( lock )
        {   //do stuff
        }
        yield();    // yield after releasing the mutex
    }
}
```

As a final pathological example of the starvation problem, consider this code:

```
public class My_pathological_thread extends Thread
{
    static String lock = "";

    public void run()
    {   synchronized( lock )
        {   while(true)
                //do stuff
        }
    }
}
```

A second, equal-priority, thread that is executing the same code can never get control since the lock is never released. The foregoing code is effectively identical to the following:

```
public class My_pathological_thread extends Thread
{
    public synchronized void run()
    {   while(true)
            //do stuff
    }

    public synchronized foo()
    {   //...
    }
}
```

All threads that call foo() are effectively blocked until run() returns (which it never does). Though you could exploit this behavior to write a method that effectively waits until run() terminates, the Thread class's join() method is a much better way to accomplish the same thing. Never synchronize run.

It's important to think about starvation even in methods of classes that do not extend Thread or Runnable, since your method could be called from a thread without you knowing it.

The **volatile** Keyword

As I mentioned earlier, assignment to variables that are 32 bits or smaller is thread safe, and you typically want write your code to leverage this behavior whenever possible to avoid unnecessary synchronization overhead. Problems can occasionally arise when your focus is too narrow, however. Consider this code:

```
class Example
{   private boolean greetings_have_been_exchanged = false;

    public void hello()
    {   greetings_have_been_exchanged = true;
    }

    public synchronized void wait_for_greeting()
    {
        greetings_have_been_exchanged = false;

        // another thread might call `hello()` here.

        if( greetings_have_been_exchanged )
        {
            // another thread did call hello(). Unfortunately,
            // code that's placed here may not be executed.
        }
    }
}
```

A superficial inspection tells us that hello() doesn't have to be synchronized because the only thing that it does is modify a boolean, and this modification is guaranteed to be atomic. The problem is in wait_for_greeting(). The JVM is likely to look at this code, notice that greetings_have_been_exchanged is set to false, never modified, and is then tested. The JVM's optimizer will assume that the code in the if statement is "dead"—that it can't possibly be executed since the test always fails, and eliminate it altogether. If you are expecting that some other thread might call hello() after the value is set to false in wait_for_greeting(), but before the value is tested, then you've got problems.

Solve this problem with the volatile keyword, which tells the optimizer that the value of greetings_have_been_exchanged might be changed by another thread at any time. Redefine the field as follows:

```
private volatile boolean greetings_have_been_exchanged = false;
```

The volatile keyword effectively turns off certain optimizations on expressions involving the volatile variable.

Exceptions and Threads

The final "gotcha" I want to mention in the current chapter is related to exceptions and threads. In particular, an exception that is not caught by a thread's run() method will indeed terminate the thread (with a printed stack trace), but it will not terminate the program. For example, the following code prints the string "above", fires off a thread that does nothing but throw an exception, waits for a few milliseconds to give the thread a chance to run, and then prints the string "below".

```
public class Exception_test
{
    public static void main(String[] args) throws InterruptedException
    {
        System.out.println("above");

        new Thread()
        {   public void run()
            {   throw new RuntimeException("Hello world");
            }
        }.start();

        Thread.currentThread().sleep( 250 );
        System.out.println("below");
    }
}
```

The following is printed when the program executes:

```
above
java.lang.RuntimeException: Hello world
        at Exception_test$1.run(Exception_test.java: 9)
below
```

There are, to my mind, two main problems with this behavior. First of all the stack trace will be incomprehensible to your average user (and may not even be visible if the application displays a graphical UI and no console window.) Second, the thread has terminated, but nobody knows it, so the program might now be unstable.

Now consider the somewhat modified version of this code in Listing 2.6. The thread normally synchronizes with the outer class by issuing a notify(), which matches the wait() on line 27. However, if the exception is thrown, the thread is terminated without issuing the notify(), and wait() never returns. Moreover, the test() method is still holding the lock it acquired on entry, so any thread that calls a synchronized method of the Exception_test class after the exception is thrown will block forever. This behavior is a variant on nested-monitor lockout, and obviously can be a problem when an exception is thrown by a thread that holds a roll-your-own lock, such as the ones I'll be discussing later in the book, or when one thread is waiting to be notified by another. Note that throwing an exception from inside a synchronized block *is* safe, however. The lock is released when you exit the synchronized block during the toss.

Listing 2.6: Exception_test.java

```
01: public class Exception_test
02: {
03:     private boolean some_condition = false;
04:     private Thread  the_thread    -
05:             new Thread()
06:             {   public void run()
07:                 {
08:                     if( some_condition )
09:                         throw new RuntimeException("Hello world");
10:
11:                     synchronized( Exception_test.this )
12:                     {   Exception_test.this.notify();
13:                     }
14:                 }
15:             };
16:
17:     public static void main(String[] args) throws InterruptedException
18:     {   Exception_test test = new Exception_test();
19:         test.test();
20:     }
21:
22:     public synchronized void test() throws InterruptedException
23:     {
24:         System.out.println("above");
25:         some_condition = true;
26:         the_thread.start();
27:         wait();
28:
29:         System.out.println("below");
30:     }
31:
32:     //...
33: }
```

Conclusion

Hopefully, I've demonstrated by now that programming in a multithreaded environment isn't as easy as the evangelist types would have you believe. Java provides platform-independent ways to use the two essential synchronization mechanisms: exclusion semaphores and condition variables. It does it in an awkward way, however, that doesn't help much when you're trying to do more than blink your logo in a simple applet. Nonetheless, all is not lost. The rest of this book presents a library of classes that solve many common threading problems, including some of the ones I've just discussed. I'll also discuss architectural solutions to many of these problems.

CHAPTER 3

The Mutex
and Lock Management

IN THE PREVIOUS TWO CHAPTERS, I focused on the pitfalls of writing multithreaded applications in Java. With this chapter, I'll show you a few solutions to the problems. I'll start out with a look at a roll-your-own mutex class that is easier to use than synchronized in some situations. In particular, it allows you to specify a timeout so that you won't have to wait forever to acquire a lock (as compared to synchronized, which provides no timeout facility). We'll also look at a lock manager class that lets you safely acquire multiple semaphores without deadlocking. Using objects of these classes rather than the built-in synchronized can save you hours of searching for unexpected deadlocks, and though these classes don't solve every possible deadlock problem, they're still pretty useful.

When **synchronized** Isn't Good Enough

There are two main problems with Java's synchronized mechanism. First, no timeout facility is supported—your threads have to wait forever to acquire the mutex. If you could specify a timeout, you could at least report a deadlock at run time if some thread has to wait an unreasonable amount of time to acquire a lock, but the synchronized keyword doesn't give you that option. Next, the object-level granularity of synchronized is simply too coarse for some situations: There is only one monitor per object, and sometimes that's not enough. Consider the following class, whose methods can be broken up into three partitions:

1. The methods in the first partition use only a subset of the fields in the class.

2. The methods in the second partition use a nonoverlapping subset; they use fields that are not used by methods in the first partition.

3. The methods in the third partition use everything.

```
class Complicated         // NOT thread safe
{
    private long a, b;
    private long x, y;

    // partition 1, methods use a and/or b

    public void use_a()      { do_something_with(a);   ); }
    public void use_b()      { do_something_with(b);   ); }
    public void use_a_and_b(){ do_something_with(a+b); ); }

    // partition 2, methods use x and/or y

    public void use_x()      { do_something_with(x);   ); }
    public void use_y()      { do_something_with(y);   ); }
    public void use_x_and_y(){ do_something_with(x+y); ); }

    // partition 3, methods use a, b, x, and y

    public void use_everything()
    {   do_something_with( a + x );
    }

    public void use_everything_else()
    {   do_something_with( b + y );
    }
}
```

As it stands, this code is a multithreading disaster. Nothing is synchronized, and we have guaranteed race conditions. (In a "race condition," you'll remember, two threads try to access the same object at the same time, and chance determines which one wins the race. Programs shouldn't work by chance.) A single-lock solution—synchronizing all the methods—would fix the problem, but then you couldn't call a method in partition 1 of the foregoing code just because some thread was using a method from partition 2. Since these two partitions don't interact with each other, the single-lock solution imposes needless access restrictions on the methods of the class. If you're accessing any method in partition 3, though, you really do want to lock out everything in the other two partitions. We really need two locks in this situation: one to lock partition-1 variables and another for partition-2 variables. The methods in partition 3 must grab both locks.

Handling Granularity with **synchronized**

The easiest way to solve the too-coarse granularity problem is by synchronizing on something other than the containing object. Rather than synchronizing the methods, you can define two local variables to use as locks and synchronize on them:

```
class Complicated_and_thread_safe
{
    private long a, b;
    private long x, y;

    private Object ab_lock = new Object();
    private Object xy_lock = new Object();

    // partition 1, functions use a and/or b

    public void use_a()      { synchronized(ab_lock){ /*...*/ } }
    public void use_b()      { synchronized(ab_lock){ /*...*/ } }
    public void use_a_and_b(){ synchronized(ab_lock){ /*...*/ } }

    // partition 2, functions use x and/or y

    public void use_x()      { synchronized(xy_lock){ /*...*/ } }
    public void use_y()      { synchronized(xy_lock){ /*...*/ } }
    public void use_x_and_y(){ synchronized(xy_lock){ /*...*/ } }

    // partition 3, functions use a, b, x, and y

    public void use_everything()
    {   synchronized(ab_lock)        // grab both locks
        {   synchronized(xy_lock)
            {   /*...*/
            }
        }
    }

    public void use_everything_else()
    {   synchronized(ab_lock)
        {   synchronized(xy_lock)
            {   /*...*/
            }
        }
    }
}
```

I have not synchronized the methods themselves in this example. (Remember, synchronizing a method is effectively the same thing as wrapping all the code in the method in a `synchronized(this){...}` block.) Instead, I'm providing a unique lock for each partition (`ab_lock` and `xy_lock`) and then explicitly synchronizing on these individual locks.

Java associates locks with objects (instance of some class that extends `Object`, so I can't use primitive-type variables as locks here. I don't want to spend unnecessary time calling constructors and doing other initialization operations on complicated objects, however. Consequently, the locks themselves are declared as the simplest possible object—an actual instance of the `Object` class (`Object` is not abstract).

In the foregoing example, it is *critical* that methods that acquire both locks always acquire them in the same order, otherwise we end up in the Wilma/Betty deadlock scenario discussed in Chapter 2. Acquiring multiple locks is a common enough problem that some operating systems have system calls for this purpose. It would be nice to have an easy way to acquire multiple locks in Java, without having to worry about the order of acquisition. The remainder of this chapter describes one way to do that.

Roll Your Own Semaphores: The **Semaphore** Interface

Listing 3.1 shows the core interface that I use for all my roll-your-own semaphore classes: the `Semaphore`. It's in the *com.holub.asynch* package, as are all the thread-related classes and interfaces that I'll be discussing.

Remember from Chapter 1 that a "semaphore" is any of various classes of objects that let two threads synchronize with each other in a predictable way. A semaphore has to have two properties to be useful:

1. It must be able to identify itself using a unique ID. The current implementation uses a unique integer for this purpose. The interface represents this requirement with the `id()` method (Listing 3.1, line 7).

2. You must be able to acquire and release the semaphore, though the semantic meaning of "acquire" and "release" can vary, depending on what sort of semaphore you're dealing with.

I've defined one symbolic constant—`Semaphore.FOREVER` (Listing 3.1, line 5). All implementations of `acquire(...)` (Listing 3.1, line 9) should treat a timeout of 0 as a request to not wait at all, but simply return `false` if the resource isn't available. Pass `Semaphore.FOREVER` as a timeout when you want to wait forever. (You'll actually wait about 292,271,023 years, but that's close enough to "forever" for me.)

The `Semaphore` interface also defines two inner classes (interfaces can contain `public static` classes in Java). Objects of the `Timed_out` class can be thrown when a semaphore times out—when a predetermined amount of time elapses and you still haven't acquired a lock, for example. Objects of class Ownership can be thrown when an object that doesn't own a mutex-like semaphore tries to release it. Unlike synchronized, my roll-your-own mutex supports a timeout. Semaphore.Timed_out is an inner class because you'll use it only in situations where you are also using Semaphore. Making Timed_out an inner class pulls it out of the package-level (global) name space so the symbol could be used for some other purpose in code that doesn't use Semaphore. Note that Timed_out extends RuntimeException, so you don't have to catch it if you don't want to.

Listing 3.1: /src/com/holub/asynch/Semaphore.java

```
01: package com.holub.asynch;
02:

    /*********************************************************************

        The implementers of the semaphore class can all be
        used by the  Lock_manager (which lets you synchronize
        several semaphores at once without worrying about
        common deadlock scenarios).

        ...............................................................

                        © 2000, Allen I. Holub
        This code may not be distributed by yourself except in
        binary form, incorporated into a java .class file. You may
        use this code freely for personal purposes, but you may not
        incorporate it into any commercial product without the
        express written permission of Allen I. Holub.

        ...............................................................

        @author Allen I. Holub
    */

03: interface Semaphore
04: {
        /*********************************************
            A useful symbolic constant to pass as a timeout
            value. It effectively waits forever (actually it
            waits for only 292,271,023 years).
        */
```

```
05:      public static final long FOREVER = Long.MAX_VALUE;
06:

         /********************************************
         Return a unique integer ID for this object.

         */

07:      public int  id      ();
08:

         /********************************************
         Acquire the semaphore. In the case of a Mutex, for
         example, you would get ownership. In the case of a
         Counting_semaphore, you would decrement the count.
         @return false if the timeout is zero and the lock
         was not acquired. Otherwise returns true.
         @throws InterruptedException if the wait to acquire
         the lock was interrupted by another thread.
         @throws Semaphore.Timed_out if the timeout interval
         expires before the semaphore has been acquired.
         */

09:      public boolean acquire(long timeout) throws InterruptedException,
10:                                             Timed_out;
11:

         /********************************************
         Release the semaphore.

         */

12:      public void release();
13:
```

```
           /*********************************************
           Thrown in the event of an expired timeout.

           */

14:    public static final class Timed_out extends RuntimeException
15:    {   public Timed_out(){ super(
16:                     "Timed out while waiting to acquire semaphore"); }
17:        public Timed_out(String s){ super(s); }
18:    }
19:

           /*********************************************
           Thrown when a thread tries to release a semaphore
           illegally, e.g., a Mutex that it has not acquired
           successfully.
           */

20:    public static final class Ownership extends RuntimeException
21:    {   public Ownership(){ super(
22:                     "Calling Thread doesn't own Semaphore"); }
23:    }
24: }
```

Managing Semaphores and Deadlock-Resistant Locking

Any semaphore that implements Semaphore can be locked in groups using the
Lock_manager class shown in Listing 3.2.

The Lock_manager has three methods of interest:

1. The static new_id() method (Listing 3.2, line 13) returns a unique int every
    time it's called. This method is called by objects of the various classes that
    implement the Semaphore interface to get the value that they'll use for their ID.

2. Use the acquire_multiple(Semaphore[],long) method (Listing 3.2, line 32)
    to safely acquire groups of semaphores. Pass it an array of objects that
    implement Semaphore. It sorts the array by ID, and then acquires the sema-
    phores one at a time in ID order. Consistent acquisition of multiple
    semaphores in ID order effectively eliminates many deadlock scenarios.

3. The `acquire_multiple(Collection,long)` method (Listing 3.2, line 39) variant on the foregoing method locks a collection (rather than an array) of semaphores.

I've used the `Arrays.sort()` method—one of the new JDK 1.2 data-structure facilities—to actually do the sorting (on line 62).

Listing 3.2: /src/com/holub/asynch/Lock_manager.java

```
01: package com.holub.asynch;
02:
03: import com.holub.asynch.Semaphore;
04: import java.util.*;
05:
```

    /**
        The `Lock_manager` class helps manage groups of locks.
        It provides a way to safely (without deadlock)
        acquire all of a set of locks.

        ....

        © 2000, Allen I. Holub
        This code may not be distributed by yourself except in
        binary form, incorporated into a java .class file. You may
        use this code freely for personal purposes, but you may not
        incorporate it into any commercial product without the
        express written permission of Allen I. Holub.

        ....

        @author *Allen I. Holub*
    */

```
06: class Lock_manager
07: {
08:     private static  Object  id_lock = new int[]{0};
09:     private static  int     id_pool = 0;
10:
11:     private Lock_manager(){};   // Make sure it can't be instantiated
12:
```

```
        /**
            Return a unique integer ID. Used by implementers
            of Semaphore to get a value to return from their id() method.
         */

13:     public static int new_id( )        // I'm deliberately using a stand-
14:     {                                  // alone lock rather than
15:                                        // synchronizing new_id() because
16:         synchronized( id_lock ) {      // I don't want to prevent a call
17:             return id_pool++;    }     // to acquire_multiple() while
18:                                        // another thread is calling
19:                                        // new_id().
20:     }
21:


        /**
            The comparator used to sort arrays of locks into
            ID order.
         */

22:     private static final Comparator compare_strategy =
23:             new Comparator()
24:             {   public int compare(Object a, Object b)
25:                 {   return ((Semaphore)a).id() - ((Semaphore)b).id();
26:                 }
27:                 public boolean equals(Object obj)
28:                 {   return obj == this;
29:                 }
30:             };
31:


        /**
            This function returns once all of the locks in the
            incoming array have been successfully acquired.
            Locks are always acquired in ascending order of ID
            to attempt to avoid deadlock situations. If the
            acquire operation is interrupted, or if it times
            out, all the locks that have been acquired will be released.
```

@param *locks* All of these locks must be acquired
before `acquire_multiple` returns. Warning: It's your
job to make sure that the `locks` array is not modified
while `acquire_multiple()` is executing.
@param *timeout* Maximum time to wait to acquire each
lock (milliseconds). The total time for the multiple
acquire operation could be (timeout * locks.length).

```
     **/

32:    public static void acquire_multiple(Semaphore[] locks, long timeout)
33:                                           throws InterruptedException,
34:                                                  Semaphore.Timed_out
35:    {   acquire( locks, timeout );
36:    }
37:
38:

       /**

           Just like acquire_multiple(Semaphore[],long),
           except that it takes a collection argument rather
           than an array argument.

        */

39:    public static void acquire_multiple(Collection semaphores,long timeout)
40:                                            throws InterruptedException,
41:                                                   Semaphore.Timed_out
42:    {   acquire( semaphores.toArray(), timeout);
43:    }
44:

       /**

           Actually do the acquisition here. The main reason
           this work can't be done in acquire_multiple() is
           that the toArray() method called in the Collection
           version returns an array of Object, and you can't
           cast an array of Object into an array of Semaphore.

        */
```

```
45:      private static void acquire( Object[] locks, long timeout )
46:                                          throws InterruptedException,
47:                                                 Semaphore.Timed_out
48:      {
49:          int current_lock = 0;
50:
51:          try
52:          {
53:              // It's potentially dangerous to work directly on the locks
54:              // array rather than on a copy. I didn't want to incur the
55:              // overhead of making a copy, however.
56:
57:              long expiration = (timeout == Semaphore.FOREVER)
58:                                  ? Semaphore.FOREVER
59:                                  : System.currentTimeMillis() + timeout;
60:                                  ;
61:
62:              Arrays.sort(locks, compare_strategy );
63:              for(; current_lock < locks.length; ++current_lock )
64:              {
65:                  long time_remaining =
66:                                  expiration - System.currentTimeMillis();
67:                  if( time_remaining <= 0 )
68:                      throw new Semaphore.Timed_out(
69:                          "Timed out waiting to acquire multiple locks");
70:
71:                  ((Semaphore)locks[current_lock]).acquire(time_remaining);
72:              }
73:          }
74:          catch( InterruptedException exception )
75:          {   // Interrupted while trying to acquire locks[current_lock]
76:              // Release all locks up to (but not including)
77:              // locks[current_lock];
78:
79:              while( --current_lock >= 0 )
80:                  ((Semaphore)locks[current_lock]).release();
81:              throw exception;
82:          }
83:          catch( Semaphore.Timed_out exception )
84:          {   // Timed out just before attempting to acquire
85:              // locks[current_lock]. Release all locks up to (but
86:              // not including) locks[current_lock];
87:
88:              while( --current_lock >= 0 )
89:                  ((Semaphore)locks[current_lock]).release();
90:              throw exception;
91:          }
92:      }
93: }
```

A Digression: Booch Utilities and Strategy

Digressing for a moment, the Arrays class is a "Booch utility"—a class that contains nothing but static methods. Utilities typically do not have state—they don't contain fields. They are really just ways to define global functions. The *java.lang.Math* class is an example.

The problem in Java is neither arrays nor primitive types are true objects. If they were, they would contain all the methods needed to manipulate them. For example, you would be able to find a cosine using:

```
double x = PI;
x.cosine();
```

You'd be able to extend double, and so forth. Java compensates for this deficiency with the java.lang.Math class. Math is a "Utility" class—a class comprised solely of static methods. Utilities are effectively ways to get global level functions in OO systems. (I'm deliberately not using the word "method" here—the members of a Utility are just plain old functions.) Utilities, then, are typically kludges that make up for some flaw in the language or some flaw in the design of a class.

The Lock_manager, though it's made up solely of static methods, is not a Utility since it does contain state information—the current ID. It is an example of the Gang-of-Four *Singleton* pattern—a true object, only one instance of which may exist. Because the information required to initialize the Lock_manager is all available at compile time, this particular Singleton is easily implemented by making everything static. The Lock_manager is a true object—it has both state and behavior. The line between a class and an object in Java is very fine indeed.

Arrays, like primitive types, aren't real classes (even though they do extend Object), so a Utility is required to make up for the design problems. You ought to be able to sort an array by asking it to sort itself, like this:

```
int array[] = new int[];
//...
array.sort();
```

No such luck.

You use the Arrays utility to supply the sort operation to the array. For example, you'd sort an array of int as follows:

```
int array[] = new int[];
//...
Arrays.sort( array );
```

The problem is complicated a bit by arrays of objects of some arbitrary class. How can a generic sort utility figure out the correct ordering of the array elements? The Object class contains an equals() function, but we'd need a greater_than() as well to do sorting.

The Strategy Pattern

To the rescue comes the Gang-of-Four *Strategy* pattern. The notion is to pass into a method or object another object that encapsulates the strategy needed to do something. There are lots of examples of Strategy in Java. A java.awt.LayoutManager, for example, encapsulates the strategy that a Frame uses for laying itself out. You can change the layout simply by changing this strategy. You don't have to define a new kind of Frame class using derivation or some other mechanism. This, in turn, makes Frame much more reusable since the behavior of a Frame can be changed without changing any of the code that comprises Frame.

The Arrays utility uses the Strategy pattern to define a comparison strategy. In Listing 3.2, the inner-class compare_strategy (Listing 3.2, line 22) field defines the comparison strategy by implementing the new (to JDK 1.2) java.util.Comparator interface and its compare() method [which works like C's strcmp(): it returns a negative number, zero, or a positive number depending on whether a is less than, equal to, or greater than b]. An instance of the Comparator is passed to the Arrays.sort() method like this:

```
Arrays.sort(locks, new Lock_comparator() );
```

The Lock_comparator object's compare() method is called by Arrays.sort() when the sort() method needs to compare objects. C programmers will recognize this approach as very similar to that of qsort(), which is passed a pointer to a compare method—another example of Strategy.

End of digression.

Implementing a Manageable Mutex Class

Let's move on and look at the other side of the locking equation: a class that implements a semaphore. The Mutex class in Listing 3.3 implements a simple mutual-exclusion semaphore that corrects some of the problems in Java's implementation of synchronized. Whether it makes sense to use it (as compared to synchronizing on a lock object, as I did earlier) really depends on the situation. The main advantages of the Mutex over synchronized are the ability to specify a timeout value and the ability to use the Lock_manager.acquire_multiple() method to acquire several mutexes without worrying about an order-of-acquisition deadlock.

You use a Mutex as follows:

```
Mutex lock = new Mutex();

lock.acquire( 10000 );  // 10-second timeout
try
{
    // guarded code goes here.
}
finally
{   lock.release()
}
```

to approximate the functionality of:

```
synchronized( lock )
{    // guarded code goes here.
}
```

The only functional difference is the timeout. It is important, by the way, to use try/finally to guarantee that the lock is released even if an exception is thrown from the guarded code. Also note that the acquire() call is outside the try block. You don't want to release the lock if you never acquired it.

Looking at the implementation, the Mutex class (Listing 3.3, line 8) starts out with the stuff needed to keep the Lock_manager happy. It implements the Semaphore interface with an id() method (Listing 3.3, line 14) that returns the value of the _id field, which in turn holds a unique value that comes from the Lock_manager.

There are two flavors of the acquire method: acquire(long) itself (Listing 3.3, line 16) and acquire_without_blocking() (Listing 3.3, line 48). The latter simply returns false if it can't acquire the mutex. If the mutex isn't owned, then it sets owner to reference the thread that called acquire_without_blocking() with the call to Thread.currentThread(), which does the obvious. The blocking version, acquire(), calls the nonblocking version and suspends itself with a wait() call if it can't get the mutex right off the bat. Note the use of a "spin lock" on line 24. (I discussed spin locks in Chapter 2.) The wait() call is inside a loop in case some other thread breaks in at an inopportune moment and gets ownership.

Interestingly, the Mutex code doesn't actually use the Mutex object's monitor to implement the lock [though it does use the monitor to make sure that two threads don't try to acquire the same mutex simultaneously. acquire() and release() are synchronized]. A local field called owner (Listing 3.3, line 10) is used to decide whether or not to block out an acquiring thread. The owner field references the Thread instance that contains the run() method for a given thread. If owner is null, then the mutex is up for grabs, otherwise, some thread owns the mutex and any other thread that tries to acquire it will block at the wait() call in acquire().

My Mutex class—as is the case with the mutex used by synchronized— implements a *recursive* mutex. The owner thread can acquire the mutex more than once, but it must release the mutex by calling release() as many times as it acquired it by calling acquire(). This facility is essential when two methods both must acquire the mutex. In the following code, for example, g() calls f(), but f() can also be called from outside—without going through g() first. If the mutex were not recursive, the thread that called g() would block when g() called f() and tried to acquire the mutex a second time. As it is, the double acquisition isn't a problem since every acquire() has a corresponding release(). The lock_count field keeps track of the number of times the mutex has been locked by its owner. The same problem arises in Java when one synchronized method calls another.

```
class some_class
{   Mutex lock = new Mutex();

    public void f()
    {   lock.acquire();
        //...
        lock.release();
    }

    public void g()
    {   lock.acquire();
        //...
        f();
        //...
        lock.release();
    }
}
```

Listing 3.3: /src/com/holub/asynch/Mutex.java

```
01: package com.holub.asynch;
02:
03: import com.holub.asynch.Semaphore;
04:
05: import com.holub.tools.Assert;          // import one or the other of
06: // import com.holub.tools.debug.Assert; // these, but not both.
07:
```

```
    /**
```
Implementation of a mutual-exclusion semaphore. It can
be owned by only one thread at a time. The thread can
acquire it multiple times, but there must be a release
for every acquire.

© 2000, Allen I. Holub
*This code may not be distributed by yourself except in
binary form, incorporated into a java .class file. You may
use this code freely for personal purposes, but you may not
incorporate it into any commercial product without the
express written permission of Allen I. Holub.*

@author *Allen I. Holub*
```
    */
```

```
08: public final class Mutex implements Semaphore
09: {
10:     private Thread  owner       = null;// Owner of mutex, null if nobody
11:     private int     lock_count = 0;
12:
13:     private final int _id   = Lock_manager.new_id();
14:     public       int id()  {   return _id;          }
15:
```

```
    /**
```
Acquire the mutex. The mutex can be acquired multiple
times by the same thread, provided that it is
released as many times as it is acquired. The calling
thread blocks until it has acquired the mutex. (There
is no timeout).

@param *timeout* If 0, then the behavior of this
function is identical to `acquire_without_blocking`.
If timeout is nonzero, then the timeout is the the
maximum amount of time that you'll wait (in milliseconds). Use `Semaphore.FOREVER` to wait forever.
@return *false* If the timeout was 0 and you did not
acquire the lock. True otherwise.
@throw *InterruptedException* If the waiting thread is
interrupted before the timeout expires.
@throw *Semaphore.Timed_out* If the specified time elapses
before the mutex on which we are waiting is released.
@see *#release*
@see *#acquire_without_blocking*

```
        */

16:     public synchronized boolean acquire( long timeout )
17:                                     throws InterruptedException,
18:                                         Semaphore.Timed_out
19:     {
20:         if( timeout == 0 )
21:         {   return acquire_without_blocking();
22:         }
23:         else if( timeout == FOREVER )                // wait forever
24:         {   while( !acquire_without_blocking() )
25:                 this.wait( FOREVER );
26:         }
27:         else                                // wait limited by timeout
28:         {
29:             long expiration = System.currentTimeMillis() + timeout;
30:             while( !acquire_without_blocking() )
31:             {   long time_remaining =
32:                             expiration - System.currentTimeMillis();
33:                 if( time_remaining <= 0 )
34:                     throw new Semaphore.Timed_out(
35:                                     "Timed out waiting for Mutex");
36:
37:                 this.wait( time_remaining );
38:             }
39:         }
40:         return true;
41:     }
```

```
42:
```

```
        /**
                A convenience method, effectively waits forever.
                Actually waits for 0x7fffffffffffffff milliseconds
                (approximately 292,271,023 years), but that's close
                enough to forever for me.
        */
```

```
43:     public void acquire() throws InterruptedException,
44:                                         Semaphore.Timed_out
45:     {   acquire( FOREVER );
46:     }
47:
```

```
        /**
                Attempts to acquire the mutex. Returns false (and
                does not block) if it can't get it.
                @return true if you get the mutex, false otherwise.
                @see #release
                @see #acquire
        */
```

```
48:     private boolean acquire_without_blocking()
49:     {
50:         Thread current = Thread.currentThread();
51:
52:         if( owner == null )
53:         {   owner = current;
54:             lock_count = 1;
55:         }
56:         else if( owner == current )
57:         {   ++lock_count;
58:         }
59:
60:         return owner == current;
61:     }
62:
```

```
      /**
            Release the mutex. The mutex has to be released as
            many times as it was acquired to actually unlock
            the resource. The mutex must be released by the
            thread that acquired it.
            @throws Semaphore.Ownership (a RuntimeException) if
            a thread other than the current owner tries to release
            the mutex. Also thrown if somebody tries to release a
            mutex that's not owned by any thread.
      */

63:    public synchronized void release()
64:    {
65:        if( owner != Thread.currentThread() )
66:            throw new Semaphore.Ownership();
67:
68:        if( --lock_count <= 0 )
69:        {   owner = null;
70:            notify();
71:        }
72:    }
73: }
```

Conclusion

So that's a simple roll-your-own semaphore. Though it's easy enough to use Java's synchronized statement directly to do most of what the Mutex does, the Mutex class gives you a timeout facility, and the associated Lock_manager can solve a class of otherwise hard-to-manage deadlock problems.

CHAPTER 4

Condition Variables and Counting Semaphores

THIS CHAPTER INTRODUCES two more semaphores and rounds out the set of basic synchronization objects that you'll need to get real work done. Like the Mutex I presented in Chapter 3, these classes duplicate the abilities of the Java language to some extent, but like the Mutex, I've fixed some problems (and added some capabilities) with the Java language implementations. I'll look at two classes: (1) a condition variable that adds to wait() the ability to not wait when the event you're waiting for has already taken place, and (2) a counting semaphore that lets you control a pool of resources without sucking up machine cycles in polling loops.

Condition Variables

I've brought up "condition variables" before in the context of wait() and notify(). The central concept is that a thread will wait until some condition becomes true. For example, a thread may need to wait for somebody to push a button before proceeding with some action, or a thread may be waiting for something to appear in an empty queue (for the queue-not-empty condition to become true).

Waiting for the Electrician (or Somebody Like Him): Condition Variables vs. wait()

I'll demonstrate why you need a condition variable with a classic Java-GUI problem: "How do I wait efficiently for some AWT event to occur?" Remember, AWT (and all the listeners) runs on its own thread. The main body of your application typically runs on another thread, however. Consider the following code, which sets up a simple TextField and an ActionListener that is notified when the user types the *Enter* key:

```
01: class Some_class extends Frame
02: {
03:     TextField input = new TextField();
04:     String    entered = "";
05:
```

```
06:     public The_wrong_way()
07:     {   input.addActionListener
08:         (   new ActionListener()
09:             {   public void actionPerformed( ActionEvent e )
10:                 {   entered = input.getText();
11:                 }
12:             }
13:         );
14:
15:         add(input);
16:         pack();
17:         show();
18:     }
19:
20:     String read_line()
21:     {   String value = entered;
22:         entered = "";
23:         return value;
24:     }
25:     //...
26: }
```

So far, so good, but let's look at the situation in more detail. When you display the Frame, AWT fires up a thread that monitors all events coming in from the operating system, including key-press events. When the *Enter* key is pressed, for example, the AWT thread gets the key-press event from the OS and, in turn, calls the listener's actionPerformed() method. The actionPerformed() messages are coming in asynchronously from the AWT event-loop thread. Put another way: the actionPerformed() method is actually running on that AWT thread.

Meanwhile, a user thread (as differentiated from the AWT thread)—perhaps the one that main() is running on—calls read_line() to find out what the user has typed. That read_line() call is running on the user thread, not the AWT thread, so it returns immediately—it doesn't wait for a new string to arrive. Meanwhile, the user thread has modified entered to an empty string to indicate that the string has been read. Both the AWT and the user thread can access the entered field simultaneously though, so this is a classic race condition. The read_line() method can be preempted by the listener (running on the AWT thread) between lines 21 and 22, after assigning entered to value, but before entered is set to an empty string.

The resulting run-time sequence of instructions is effectively:

```
String value = entered;        // Runs on user thread
entered = input.getText();     // Runs on AWT thread
entered = "";                  // Runs on user thread.
```

Note that the opposite situation—the user thread calling read_line() while the AWT thread is in the middle of actionPerformed()—is not a synchronization problem because assignment to a reference is atomic in Java. The read_line() method might return an empty string even if there is text in the TextField, however.

In any event, the behavior of the system isn't really correct: I don't want
`read_line()` to return garbage if nothing has been entered—I want it to block until
there is something reasonable to read.

Now let's look at some solutions. The race-condition problem can be solved
with some synchronization:

```
class Some_class extends Frame
{
    TextField input = new TextField();
    String    entered = "";

    public Some_class()
    {   input.addActionListener
        (   new ActionListener()
            {   public void actionPerformed( ActionEvent e )
                {   synchronized( Some_class.this )
                    {   entered = input.getText();
                    }
                }
            }
        );

        add(input);
        pack();

        show();
    }

    String synchronized read_line()
    {   String value = entered; //#before
        entered = "";           //#after
        return value;
    }
    //...
}
```

The inner-class method must synchronize explicitly on the outer-class object—
the object that contains the data that is being accessed. Simply synchronizing
`actionPerformed()` doesn't work because you'll be synchronizing on the monitor
of the anonymous inner-class object, but the field you want to guard is in the
outer-class object.

Moving on to the I-don't-want-to-read-garbage problem, our user thread
needs to know *when* an entire line has been typed to be sure that `read_line()` will
return a complete line of input, but (and this is the big "but"), there is no direct
communication between the two threads involved in this transaction. The code
running on the AWT thread (`actionPerformed()`) doesn't tell the user thread that an
entire-line-has-been-typed event has occurred.

So how does the caller of read_line() know that the string has changed? One (hideously bad) solution is to sit in a tight polling loop, calling read_line() and checking the current return value against null:

```
class Some_class extends Frame
{   TextField input  = new TextField();
    String   entered;

    public Some_class()
    {   input.addActionListener
        (   new ActionListener()
            {   public void actionPerformed( ActionEvent e )
                {   synchronized( Some_class.this )
                    {   entered = input.getText();
                    }
                }
            }
        );
        add(input);
        pack();
        show();
    }
    String synchronized read_line()
    {   while( entered == null ) /*spin*/;     // UGH!
            return entered;
    }
    //...
}
```

This code is enormously wasteful of machine resources though. The time spent in that polling loop [the while statement in read_line()] is time better spent doing other tasks.

Send in the Cavalry: Using a Condition Variable

So what's the right way for two threads to communicate with each other (that's a rhetorical question)? Use a semaphore. Think Napoleon, flags, mountain tops. To the rescue comes a semaphore known as a *condition variable*. To rehash from previous chapters: The basic notion of a condition variable is that some thread waits (is suspended) on the condition variable until the condition that it represents becomes true. Every Java object has a condition variable built into it—in the same way that it has the mutex used to guard the monitor. You wait for the condition to become true by calling wait() and you set the condition true by calling notify(). (The notify() call doesn't work in quite this way—I'll talk more about this in a moment.) It's easy enough to do a roll-your-own condition variable that solves the current thread-communication problem by using wait() and notify(). Listing 4.1 demonstrates how to do this. An object that I'll use as a condition variable, called `text_has_been_entered` (we are going to wait for the text-has-been-entered condition to become true), is declared up at the top of the class definition. Roll-your-own locks of this sort are typically declared as actual instances of the `Object` class [created with `new Object()`] or are one-element arrays of some primitive type such as `int`. I've measured the creation time and found that the two alternatives are about par, though I wouldn't be surprised if the time required to create an `Object` was longer than the time required for an array in some JVMs.

The `actionPerformed()` method on line 14 doesn't read the text at all; it simply notifies the condition variable, setting the condition to "true." Note that Java requires you to "be in the monitor" for an object before you can call `wait()` or `notify()` on that object. (You must be holding the lock associated with the object, by being in either a `synchronized` function of that object's class or a stand-alone `synchronized` statement whose argument is the object on which you're synchronizing.) The `synchronized(text_has_been_entered)` statement on line 16 is mandatory, since entering the `synchronized` block puts us into the monitor of the object referenced by `text_has_been_entered`.

Meanwhile, the thread that calls `read_line()` is waiting for the condition to become true. When this happens, the new text value is read and returned. The `read_line()` method itself is `synchronized` so that two threads can't attempt to read the same line simultaneously. It's now possible to have a simple loop like the one in `main()`:

```
while( (input = source.read_line()) != null )
    System.out.println("Got: " + input );
```

which blocks until a new input line arrives.

Listing 4.1: /text/books/threads/ch4/Input_source.java

```
01: import java.awt.*;
02: import java.awt.event.*;
03:
04: public class Input_source extends Frame
05: {
06:     int[]   text_has_been_entered = new int[1]; // The condition variable
07:
08:     TextField input = new TextField();
09:
10:     public Input_source()
11:     {
12:         input.addActionListener
13:         (   new ActionListener()
14:             {   public void actionPerformed( ActionEvent e )
```

```
15:                     {
16:                         synchronized( text_has_been_entered )
17:                         {   text_has_been_entered.notify();  // set the condition true
18:                         }
19:                     }
20:                 }
21:             );
22:
23:         add(input);
24:         pack();
25:         show();
26:     }
27:
```

```
        /**
            A blocking function that works like readLine(),
            but gets its text from the current window's text
            area. The function doesn't return until sombody
            types a line of text, whereupon it returns the line.
            Returns null if the user types an empty line.
        */
```

```
28:     synchronized String read_line() throws InterruptedException
29:     {
30:         synchronized( text_has_been_entered )
31:         {   text_has_been_entered.wait(); // wait for the condition to become true
32:         }
33:
34:         String entered = input.getText();
35:         input.setText("");
36:         return (entered.length() == 0) ? null : entered;
37:
38:     }
39:
40:
41:     static public void main( String[] args ) throws Exception
42:     {   Input_source source = new Input_source();
43:         String input;
44:
45:         while( (input = source.read_line()) != null )
46:             System.out.println("Got: " + input );
47:
48:         System.exit(0);             // kill the AWT Thread on exit
49:     }
50: }
```

Another interesting use of a condition variable is in daemon-thread management. A *daemon* thread is one whose running status is not considered when the JVM decides whether to shut down an application. That is, the JVM shuts down when all of the non-daemon threads terminate. Daemons are useful for ongoing background processing, such as socket accept loops.

The main problem with daemons is that they are shut down rather abruptly when the JVM terminates. If the daemon has side effects—if it creates a temporary file or opens a database connection, for example—there's no way to guarantee that it will clean up after itself. It might be terminated after creating the temporary file, but before it has a chance to delete the file. Unfortunately, you can't turn daemon status on and off—it must be specified before the thread starts running.

You can solve the premature termination problem by using a non-daemon thread as a kind of lock. The daemon creates the non-daemon auxiliary thread, waits for it to start up, does its work, then kills the auxiliary thread. You simply wait for the auxiliary thread to start up, do whatever you have to do, then kill the auxiliary thread. The main difficulty is that Java doesn't support a start-up version of join() that waits until another thread is running—start() can return before the system calls the other thread's run() method.

That's where the condition variable comes into play. The Wait_for_start class (in Listing 4.2) demonstrates the technique. Wait_for_start is a generic daemon-thread class that runs code that you provide continuously until its interrupted. You specify a Runnable object in the Wait_for_start object's constructor, and the code in that Runnable object's run() method is guaranteed not to be interrupted by a premature JVM shutdown. A second Runnable object specifies the delays between calls. Here's an example that prints "Hello world" once a second:

```
Daemon beelzebub =  new Daemon
                  (   new Runnable()             // operation
                      {   public void run()
                          {    System.out.println("Hello world");
                          }
                      },
                      new Runnable()             // delay
                      {   public void run()
                          {    Thread.currentThread.sleep(1000);
                          }
                      },

                  );
beelzebub.start();
```

Looking at the implementation, the daemon uses a condition variable (Listing 4.2, line 21) to find out when the auxiliary thread is running. The daemon's run() method creates an auxiliary thread to serve as a lock on the JVM (on line 23), starts it up (on line 34, and then waits for the auxiliary thread to actually start running (on line 35). The auxiliary thread releases the daemon from its wait at the top of its run() (on line 25), then then goes to sleep. Since the auxiliary thread isn't a daemon, the JVM won't shut down until the auxiliary thread's run() terminates, which it won't do until it's notified. When the daemon is done with whatever its doing, the daemon wakes up the auxiliary thread with a notify() call (line 43), thereby terminating the auxiliary thread. At this juncture, the JVM is free to shut down the application.

Listing 4.2 (Wait_for_start.java): Keeping a Daemon Alive with a Condition Variable

```
01: import com.holub.asynch.Condition;
02: import java.util.Date;
03:
```

```
    /**
        A generic daemon thread that uses the wait-for-start strategy.
        Runs until interrupted, but guarantees that the operation
        that you provide in the constructor will not be terminated
        by a premature JVM shut down.
        @param operation The operation to perform on the thread
        @param delay The run() method of this object is called
        at the end of the iteration. It can terminate the daemon
        by calling Thread.currentThread().interrupt().
    */
```

```
04: final class Wait_for_start extends Thread
05: {
06:     Runnable operation;
07:     Runnable delay;
08:
09:     public Wait_for_start( Runnable operation, Runnable delay )
10:     {   setDaemon(true);
11:         this.operation = operation;
12:         this.delay     = delay;
13:     }
14:
15:     public void run()
16:     {
17:       try
18:       {
19:         while( !isInterrupted() )
20:         {
21:             final Condition lock_is_running = new Condition( false );
22:
23:             Thread lock = new Thread()
24:                             { synchronized public void run()
25:                               {   lock_is_running.set_true();
26:                                   try
27:                                   {   wait();
28:                                   }
29:                                   catch(InterruptedException e)
30:                                   {   // eat it
31:                                   }
32:                               }
33:                             };
```

```
34:             lock.start();
35:             lock_is_running.wait_for_true();
36:
37:             operation.run();
38:
39:             // The deamon will not be killed by the JVM
40:             // until the following notify is executed.
41:
42:             synchronized( lock )
43:             {   lock.notify();   // Allow the lock thread to terminate.
44:             }
45:
46:             delay.run();
47:         }
48:     }
49:     catch( InterruptedException e )
50:     { // ignore it, we terminate this thread by interrupting it.
51:     }
52: }
53: //-------------------------------------------------------------------
54: public static class Test
55: {   public static void main( String[] args )
56:                                     throws InterruptedException
57:     {   new Wait_for_start
58:             (   new Runnable()  // operation
59:                 {   public void run()
60:                     {   System.out.println( new Date() );
61:                     }
62:                 },
63:                 new Runnable()  // delay
64:                 {   public void run()
65:                     {   try
66:                         {   Thread.currentThread().sleep(1000);
67:                         }
68:                         catch(InterruptedException e){}
69:                     }
70:                 }
71:             ).start();
72:
73:             Thread.currentThread().sleep(5000);
74:     }
75: }
76: }
```

Though using a condition variable for synchronization is a useful technique, its not actually necessary in the current application. The Daemon class in Listing 4.3 demonstrates an alternative technique. Here, I had the daemon thread simply create a non-daemon thread to execute the operation.

Listing 4.3 (/src/com/holub/asynch/Daemon.java):
Keeping a Daemon Alive without a Condition Variable

```
01: package com.holub.asynch;
02: import com.holub.asynch.Condition;
03: import java.util.Date;
04:
```

/**

A generic deamon thread. Execute the "operation" object's
run() method repeatedly until interrupted. Guarantees
that the operation that you provide in the constructor
will not be terminated by a premature JVM shut down,
however. For example, the following code prints the time
once a second. The program won't shut down while the time
is actually being printed, but it can shut down at other times:

```
new Daemon
(   new Runnable()  // operation
    {   public void run()
        {   System.out.println( new Date() );
        }
    },
    new Runnable()  // delay
    {   public void run()
        {   try
            {   Thread.currentThread().sleep(1000);
            }
            catch(InterruptedException e){}
        }
    }
).start();
```

Note that the delay operation runs in parallel to the operation
performed on the thread.
@param *operation* The operation to perform on the thread
@param *delay* The run() method of this object is called
at the end of the iteration. It can terminate the daemon
by calling Thread.currentThread().interrupt().

*/

```
05: final class Daemon extends Thread
06: {
07:     final Runnable operation;
08:     final Runnable delay;
09:
10:     public Daemon( Runnable operation, Runnable delay )
11:     {   setDaemon(true);
12:         this.operation = operation;
13:         this.delay     = delay;
14:     }
15:
```

```
16:     public void run()
17:     {
18:         while( !isInterrupted() )
19:         {   new Thread()
20:             {   public void run()
21:                 {   operation.run();
22:                 }
23:             }.start();
24:
25:             delay.run();
26:         }
27:     }
28:
29:     //------------------------------------------------------------
30:     public static class Test
31:     {   public static void main( String[] args )
32:                                         throws InterruptedException
33:         {
34:             new Daemon
35:                 (   new Runnable()  // operation
36:                     {   public void run()
37:                         {   System.out.println( new Date() );
38:                         }
39:                     },
40:                     new Runnable()  // delay
41:                     {   public void run()
42:                         {   try
43:                             {   Thread.currentThread().sleep(1000);
44:                             }
45:                             catch(InterruptedException e){}
46:                         }
47:                     }
48:                 ).start();
49:
50:             Thread.currentThread().sleep(5000);
51:         }
52:     }
53: }
```

Implementing a Condition Variable

A subtle problem occurs when using Java's built-in condition variable, however. What if you call read_line() just after the value has changed rather than before? You'll just wait until the value is changed again, missing the first value entirely. The problem is that the built-in condition variable doesn't really have a notion of state associated with it. What we really need in order to solve the current problem is a true condition variable—one that blocks only if we try to wait() when the condition is false, and that doesn't block at all if the condition is true. Listing 4.4 shows a simple implementation of such a beast. There's not much to it—the vast majority of the file is comments. The main thing is the _is_true flag, declared at the top of the class, which stores the state of the condition for which we're testing. You can set the condition to true or false by calling `set_true()` or `set_false()`. You can test the current state without blocking by calling is_true() or is_false(). You can block, waiting for the condition to become true by calling `wait_for_true()`, which doesn't block at all if the condition happens to be true when you call it. The only complexity is the spin lock on line 33, which uses the current system time to determine whether or not its timeout has expired. (Spin locks were discussed in Chapter 2.)

Listing 4.4 (/src/com/holub/asynch/Condition.java): A Condition Variable

```
01: package com.holub.asynch;
02:
```

```
/**
```
This class implements a simple "condition variable."
The notion is that a thread waits for some condition
to become true. If the condition is false, then no wait occurs.
Be very careful of nested-monitor lockout here:
```
    class lockout
    {  Condition godot = new Condition(false);

       synchronized void f()
       {
           some_code();
           godot.wait_for_true();
       }

       synchronized void set() // Deadlock if another thread is in f()
       {   godot.set_true();
       }
    }
```

You enter f(), locking the monitor, then block waiting
for the condition to become true. Note that you have
not released the monitor for the "lockout" object. [The
only way to set godot to true is to call set(), but you'll
block on entry to set() because the original caller to
f() has the monitor containing "lockout" object.]

Solve the problem by releasing the monitor before waiting:

```
    class okay
    {  Condition godot = new Condition(false);

       void f()
       {   synchronized( this )
           {   some_code();
           }
```

```
                godot.wait_for_true();   // Move the wait outside the monitor
            }

            synchronized void set()
            {   godot.set_true();
            }
        }
```

or by not synchronizing the set() method:

```
        class okay
        {   Condition godot = new Condition(false);

            synchronized void f()
            {   some_code();
                godot.wait_for_true();
            }

            void set()                    // Remove the synchronized statement
            {   godot.set_true();
            }
        }
```

The normal wait()/notify() mechanism doesn't have this problem since wait() releases the monitor, but you can't always use wait()/notify().

```
    */

03: public class Condition implements Semaphore
04: {
05:     private boolean _is_true;
06:

    /**
        Create a new condition variable in a known state.
    */
```

```
07:     public Condition( boolean is_true ){ _is_true = is_true; }
08:
```

```
/**
    Set the condition to false. Waiting threads are not affected.
    Setting an already false condition variable to false is
    a harmless no-op.
*/
```

```
09:     public synchronized void set_false(){ _is_true = false; }
10:
```

```
/**
    Set the condition to true, releasing any waiting threads.
*/
```

```
11:     public synchronized void set_true() { _is_true = true; notifyAll();}
12:
```

```
/**
    For those who actually know what "set" and "reset"
    mean, I've provided versions of those as well.
    (Set and "set to true" mean the same thing. You
    "reset" to enter the false condition.)
*/
```

```
13:     public final void set()  { set_true(); }
14:     public final void reset(){ set_false(); }
15:
```

```
/**
    Returns true if the condition variable is in the "true" state.
    Can be dangerous to call this method if the condition
    can change.
*/
```

```
16:     public final boolean is_true(){return _is_true;}
17:
```

```
/**
    Release all waiting threads without setting the condition to true.
    This method is effectively a "stateless" or "pulsed" condition
    variable, as is implemented by Java's wait() and notify() calls.
    Only those threads that are waiting are released and subsequent
    threads will block on this call. The main difference between
    raw Java and the use of this  function is that wait_for_true(),
    unlike wait()  indicates a timeout with an exception toss. In Java
    there is no way  to distinguish whether wait() returned because
    of an expired  timeout or because the object was notified.
*/
```

```
18:        public final synchronized void release_all(){ notifyAll(); }
19:

           /**
               Release one waiting thread without setting the condition to true.
            */

20:        public final synchronized void release_one(){ notify(); }
21:

           /**
               Wait for the condition to become true.
               @param timeout Timeout, in milliseconds. If 0, method returns
               immediately.
               @return false if the timeout was 0 and the condition was
               false, true otherwise.
            */

22:        public final synchronized boolean wait_for_true( long timeout )
23:                                              throws InterruptedException,
24:                                                      Semaphore.Timed_out
25:        {
26:            if( timeout == 0 || _is_true )
27:                return _is_true;
28:
29:            if( timeout == Semaphore.FOREVER )
30:                return wait_for_true();
31:
32:            long expiration = System.currentTimeMillis() + timeout ;
33:            while( !_is_true )
34:            {
35:                long time_remaining = expiration-System.currentTimeMillis();
36:                if( time_remaining <= 0 )
37:                    throw new Semaphore.Timed_out(
38:                        "Timed out waiting to acquire Condition Variable"),
39:
40:                wait( time_remaining );
41:            }
42:
43:            if( !_is_true )                // assume we've timed out.
44:                throw new Semaphore.Timed_out();
45:
46:            return true;
47:        }
48:

           /**
               Wait (potentially forever) for the condition to
               become true.This call is a bit more efficient than
               wait_for_true(Semaphore.FOREVER);
            */
```

```
49:     public final synchronized boolean wait_for_true()
50:                                         throws InterruptedException
51:     {   while( !_is_true )
52:             wait();
53:         return true;
54:     }
55:
56:     //-----------------------------------------------------------------
57:     // Support for the Semaphore interface:
58:     //-----------------------------------------------------------------
59:
60:     private final int  _id = Lock_manager.new_id();
61:
```

```
        /**
            The id() method returns the unique integer identifier
            of the current condition variable. You can use this ID
            to sort an array of semaphores in order to acquire
            them in the same order, thereby avoiding a common
            deadlock scenario.
        */
```

```
62:     public        int  id() { return _id; }
63:
```

```
        /**
            Identical to  wait_for_true(long).
        */
```

```
64:     public boolean acquire(long timeout) throws InterruptedException,
65:                                         Semaphore.Timed_out
66:     {   return wait_for_true( timeout );
67:     }
68:
```

```
        /**
            Identical to  set_true().
        */
```

```
69:     public void release()
70:     {   set_true();
71:     }
72: }
```

Listing 4.5, following, is basically Listing 4.1 rewritten to use a Condition object. Now, a call to read_line() after the user enters the text works just fine because the condition will be in the true state, and wait_for_true() won't block. Notice that read_line() has to explicitly set the condition back to false after it has read the line so that we *will* block once the line has been read.

There are still a few problems in Listing 4.5 that have to be fixed to make this example work in the real world. For example, there's no way for a program to know if the user overtypes a string when nobody fetches the original string before it is overwritten. Input strings should be queued up as they come in and read_line() should return a string from the queue if there is one, blocking only if the queue is empty. Listing 4.5 serves to illustrate the problem at hand without addressing these other issues, however.

Returning to Listing 4.4, support for the Semaphore interface is provided at the bottom of listing. As with the Mutex, the id() method (Listing 4.4, line 62) just returns a static field that was initialized by the Lock_manager. The acquire(...) method (Listing 4.4, line 64) waits for the condition to become true, and assumes that a time-out has occurred if the condition still isn't true once the wait is over. Note that this is not a nested-monitor lockout because the actual wait call in wait_for_true() releases the monitor before it waits. Finally release() sets the condition true to release any waiting threads. The release() method doesn't have to be synchronized because all it does is call a synchronized method, but there is an important subtlety.

Listing 4.5: /text/books/threads/ch4/Input_source_fixed.java

```
01: import java.awt.*;
02: import java.awt.event.*;
03: import com.holub.asynch.Condition;
04:
05: public class Input_source_fixed extends Frame
06: {
07:     Condition    text_has_been_entered = new Condition(false); // Initial condition is false
08:
09:     TextField input = new TextField();
10:
11:     public Input_source_fixed()
12:     {
13:         input.addActionListener
14:         (   new ActionListener()
15:             {   public void actionPerformed( ActionEvent e )
16:                 {   text_has_been_entered.set_true(); // set the condition true
17:                 }
18:             }
19:         );
20:
21:         add(input);
22:         pack();
23:         show();
24:     }
25:
```

```
       /**
           A blocking function that works like readLine(), but gets its
           text from the current window's text area. The function doesn't
           return until somebody types a line of text, whereupon it returns
           the line. Returns null if the user types an empty line.
       */

26:    synchronized String read_line() throws InterruptedException
27:    {
28:        text_has_been_entered.wait_for_true();
29:        text_has_been_entered.set_false();
30:
31:        String entered = input.getText();
32:        input.setText("");
33:        return (entered.length() == 0) ? null : entered;
34:
35:    }
36:
37:
38:    static public void main( String[] args ) throws Exception
39:    {   Input_source_fixed source = new Input_source_fixed();
40:        String input;
41:
42:        while( (input = source.read_line()) != null )
43:            System.out.println("Got: " + input );
44:
45:        System.exit(0);          // kill the AWT Thread on exit
46:    }
47: }
```

There is one downside to a roll-your-own condition variable. Because locks aren't released automatically, nested-monitor lockout becomes a real possibility. Don't wait for a condition inside a synchronized method if the only way to set the condition true is to call another synchronized method of the same class. In the following code, the only way to set the condition to a "true" state is to call set(), but a call to set() will block if a second thread is in never_returns(), waiting for the condition to become true. The only way that this code will work is if you set the condition before you wait, but what's the point of that?

```
class lockout
{   Condition godot = new Condition(false);

    synchronized void never_returns()
    {   some_code();
        godot.wait_for_true();
    }

    synchronized void set() // DEADLOCKS if a second thread is in
```

```
    {   godot.set_true();    // never_returns(), waiting for the
    }                        // condition to change state.
}
```

Condition Sets: Waiting for Multiple Conditions

One problem with the simple condition-variable implementation we just examined is the problem of waiting for more than one condition to become true (that is, waiting for the logical AND of several conditions). You can use one of the Lock_manager.wait_for_multiple() variants for this purpose, but there's a problem. The Lock_manager just acquires the conditions in sorted order, one at a time. but this strategy doesn't work in very dynamic situations. Consider this case:

1. The lock manager is waiting for three conditions (a, b, and c) to become true.

2. It successfully acquires a and b, but c is false so it blocks.

3. A thread comes along and resets a (to false).

4. A thread comes along and sets c (to true).

5. The lock manager acquires c and returns from acquire_multiple(), even though only two of the conditions are true at this juncture (b and c).

I've solved that problem with the Condition_set class Listing 4.6. You must get the Condition objects that comprise a set from the Condition_set itself using the Condition_set's element method (Listing 4.6, line 27), rather than using new. The element() creates an instance of the private inner class Lockable_condition, which implements Condition with a single twist: an object of class Lockable_condition synchronizes on the Condition_set object that creates it in its set_true() and set_false() methods. To see why that is helpful, look at acquire(...) (Listing 4.6, line 33). This method calls Lock_manager.acquire_multiple() to get all the conditions, but then it locks
the Condition_set itself and checks to see if the conditions are all still true. The Lockable_condition's set_true() and set_false() methods are synchronized on the outer-class object, so it's not possible for any of the condition variables in the set to change state while this second test is going on. If the second test fails, then acquire() goes back to waiting, otherwise it returns success.
Filling in the rest of the details, a condition set can be created so that the acquire(...) method (Listing 4.6, line 33) waits for *all* of the conditions in the set to become true (if you specify Condition_set.ALL in the constructor call) or if any of the conditions become true (if you specify Condition_set.ANY). You can override this default behavior by calling acquire_all(...) (Listing 4.6, line 41) or acquire_any(...)

(Listing 4.6, line 75) directly. Again, most of the complexity in these last two methods is in implementing the spin-lock timeout correctly.

My solution to the acquire-all case still isn't foolproof in that one of the conditions could return to the false state after the second test is made, but before `acquire()` returns. There's little point in fixing this problem, because the same thing could happen after `acquire()` returns, but before we do anything else. The current implementation *does* guarantee that at some point in the immediate past, all of the conditions were true at the same time.

The other main problem with the existing implementation is that it's not possible for a given condition to simultaneously be in more than one set. Implementing this behavior would add considerable complexity to the class, however, and I decided that it just wasn't worth the effort.

Listing 4.6: /src/com/holub/asynch/Condition_set.java

```
001: package com.holub.asynch;
002:
003: import java.util.*;
004:
005: import com.holub.asynch.Semaphore;
006: import com.holub.asynch.Condition;
007: import com.holub.io.Std;
008:
```

```
    /**
```
A set of condition variables that can be tested as a single unit.

....

....

```
    @author Allen I. Holub
    */
```

```
009: public final class Condition_set implements Semaphore
010: {
011:     private final int  _id = Lock_manager.new_id();
012:     public        int  id(){ return _id; }
013:
014:     public static class Mode{ private Mode(){} }
```

```
015:     public static final Mode ALL = null;
016:     public static final Mode ANY = new Mode();
017:
018:     private Collection  locks              = new Vector();
019:     private Mode         acquisition_mode = ALL;
020:
```

```
         /**
             Create a condition set whose acquire() method uses the
             specified acquisition mode.
             @param acquisition_mode If Condition_set.ALL, then
             acquire() blocks until all condition variables in
             the set are in the true state.
             If Condition_set.ANY, then acquire() blocks until any
             of the condition variables in the set are in the true state.
         */
```

```
021:     public Condition_set( Mode acquisition_mode )
022:     {    acquisition_mode = acquisition_mode;
023:     }
024:
```

```
         /**
             A convenience method, works like
             Condition( Condition_set.ALL ).
         */
```

```
025:     public Condition_set(){}
026:
```

```
         /**
             Return a Condition object that's a member of the current
             set. You can not insert Condition objects into a set,
             rather you must ask the Condition_set to manufacture them
             for you by using this method.
             @param is_true if true, the created Condition object
             will be in the true state.
         */
```

```
027:     Condition element( boolean is_true )
028:     {    Lockable_condition member = new Lockable_condition( is_true );
029:         locks.add( member );
030:         return member;
031:     }
032:
```

```
         /**
             Block until either all or any of the members of the
             condition set are true. The behavior (all vs. any) is
             controlled by the constructor argument.
         */
```

```
033:    public boolean acquire( long timeout ) throws InterruptedException,
034:                                                    Semaphore.Timed_out
035:    {
036:        return ( acquisition_mode == ALL )  ? acquire_all( timeout )
037:                                            : acquire_any( timeout )
038:                                            ;
039:    }
040:
```

/**

Blocks until *all* of the condition variables in the
Condition_set become true. If all of them are already
true when this method is called, then return immediately. The Condition_set, and all Condition objects
that the Condition_set creates, will be locked while
this test is going on.
@param *timeout* blocks for, at most, this many milliseconds. Must be a nonzero positive number.
@throws *InterruptedException* is a Thread#interrupt
message is sent to the current thread.
@throws *Semaphore.Timed_out* if the method times out.
@throws *Java.lang.IllegalArgumentException* if the
timeout argument is <= 0.

   */

```
041:    public boolean acquire_all( long timeout )
042:                                        throws  InterruptedException,
043:                                                Semaphore.Timed_out
044:    {
045:        if( timeout <= 0 )
046:            throw new IllegalArgumentException(
047:                        "timeout <= 0 in Condition_set.acquire_all()");
048:
049:        long expiration = System.currentTimeMillis() + timeout ;
050:
051:        waiting:
052:            while( true )
053:            {
054:                Lock_manager.acquire_multiple( locks, timeout );
055:                synchronized( this )
056:                {   for( Iterator i = locks.iterator(); i.hasNext(); )
057:                    {   if( !((Condition) i.next()).wait_for_true(0) )
058:                        {
059:                            timeout = expiration -
060:                                            System.currentTimeMillis();
061:
062:                            if( timeout <= 0 )
063:                                throw new Semaphore.Timed_out(
064:                                  "Timed out waiting for Condition set");
065:
066:                            continue waiting;
```

```
067:                             }
068:                         }
069:                     }
070:                     break;
071:                 }
072:             return true;
073:     }
074:
```

```
       /**
           Blocks until any of the condition variables in the
           Condition_set become true. If any of them are already
           true when this method is called, then returns immediately.
           @param timeout blocks for, at most, this many milli-
           seconds. The timeout may be zero if you want to check
           without blocking.
           @throws InterruptedException is a Thread#interrupt
           message is sent to the current thread.
           @throws Semaphore.Timed_out if the method times out.
        */
```

```
075:     public synchronized boolean acquire_any( long timeout )
076:                                         throws InterruptedException,
077:                                         Semaphore.Timed_out
078:     {
079:         for( Iterator i = locks.iterator(); i.hasNext(); )
080:             if( ((Condition) i.next()).is_true() )
081:                 return true;
082:
083:         if( timeout == 0 )
084:             return false;
085:
086:         wait( timeout );          // wait for one to become true
087:
088:         for( Iterator i = locks.iterator(); i.hasNext(); )
089:             if( ((Condition) i.next()).is_true() )
090:                 return true;
091:
092:         throw new Semaphore.Timed_out(); // none of them were true, must
093:                                          // have timed out.
094:     }
095:
096:     private boolean modified;
097:
```

```
         /**
             Releases (sets to "false") all condition variables
             in the set.
          */

098:     public synchronized void release()
099:     {   for( Iterator i = locks.iterator(); i.hasNext(); )
100:             ((Lockable_condition) i.next() ).release();
101:     }
102:


         /**
             A private class that extends a standard condition
             variable to support locking on a Condition_set. This
             way you cannot modify the state of a Condition_set
             while a test operation is in progress.
          */

103:     private final class Lockable_condition extends Condition
104:     {
105:         public Lockable_condition(boolean is_true){ super(is_true); }
106:
107:         public void set_false() {synchronized(Condition_set.this)
108:                                     { super.set_false();
109:                                     }
110:                                 }
111:         public void set_true()  {synchronized(Condition_set.this)
112:                                     { super.set_true();
113:                                       Condition_set.this.modified = true;
114:                                       Condition_set.this.notifyAll();
115:                                     }
116:                                 }
117:     }
118:


         /**
             A simple test class. Should print:

             % java com.holub.asynch.Condition_set\$Test

             setting a
             setting b
             resetting b
             setting c
             setting b
             Got 'em all
             setting f
```

```
                    Got one as it's set
                    Got one initially


          */

119:    public static final class Test
120:    {
121:        static Condition_set conditions = new Condition_set();
122:        static Condition a = conditions.element( false );
123:        static Condition b = conditions.element( false );
124:        static Condition c = conditions.element( false );
125:
126:        static Condition_set or_set = new Condition_set(
127:                                            Condition_set.ANY);
128:        static Condition d = or_set.element( false );
129:        static Condition e = or_set.element( false );
130:        static Condition f = or_set.element( false );
131:
132:        public static void main( String[] s ) throws Exception
133:        {
134:            new Thread()                    // ALL
135:            {   public void run()
136:                {   try{ sleep(100); }catch(InterruptedException e){}
137:                    Std.out().println("setting a"); a.set_true();
138:                    Std.out().println("setting b"); b.set_true();
139:
140:                    // give acquire multiple a chance to get the
141:                    // two that we just set--it will block waiting
142:                    // for c--then change the state of b back to false
143:
144:                    try{ sleep(100); }catch(InterruptedException e){}
145:                    Std.out().println("resetting b"); b.set_false();
146:
147:                    Std.out().println("setting c"); c.set_true();
148:                    Std.out().println("setting b"); b.set_true();
149:                }
150:            }.start();
151:
152:            conditions.acquire( 1000 * 5 );
153:            System.out.println("Got 'em all");
154:
155:            //--------------------------------------------------
156:
157:            new Thread()                    // ANY
158:            {   public void run()
159:                {   try{ sleep(1000); }catch(InterruptedException e){}
160:                    Std.out().println("setting f");
161:                    f.set_true();
162:                }
163:            }.start();
164:
```

```
165:                or_set.acquire_any( 1000 * 5 );
166:                System.out.println("Got one as it's set");
167:
168:                or_set.acquire_any( 1000 * 5 );
169:                System.out.println("Got one initially");
170:            }
171:        }
172: }
173:
174: // Implementation note. It's been pointed out to me that I could
175: // implement a condition set using a semaphore, where a true
176: // condition was indicated by acquiring the semaphore.
177: // (You couldn't wait on individual conditions in this case---
178: // only on the set as a whole.) I'll leave this implementation
179: // as an "exercise for the reader."
```

Counting Semaphores for Managing Resource Pools

The final basic semaphore that I want to look at is the "Dijkstra" counting semaphore. This one has no direct analog in Java, so it's among the more useful of the
com.holub.asynch classes. *Counting semaphores* are used to keep track of the avail-
ability of a resource within a pool of limited size. For example, you might have four
connections open to a database server that are simply recycled to perform multiple
queries. This way you won't incur the overhead of opening a connection every time
you make a query. Threads that want to make queries should block (should be suspended, waiting) if no connections are available. They should be reactivated (released
from their wait) when a connection becomes available. A counting semaphore can
solve this problem (though other solutions, such as a thread-safe stack whose pop
method blocks if the stack is empty, are also possible).

Counting semaphores are initialized with a count—typically the number of
objects available in the pool. Every time you acquire the semaphore, the count is
decremented; every time you release the semaphore, it is incremented. On acquisition, if the count (after the decrement) is nonzero, nothing happens, and you get
your slot in the pool. If the count is zero, however, the acquiring thread blocks
until some other thread releases the semaphore, thereby incrementing the count.

Counting semaphores typically have maximum counts as well as initial counts.
A semaphore initialized with a count of 0, but with a maximum of 10, is effectively
saying that 10 objects can be in the pool, but none of them are available right now.
A *reverse-sensing semaphore* (which I haven't implemented) is also occasionally
useful. This one blocks unless the count is zero. Use it when you need to acquire
the entire pool before you can do anything useful, or if you need to do something
when the pool becomes empty (such as add extra elements). Listing 4.7 shows my
Counting_semaphore implementation. It implements the Semaphore interface, so slots
in multiple pools can be acquired safely by using last chapter's Lock_manager class.
As was the case with the Condition class, the counting semaphore is built around
Java's wait() and notify() methods. The acquire(...) method (Listing 4.7, line 71)

blocks if enough slots aren't available. The release() method (Listing 4.7, line 127) notifies waiting threads that a slot has become available.

Releasing waiting threads is tricky because more threads can be waiting than there are available slots. Though the release() method indeed calls notifyAll() to release the waiting threads, the too-many threads problem is solved by acquire(): The notifyAll() bumps all the waiting threads out of the wait() (on line 84), but this wait is in a spin lock that is testing for available slots. If no slots are available, the thread goes back to waiting. There's no way to predict which of the waiting threads will get the slot, though.

I've implemented a version of acquire() that lets you get multiple slots at once, but it does so by calling the single-slot acquire multiple times rather than by waiting for the specified number of slots to become available. The problem is that the number of slots that you need may become available one at a time, but they may also be grabbed by other threads before the total number you need becomes available. By forcing you to acquire slots one at a time, the odds of getting the total number of slots you need are actually higher than if you waited until the semaphore's internal count came up to the total. You'll be able to suck the slots up one at a time as they become available. I do have a version of release(int) (Listing 4.7, line 129) that lets you free up multiple slots all at once, however.

The Counting_semaphore's constructor includes an enforce_ownership argument that, if true, causes the semaphore to keep track of how many slots a given thread has allocated and complain (with a Semaphore.Ownership exception toss) if that thread tries to release more slots than it has acquired. This behavior can be disabled with a false argument, since there is some overhead involved in associating slots with threads, and you might decide that the "honor system" will work. (If enforce_ownership is false, a thread is on its honor to free up only the slots that it has previously acquired.)

A Counting_semaphore.Too_many_releases object will be thrown if some thread tries to bring the total available-slot count above the maximum, but a thread could still incorrectly release the wrong number of slots without triggering the exception toss.

Listing 4.7: /src/com/holub/asynch/Counting_semaphore.java

```
001: package com.holub.asynch;
002:
003: import java.util.*;
004: import com.holub.asynch.Semaphore;
005: import com.holub.asynch.Lock_manager;
006:

    /**
        A counting-semaphore.
```

@author *Allen I. Holub*
```
        */
```

```
007: public final class Counting_semaphore implements Semaphore
008: {
009:     private int        available_slots; // Currently available slots.
010:     private int        maximum_slots;  // Maximum   available slots.
011:     private Runnable   notify_on_empty;
012:     private boolean    enforce_ownership;
013:
```

```
        /****************************************************************
```
The "owners" list keeps track of the number of slots
allocated by a given thread. It's used only if
`enforce_ownership` is true. The class keeps a hash table
keyed by `Thread` object, where the associated value number
of slots allocated by that thread. If a given thread
isn't in the table, then it has no slots allocated to it.
```
        */
```

```
014:     private final class Owner_list
015:     {
016:         private Map owners = new HashMap();
017:
```

```
        /**
```
HashMap objects must contain `Object` values, not raw
`int`s, so wrap the `int` in a class so that it can go into
the table.
```
        */
```

```
018:         private class Count{ public int count = 0; }
019:
```

```
        /**
```
Increment the slot count associated with the
current thread.
```
        */
```

```
020:        public void add_slot_for_current_thread()
021:        {
022:            Thread requester = Thread.currentThread();
023:            Count  current   = (Count)owners.get(requester);
024:
025:            if( current == null ) // thread hasn't allocated any slots
026:                owners.put( requester, current = new Count() );
027:
028:            ++current.count;
029:        }
030:
```

/**
   Reduce the slot count associated with the current
   thread by `number_of_slots` and throw an exception
   if the count goes negative.
*/

```
031:        public void remove_slots_for_current_thread(int number_of_slots)
032:                                            throws Semaphore.Ownership
033:        {
034:            Thread requester = Thread.currentThread();
035:            Count  current   = (Count)owners.get(requester);
036:
037:            if( current == null )    // all slots associated with thread
038:            {                        // have been freed or thread never
039:                                     // had any slots to begin with.
040:                throw new Semaphore.Ownership();
041:            }
042:
043:            if( (current.count -= number_of_slots) <= 0 )
044:                owners.remove(requester);
045:
046:            if( current.count < 0 ) // Too many slots were freed.
047:                throw new Semaphore.Ownership();
048:        }
049:    }
050:
051:    Owner_list owners = new Owner_list();
052:
```

/***
   Create a counting semaphore with the specified initial
   and maximum counts. The `release()` method, which
   increments the count, is not permitted to increment
   it past the maximum. If the `initial_count` is larger
   than the `maximum_slots`, it is silently truncated.
   @param *initial_count* The number of elements initially
   in the pool.

```
                   @param maximum_slots The maximum number of elements
                   in the pool.
                   @param notify_on_empty The run() method of this object
                   when the count goes to zero. You can use this facility
                   to implement pools that grow when all resources are
                   in use. [See increase_maximum_slots()]
                   @param enforce_ownership If true, then a given thread
                   can release only the number of slots that it has
                   previously acquired. One thread cannot release a slot
                   acquired by another thread.
                   @see release
               */

053:    Counting_semaphore(int initial_count, int       maximum_slots,
054:                                           boolean  enforce_ownership,
055:                                           Runnable notify_on_empty)
056:    {
057:        this.notify_on_empty    = notify_on_empty;
058:        this.maximum_slots      = maximum_slots;
059:        this.enforce_ownership  = enforce_ownership;
060:        this.available_slots    = (initial_count > maximum_slots)
061:                                        ? maximum_slots : initial_count;
062:    }
063:


        /***************************************************************
            Create a counting semaphore with a maximum count of
            Integer.MAX_VALUE. Strict ownership is enforced.
         */

064:    Counting_semaphore( int initial_count )
065:    {   this( initial_count, Integer.MAX_VALUE, true, null );
066:    }
067:


        /***************************************************************
            Required override of Semaphore.id(). Don't call this
            function.
            @see Lock_manager
         */

 68:    public      int  id() { return _id; }
 69:    private final int  _id = Lock_manager.new_id();
 70:


        /***************************************************************
            Acquire the semaphore, decrementing the count of
            available slots. Block if the count goes to zero.
```

If this call acquires the last available slot, the
run()method of the Runnable object passed to the
constructor is called. You can use this method to
increase the pool size on an as-needed basis.
[See increase_maximum_slots().]
@throws *InterruptedException* if interrupted while
waiting for the semaphore.
@return *false* if timeout is 0 and we didn't get the
slot. Otherwise, return true.

```
      */

071:     public synchronized boolean acquire(long timeout)
072:                                         throws InterruptedException,
073:                                                Semaphore.Timed_out
074:     {   if( timeout == 0 && available_slots <= 0 )
075:             return false;
076:
077:         long expiration = System.currentTimeMillis() + timeout ;
078:         while( available_slots <= 0 )
079:         {   long time_remaining = expiration-System.currentTimeMillis();
080:             if( time_remaining <= 0 )
081:                 throw new Semaphore.Timed_out(
082:                     "Timed out waiting to acquire Condition Variable" );
083:
084:             wait( time_remaining );
085:         }
086:
087:         if( enforce_ownership )
088:             owners.add_slot_for_current_thread();
089:
090:         if( --available_slots == 0 && notify_on_empty != null )
091:             notify_on_empty.run();
092:
093:         return true;
094:     }
095:


    /******************************************************************
```

Acquire the specified number of slots. If you need to
acquire multiple slots and some other semaphore as well,
use Lock_manager.acquire_multiple(), and put multiple
references to a single Counting_semaphore in the array
passed to acquire_multiple().
@param *timeout* maximum time (milliseconds) to wait for
any one of the slots. The total time to wait is
(timeout * number_of_slots).
@throw *Semaphore.Timed_out* if a timeout is encountered
while waiting for any of the slots.

```
      */
```

```
096:       public synchronized boolean acquire_multiple_slots( int slots,
097:                                                    long timeout)
098:                                         throws InterruptedException,
099:                                                 Semaphore.Timed_out
100:       {
101:           if( timeout == 0 )
102:           {   if( available_slots < slots )
103:                   return false;
104:
105:               if( (available_slots -= slots)<=0 && notify_on_empty!=null)
106:                   notify_on_empty.run();
107:           }
108:           else
109:           {   while( --slots >= 0 )
110:                   acquire(timeout);
111:           }
112:
113:           return true;
114:       }
115:
```

```
/****************************************************************
```
Increase the pool size by this_many slots. If the
available-slots count is zero, then waiting threads
are released (up to the maximum specified by the
new size). That is, this call modifies the maximum-
available-slots count and then effectively performs
a release(this_many) operation.
@param *this_many* Number of slots to add to the pool.
An IllegalArgumentException is thrown if this number
is negative.
```
 */
```

```
116:       public synchronized void increase_maximum_slots_by( int this_many )
117:       {
118:           if( this_many < 0 )
119:               throw new IllegalArgumentException("Negative Argument");
120:
121:           maximum_slots += this_many;
122:           release( this_many );
123:       }
124:
```

```
/****************************************************************
```
Return the current pool size (the maximum count),
as passed into the constructor or as modified by
increase_maximum_slots().
```
 */
```

```
125:      public int maximum_slots(){ return maximum_slots; }
126:
```

```
          /*************************************************************
              Release the semaphore and increment the count.
              This one is the generic release required by the
              Semaphore interface, so all it can do is throw an
              exception if there's an error.
              @throws Counting_semaphore.TooManyReleases
              (a RuntimeException)if you try to release a semaphore
              whose count is already at the maximum value.
           */
127:      public synchronized void release(){ release(1); }
128:
```

```
          /*************************************************************
              Release "increment" slots in the semaphore all at once.
              @param increment The amount to increment the count. If
              this value is zero, the current count is returned and
              no threads are released. An IllegalArgumentException
              is thrown if increment is negative.
              @throws Counting_semaphore.TooManyReleases
              (a RuntimeException)if the current value + count is
              greater than the maximum. The semaphore will not have
              been modified in this case.
              @throws Semaphore.Ownership (a RuntimeException) if
              a given thread tries to free up more slots than it has
              acquired (and enforce_ownership was specified in the
              constructor).
              @return the value of the count after the increment is added.
           */
129:      public synchronized int release( int increment )
130:      {
131:          if( increment < 0 )
132:              throw new IllegalArgumentException("Negative Argument");
133:
134:          if( increment > 0 )
135:          {
136:              int original_count = available_slots;
137:              int new_count       = available_slots + increment;
138:
139:              if( enforce_ownership )
140:                  owners.remove_slots_for_current_thread(increment);
141:
142:              if( new_count > maximum_slots )
143:              {   throw new TooManyReleases();
144:              }
145:
```

```
146:            available_slots = new_count;
147:            if( original_count == 0 )
148:                notifyAll();
149:        }
150:        return available_slots;
151:    }
152:

        /**
            Thrown if you try to release more than the maximum
            number of slots.
         */

153:    public static final class TooManyReleases extends RuntimeException
154:    {   private TooManyReleases()
155:        {   super("Released semaphore that was at capacity");
156:        }
157:    }
158: }
```

Though the current implementation doesn't support a reverse-sensing semaphore, it does provide the hooks you need to increase the pool size on an as-needed basis. You can pass the constructor a reference to a Runnable object whose run() method is called when the number of available slots in the pool goes to zero. This method can then call increase_maximum_slots_by(...) to increase the maximum-number-of-slots count. Increasing the size of a pool whose available-slot count is zero automatically releases any threads who are waiting for newly-added slots.

Wrapping Up

So that's the basic set of "primitive" synchronization objects. You've seen how to use the built-in condition variable to communicate between threads generally (and the AWT event thread in particular). You've also seen that, though you can do a lot of what a condition variable does just by using wait() and notify(), you can't do everything. The Condition class adds the essential ability to not wait when the condition is already true. The Counting_semaphore isn't implemented as a Java primitive at all, so it can be particularly useful when you really need it to manage pooled resources.

Subsequent chapters move on to look at more complicated synchronization objects, such as a Timer class that makes it easy to fire events on a regular schedule. The Timer implementation also demonstrates how to write code that needs to suspend, resume, and stop threads without using the (now deprecated) suspend(), resume(), and stop() methods.

CHAPTER 5

Timers, Alarms, and Swing Thread Safety

THIS CHAPTER DISCUSSES the first of several classes that are useful in multithreaded programming, but which aren't semaphores. In particular, I'll talk about *timers*—objects that help execute some operation at a fixed interval or at some point in the future. I'll discuss both the timer that is part of the Swing package (called Timer) and also a roll-your-own variety of my own (called Alarm) that is useful when the Swing Timer isn't available or appropriate. My Alarm implementation is the most complicated of the classes in the book, and it demonstrates several important Java-programming techniques, such as how to write code that needs to suspend and resume threads without using the (now deprecated) suspend() and resume() methods. Along the way, I'll talk about how to kill a thread gracefully without using the (also deprecated) stop() method.

Why a Timer?

Timers have a multitude of applications. Animation loops (which must refresh at regular intervals) and clocks come to mind immediately, but other applications are legion: You might set a timer on an I/O operation that gives the user a cancel option after a set time has elapsed, for example. Or consider the case of a thread that must notify a large list of observers that some event has occurred: Using a timer to notify one observer from the list on each "tick" of the timer can give other threads a chance to run while notifications are in progress. A server might need to "ping" a client at regular intervals to make sure the client is still alive. You get the idea.

A simple timed wait can serve for some of these purposes, but it often doesn't do the trick. For example, each loop iteration in the following could take a different amount of time to execute, depending on which way the test goes and how long the database server takes to process requests:

```
//...
while( running )
{
    if( some_condition )
        notify_any_observers( FAILED );
    else
```

```
            {
                open_a_database();
                make_1000_queries();
                process_the_results():
                generate_a_billion_reports();
                notify_any_observers( SUCCESS );
            }

            Thread.currentThread.sleep( FIVE_MINUTES );
        }
        //...
```

The foregoing code works fine if you want five minutes to elapse between operations. On the other hand, if your intent was to perform an operation every five minutes on the dot, the foregoing code fails miserably. (There are also lock-related problems with using `sleep()` in the previous code. Any locks acquired before `sleep()` executes will remain locked while the method is sleeping. You can sometimes use `wait()` instead of `sleep()`, since `wait()` releases the lock on the object that acts as the wait target, but a simple `wait()` won't work if you're holding multiple locks. Be careful.)

Swingin' Threads: Swing Isn't Thread Safe

Timers solve the do-it-every-five-minutes-on-the-dot problem by initiating events at regular intervals or at a predetermined time in the future. Java does have one timer implementation built in: the `javax.swing.Timer` class. Unfortunately, the Swing `Timer` is designed as Swing-specific solution—it's only available if Swing is installed on the client system—to a Swing-specific problem. Swing itself is not thread safe. The Swing timer, consequently, doesn't solve the general problem of timing. That is why we need the `Alarm` class, discussed later.

The Swing thread-safety issue is an important one. Swing, like AWT, uses a single thread to field all UI events that come in from the operating system. This thread pulls OS events from some sort of event queue, figures out what the OS is trying to tell it, and then notifies listeners interested in the event. For example, the event thread could dequeue a `WM_MOUSEMOVE` message from the Windows message queue, in response to which Swing will send `mouseMoved()` messages to all interested `MouseMotionListener` objects.

These event-handler methods [such as `mouseMoved()`] *actually run on the Swing (or AWT) thread*—the one that is dequeueing the OS-level events. This single-threaded approach is a big issue, because the UI is effectively locked while the event-handler messages are executing. That is, no OS-level messages (such as button presses) are serviced while listener notifications are in progress. Consequently, button presses and so forth (such as clicks on the Cancel button) will be ignored while the handler executes. To keep your UI responsive to user input, these event-handler functions should be very short and very fast. They *must* spawn off threads to do time-consuming operations. That's what I meant in the first chapter when I said all Java programs that create a graphical UI are multithreaded, whether you like it or not. It is not okay for the UI to become unresponsive simply because you're executing some listener method.

To make matters more interesting, virtually none of the Swing class's methods are thread safe—they are simply not designed to handle the case of two threads accessing them simultaneously. The performance hit required to make Swing thread safe (not to mention the extra complexity) are just unacceptable. (Most of the AWT classes *are* thread safe—it's just the Swing classes that I'm talking about.) The lack of thread safety means that once you "realize" a window (make it visible on the screen by calling setVisible(), pack(), or equivalent) you cannot safely invoke a Swing method on that Component from anywhere but Swing's own event-handler thread. (You *can* safely manipulate Swing objects *before* the first window is realized, just not after.)

The foregoing notwithstanding, there are a few messages that you *can* pass safely to a "realized" Swing object, but these thread-safe methods are not listed in any particular place in the documentation, and there are only a handful of them. Table 5.1 is my best attempt at listing those methods that can be called safely from any thread in your program. Everything else is off limits. (I make no claims that this is an exhaustive list—these are the ones I could find by rooting around in the documentation as I was writing the book.)

Table 5.1. Thread-safe Methods in Swing

JComponent	repaint()
	revalidate()
	invalidate()
JTextArea	insert()
	append()
	replaceRange()
JEditorPane	replaceSection()
	setText()
JTextPane	replaceSection()
	insertIcon()
	setLogicalStyle()
	setCharacterAttributes()
	setParagraphAttributes()

Note: Listener lists can be modified from any thread.

Because repaint() and invalidate() are on the list, you can safely update a window by changing the underlying data and then asking the window to redraw itself, but that is the *only* reliable way to cause a window to change appearance by sending it a direct message. Even a message as innocuous as setEnable(false) is out of the question in a multithreaded scenario.

The lack of thread safety is sometimes a non-issue because Swing methods are, more often than not, called from a listener running on Swing's own event-handler thread. For example, a listener's event handler like mouseMoved() might actually draw a line on some Component by writing directly to the Component's Graphics object. This operation is safe because mouseMoved() is running on Swing's own thread, so the drawing request to the Graphics object will effectively be synchronous. Similarly, as mentioned earlier, you often change a window's appearance by changing the underlying data model and then sending an invalidate() or repaint() message to the window, causing it to redraw itself to reflect the new state. Both invalidate() and repaint() are thread safe, however, so this strategy works fine. (The invalidate() and repaint() methods put a request on the Swing input queue, which is serviced when Swing gets around to it. The resulting paint() call runs on the Swing thread, of course.)

On the other hand, it's often unacceptable to redraw a large window just to reflect a change in state of a small piece of that window (say a counter that is being updated dynamically). The window will flicker horribly if you redraw the whole thing too often, and the net effect is pretty annoying. It's this situation that brings thread safety to the fore.

The *invokeLater()* and *invokeAndWait()* Methods

Fortunately, Swing provides two mechanisms to safely ask any Swing object to do anything. The first two methods of interest are used when some thread of your own devising needs to communicate with some realized Swing component. For example, the main thread of an application could fire up a window, do some stuff, then want to update some field in that window. To solve this problem, You need to encapsulate your code into a Runnable object, and then pass that object to Swing by calling SwingUtilities.invokeLater() or SwingUtilities.invokeAndWait(). Swing puts the Runnable object onto the Swing event queue, and exercises the object's run() method when the object appears at the head of the queue (at some indeterminate time in the future).

For example, a thread could change the cursor in a thread-safe way as follows:

```
Component some_window = ... ;
//...
```

```
// change the cursor to the wait cursor:
SwingUtilities.invokeLater
(    new Runnable()
     {    public void run()
          {    some_window.setCursor( new Cursor(WAIT_CURSOR) )
          }
     }
);
```

The asynchronous `invokeLater()` message just puts the `Runnable` object onto the event queue and then returns. The object's `run()` method, which changes the cursor type, executes when Swing gets around to calling it. Since the `run()` methods run synchronously with other Swing methods on the Swing event-handler thread, the thread safety of the individual Swing methods is irrelevant. The similar `invokeAndWait()` method blocks until the `run()` function has been executed, but is otherwise the same as `invokeLater()`.

Software-engineering note: This use of `Runnable` is a good example of the Gang-of-Four *Command* pattern. The `Runnable` object encapsulates a command that the Swing event thread executes. It's the OO equivalent of a function pointer—a way to pass an operation to an object. Don't be misled by the fact that you use a `Runnable` object to pass the request to Swing. The `run()` method does not run on its own thread; it runs on the Swing event handler. The `Runnable` interface is convenient for the current application—it has a method that you can call when you want to get something done but using `Runnable` is just a convenience that allows the Swing designers not to introduce a similar interface into the language.

Remember, your `Runnable` object's `run()` method executes on the Swing event thread, so it has the same UI-lock-up problems as a listener. Your program's user interface will not respond at all to any user input until `run()` returns. As is the case with listeners, it's best for these methods either to be very short or to fire up their own threads to do time-consuming background operations.

Using the Swing Timer

Swing also supports a `Timer` class, but in writing this book I was hard pressed to come up with a reasonable UI-related use for it. But the `Timer` is available should you need to update some piece of a UI at a fixed interval or at some known future time, and you don't want to redraw the entire window by issuing a `repaint()` or `update()`.

The swing `Timer` class executes requests (passed in as Gang-of-Four *Command* objects) on Swing's own event-processing thread at fixed intervals. I think of this kind of timer as "proactive." You set up a timer interval and register one or more `ActionListener` objects with it. The `Timer` then sends an `actionPerformed()` message to each listener when the interval elapses. (All the listeners are notified at once, not one per interval.) These notifications are executed from the Swing event loop, so they can happily call Swing methods without worrying about thread synchronization. Listing 5.1 demonstrates how to use a `Timer` by printing the time once a second.

The Timer is initialized with a time interval (1000 milliseconds) and is provided an ActionListener to notify when the interval expires. The listener's actionPerformed() method both prints the current time and advances the elapsed-time counter. After five seconds (and five calls to actionPerformed()), the condition variable (discussed in the previous chapter) is set to true, thereby releasing any threads that are waiting for the timer to finish. The main thread, creates creates a Swing_timer, whose constructor starts the clock and then blocks, waiting for the done condition to become true. The constructor doesn't return until five seconds have elapsed.

Sun's Timer is a bit more flexible than I've shown; it can also work in a one-shot mode where the listeners are notified only once, for example. The Timer also supports methods that let you add additional listeners, change the timer interval, and so forth.

Listing 5.1 (Swing_timer.java): Using javax.swing.Timer

```
01: import java.util.*;
02: import java.awt.event.*;
03:
04: import com.holub.asynch.Condition;
05:
06: public class Swing_timer
07: {
08:     private Condition done        = new Condition(false);
09:     private int       elapsed_time = 0;
10:
11:     // Create a one-second timer:
12:
13:     javax.swing.Timer clock =
14:         new javax.swing.Timer
15:         (   1000,
16:             new ActionListener()
17:             {   public void actionPerformed( ActionEvent e )
18:                 {   synchronized( Swing_timer.this )
19:                     {   System.out.println( (new Date()).toString() );
20:                         if( ++elapsed_time == 5 )
21:                             done.set_true();        // Notify other threads
22:                                                     // that timer has finished.
23:                     }
24:                 }
25:             }
26:         );
27:
28:     Swing_timer() throws InterruptedException
29:     {   clock.start();
30:         done.wait_for_true(); // wait for timer to finish
31:     }
32:
```

```
33:     public static void main(String[] args) throws InterruptedException
34:     {   new Swing_timer();
35:     }
36: }
```

So, How Does It Work?

It's interesting to delve into the inner workings of the Timer. (The sources are in the JDK's *src.jar* file, installed in the JDK root directory, if you tell the JDK installer program to install it.)

You would expect the timer to fire off a thread whose run() method would first wait for the time interval to elapse, and then notify the listeners. Then this thread would either terminate or loop back up and wait again, depending on whether or not the timer is a one-shot. That's more or less how my Alarm class, which I'll present in a moment, works.

Swing's Timer doesn't work this way, however. What you don't see on the surface is a second package-access class, called a TimerQueue. This class is an example of the Gang-of-Four *Singleton* pattern—only one instance of it ever exists. It's the TimerQueue object that encapsulates the "wait" thread. The Timer object actually doesn't do any timing at all. It just stores its time interval or expiration time internally. When you start up the Timer object, the Timer simply adds itself the list of timers maintained by the TimerQueue object. Timers are ordered by expiration time within the queue, and the TimerQueue puts itself to sleep until the expiration time associated with the object at the head of the queue arrives. The TimerQueue object then passes the ball back to the expired Timer, asking it to notify its listeners.

At this juncture, the Timer object calls Swing's invokeLater() method (discussed earlier) and passes it a Runnable object whose run() method sends actionPerformed() messages to the Timer's ActionListener objects. It is important to observe that this notification happens on Swing's event-processing thread, so the actionPerformed() method can happily call Swing functions without worrying about thread safety. That's, in fact, the whole point of Swing's incorporation of a Timer class, to allow the UI to be safely updated at fixed intervals.

By default, if several references to the *same* Timer object are waiting in the notification queue, all but one are ignored. (Notification requests can build up in this way if the application is busy servicing normal OS-event handlers.) This way, a listener doesn't get multiple notifications coming on top of each other. This behavior can be suppressed by passing the Timer object a setCoalesce(false) message.

Why Use a Swing Timer (or Not)

The main advantage to Swing's approach (over and above the thread-safety issue) is that the number of threads that exist at a given moment is small, since all real work is done on the Swing event thread and all timers share the same `TimerQueue`.

There are lots of disadvantages, though:

- If your program doesn't have a GUI, or if it is using 1.1 AWT instead of Swing, then it can't use a Swing `Timer`.

- The notification is performed on Swing's event thread. This is great in the context of sending messages to Swing components, but is a problem everywhere else. If the event queue is full of operating-system events like mouse moves, it could take quite a while for your `ActionPerfomed()` method to be called. In other words, the time interval is really a minimum, and there is no way to be sure that a `Timer` will actually perform the operations you send to it when you want them to be performed.

- Since `actionPerformed()` executes on the Swing event thread, the UI is locked up while `actionPerformed()` method is executing. It's a bad idea to lock up the UI by doing something that is not related to the UI.

The synchronization problems that I discussed in the previous chapter in the context of AWT are an issue here as well: The `actionPerformed()` methods run on Swing's event thread, which is typically not the thread that is waiting for the time to expire. This means you must remember to synchronize the listener on the outer-class object (as I've done on line 18 in Listing 5.1). You must also use condition variables or a wait/notify strategy to synchronize the waiting thread and the notifying thread. For the reason I discussed in the previous chapter, it is this last set of problems that are the most bothersome in practice. That's why I didn't use Swing's architecture when I came up with my own timer class.

Roll Your Own Timer: Implementing the **Alarm** Class

My own timer class, called `Alarm`, is different from the Swing `Timer` in several ways. First, it doesn't have to use listeners at all (though it can). You typically wait for the timer to expire by calling a blocking function that suspends the calling thread until the next timer tick occurs. This strategy has two advantages when compared to Swing's `Timer`.

First, it's more in line with an object-oriented way of thinking. In OO systems, you tend to think in terms of objects sending each other synchronous messages (which don't return until they've finished doing whatever they do) or asynchronous messages (which return immediately, while whatever they do goes on in the background). You're thinking messages here, not threads. Consequently, a synchronous "wait for expiration" request makes more sense in an object model than a method that magically gets called for no apparent reason in the middle of some scenario.

Second, it's easier to code my Alarm than it is a Swing Timer. You don't have to worry about the listener-related synchronization problems, and you don't have to mess with wait() and notify() or a condition variable to find out when the Timer has ticked. The Swing approach makes more sense when you can do everything you need to do in the actionPerformed() method, but I've found that most of the applications for timers that I've come up with lend themselves more to a blocking-wait strategy. In any event, I've provided a notification mechanism if you prefer.

Here's the earlier print-the-time-once-a-second example from Listing 5.1 rewritten to use my Alarm class and a blocking-wait strategy:

```
static public void main( String[] args )
{
    Alarm clock = new Alarm(1000, Alarm.CONTINUOUS);
    clock.start();

    for( int i = 3; --i>= 0; )
    {   System.out.println( new Date().toString() );
        clock.await( Alarm.FOREVER );    // wait for the next clock tick,
    }                                    // with a standby timeout of
                                         // FOREVER.
    clock.stop();
}
```

The clock is running while the Date() object is being created and printed: The time required to get and print the time is not added to the 1000-millisecond interval specified in the Alarm's constructor call. If the loop takes longer than 1000 milliseconds to execute, the program will miss a timer tick (which can be either good or bad, depending on the situation). Contrast this with the Swing approach, where timer ticks can be missed because the I/O system is too busy to notify the listeners. It's not that one situation is better or worse, but there is a difference.

Note that I've synchronized the Alarm's await(...) method (Listing 5.2, line 80), rather than Object's wait() method, in the previous code. The await() method does not block if you wait on an expired one-shot timer (a timer that "ticks" once, then stops running). You can use wait() if you want, but wait() always blocks until the next clock tick.

I find the code that uses an Alarm is both easier to write and easier to read than Listing 5.1. It also doesn't require any condition variables for synchronization, because the Alarm object isn't sending messages to the main thread asynchronously; rather, the main thread simply waits for the timer to expire with a blocking call. There are still two threads, but the timer thread is doing nothing but timing—it has no access to the code in the class that contains main(). Therefore, the main thread does not have to synchronize access to any fields because only one thread accesses those fields.

If you really need a Swing-style event-based notification, the Alarm class supports that as well. Just add an ActionListener to the thread with a call to addActionListener() and remove the listener with a call to removeActionListener(). Here's an example:

```
clock = new Alarm( 1000 );  // 1-second continuous timer
Alarm.Notifier notifier = new Alarm.Notifier( clock );

notifier.addActionListener
(   new ActionListener()
    {   public void actionPerformed()
        {   System.out.println( new Date().toString() );
        }
    }
);

clock.start();
```

The listeners are notified on each timer tick using a queued-notification strategy. That is, on each clock tick, a request to notify all listeners is placed on a queue that is serviced by a thread other than the Alarm's own timing thread. These requests are then serviced in order by the notification thread. The notification thread isn't created until a listener is registered, and it destroys itself automatically when no listeners are left to notify. If the total time required to notify the listeners is longer than the timing interval, then the time that elapses between the clock tick and the notifications associated with that tick will get progressively longer because the requests will back up in the queue, waiting to be serviced.

Because a second thread is used for notification, the time spent executing actionPerformed() methods doesn't impact the Alarm's timing. The Alarm doesn't use the Swing thread to run these listener methods, so you don't have to worry about locking up the UI if a listener takes too long to do its work, but by the same token, you do have to call SwingUtilities.invokeLater() or SwingUtilities.invokeAndWait() from your actionPerformed() method to safely talk to Swing. Also, the notification thread is a "Daemon." The fact that it's running will not keep the program alive. The Alarm itself has a reference to it, so as long as you have a reference to the Alarm object with which listeners have been registered, the notifier thread will hang around (not doing anything).

You can also "reset" an Alarm object at any time. If you pass a start() message to a running timer, the timing starts over again from the moment that second start() is received. This facility lets you implement a "dead-man" timer, which goes off only if something *doesn't* happen within a predetermined time. For example, a server that expects to be contacted by a client at least every five minutes can use this mechanism to detect that the client isn't functioning properly. The server will create a ONE_SHOT timer with a five-minute timeout. Every time a client connects, the server sends a start() message to the timer. The timer won't fire unless five minutes elapses without a client having connected.

The Static Structure of an Alarm

The source code for the Alarm class is in Listing 5.2. There's a lot to talk about here. Figure 5.1 shows the static model for the Alarm. In addition to the Alarm class itself, there are three inner classes of interest.

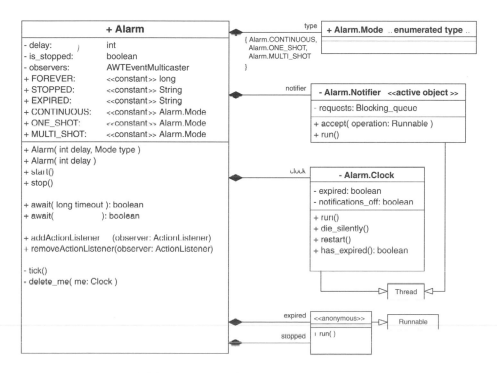

Figure 5.1. Static Model for the Alarm Class

The Alarm.Mode class has no members and is used to define various symbolic constants that indicate how the Alarm works. (These are defined on lines 18, 20, and 22 of Listing 5.2. In CONTINUOUS mode, the Alarm runs continuously, firing off events (or releasing any waiting threads) at regular intervals. A ONE_SHOT Alarm runs only once, then shuts itself down, freeing all support-level threads. You can restart the timer by calling start() a second time. A MULTI_SHOT timer works like just like a ONE_SHOT; it doesn't free the underlying timer thread, however. Use a MULTI_SHOT when you know you're going to fire up the Alarm again and don't want to incur the thread-creation overhead.

All three of these symbolic constants are instances of the Mode class, defined on line 16. This class demonstrates the proper way to do a constrained, enumerated type in Java. Because the Mode class's constructor is private, only two instances of Mode will ever exist: Alarm.ONE_SHOT, and Alarm.MULTI_SHOT (I use the value null for Alarm.CONTINUOUS.) Consequently, the values of a Mode are constrained, as is only proper for an enumerated type. Because the Mode class itself is public, other classes can access a Mode, declare references to Mode objects, among other things, but the private constructor prevents other classes from creating a new Mode. A method can now take a Mode argument (as does the constructor on line 36), and the compiler—not the runtime system— guarantees that that argument will always be a legitimate mode. There are no other possibilities. Had I used a static final int to define the modes, it would be possible to pass the constructor an illegal value for the Mode argument.

Two more symbolic constants, STOPPED and EXPIRED, are defined on lines 31 and 33. These are the "action command" Strings attached to the ActionEvent objects sent to registered listeners when the timer fires. Because the action commands are outputs from the Alarm (as compared to inputs), the values are effectively constants, and a full-blown enumeration like Mode isn't required here.

The next fields of interest are stopped (Listing 5.2, line 136), expired (Listing 5.2, line 145), and observers (Listing 5.2, line 28). The first two fields reference anonymous-inner-class implementations of Runnable in such a way that the run() method will send a STOPPED or EXPIRED message to any registered listener when the clock ticks or the Alarm is shut down. The definition for stopped looks like this:

```
private static final Runnable stopped =
    new Runnable()
    {   public void run()
        {   if( observers != null )
                observers.actionPerformed(
                    new ActionEvent(Alarm.this,0, STOPPED ));
        }
    };
```

The observer field, which is referenced from the run() method, references an AWTEventMulticaster that actually sends the actionPerformed() messages to the listeners. (If you haven't used an AWTEventMulticaster, this class effectively implements a list of listeners. When you send some sort of AWT event, such as actionPerformed(), to the multicaster, it relays the event to all the listeners in the list. I discuss multicasters in depth in Chapter 6.)

Finishing up with the Alarm class's fields, the is_stopped flag (Listing 5.2, line 11) lets me distinguish between a timer that has expired and one that has been stopped by the user. I need this flag because those threads that are waiting on the Alarm are notified both on expiration and when the Alarm is sent a stop() request. This flag lets me return different values from await() so that the waiting threads can distinguish the normal-expiration case from the timer-being-stopped case.

Two additional (private) inner classes are used by the Alarm to do its work. An instance of the Clock class (Listing 5.2, line 174) (which is also a Thread) actually does the timing. It's important to note that the Alarm itself *uses* a Thread (a Clock instance) to do its timing, but the Alarm itself is *not* a thread. Using an auxiliary class for timing makes it easier to reset the timer and also allows for better organization of the code. The Alarm object resets the time by killing the existing Clock thread, throwing away the object, and then creating a new Clock with the original timing interval. Implementing this sort of restart with a single class is difficult as there is no way to change the time associated with a sleep() call without breaking out of the sleep operation.

Another reason for using an auxiliary class for the timer thread (as compared to making the Alarm itself a Thread), is that it's occasionally convenient to wait on a timer that hasn't been started yet. For example, you might have a thread that performs a timeout action that permanently waits on a MULTI_SHOT Alarm whose delay interval is the timeout time. The Alarm isn't fired up until the event is initiated, however. Using two objects lets me hold off on creating the timing thread until it's actually needed.

The second important auxiliary class is the Notifier (Listing 5.2, line 109) class (also a Thread), which notifies listeners about "tick" events. The Notifier class is implemented as a single object that exits only when listeners are registered with a given Alarm. It keeps a queue of Runnable objects, passed from the Alarm when the Alarm "ticks," and executes those Runnable object's run() functions on the thread associated with the Notifier itself, as compared to the Alarm. This way the Alarm object can notify other objects about tick events without its own timing being affected—the notifications happen on the Notifier object's thread, not the clock's.

Dissecting a Notification

Delving further into the operation of this thing, the hideously complicated dynamic-model diagram in Figure 5.2 shows you the message sequence during the normal operation of an Alarm that notifies a listener when it goes off. (This scenario is something of a worst-case in terms of complexity.)

Starting with the client object in the upper-left corner: The client creates a new instance of Alarm (called an_Alarm), and passes it the time interval (delay) and the operational mode (either CONTINUOUS, ONE_SHOT, or MULTI_SHOT). The client then manufactures a Runnable object of some sort to be notified when the timer ticks, and adds it to the Alarm's listener list. The equivalent code might look like this:

```
an_alarm = new Alarm(1000,ONE_SHOT);
an_alarm.addActionListener
(    new Runnable()
     {    // Do this when timer goes off.
     }
);
```

UML Sequence Diagrams

A UML "sequence" diagram shows you the objects involved in some "scenario," and the messages these objects pass to one another as the scenario plays out. The "scenario" here is "Create an Alarm and notify a listener when the Alarm fires." The vertical lines with boxes on top of them are the objects. The name in the box is the name of the object, not of the object's class. It corresponds directly to the name of a field in a class, an argument to a method, or a local variable of some method. The horizontal lines represent messages, with the arrow head pointing at the receiving object. The different arrowheads have specific meanings: for example, a half stick-style arrow is an "asynchronous" message—one whose handler returns immediately after initiating a background operation. A solid arrowhead is a "synchronous" message—one whose handler doesn't return until the requested operation completes. The vertical axis represents time. The message closest to the top of the diagram is sent first, then the message below that one is sent, and so forth. The boxes with turned-down corners are comments.

The an_alarm object then adds the Runnable observer to its list of observers, calling addActionListener(...) (Listing 5.2, line 92). Since this is the first observer to be added, an_alarm creates an instance of Notifier called notifier, sets its daemon status, and starts it up. The notifier thread is now running. The first thing the notifier thread does (in run() (Listing 5.2, line 124)) is call dequeue() on its request queue. The request object is an instance of Blocking_queue, a queue whose dequeue() operation blocks (suspends the thread that calls it) until the queue isn't empty. Blocking queues are handy for inter-thread communication, and we'll look at an implementation in Chapter 8. (I couldn't eliminate all the forward references—sorry.) Finally, the client starts up the timing process by sending an_alarm a start() message.

Control now passes to an_alarm (start() (Listing 5.2, line 46)), which creates and starts up a timing element—the clock object—in response to receiving the start() message. Eventually, a run() event comes in from the operating system, and the clock enters its main control loop [while(!interrupted), in run() (Listing 5.2, line 185). The clock immediately puts itself to sleep for delay milliseconds. (The delay argument to sleep() is the same delay that's passed into the constructor.) Once the delay expires, clock sends a tick() message to an_alarm() to cause it to notify any interested parties that the timer has ticked. (This message is not sent in every scenario, but it does apply to the current one—I'll come back to tick in a moment.) What happens next depends on the operating mode. If we use a multi-shot timer, then the clock enters a wait(). The equivalent notify is sent when the clock is restarted by sending a start() message to an_alarm; we don't do that in the current scenario, however. If the clock is a one-shot, it sends a delete_me() message to an_alarm(), which causes an_alarm() to null out its clock reference so the memory can be garbage collected. As it says in the comment, the clock thread terminates itself after it sends the delete_me() message [*if* it sends the delete_me() message]. If this is a continuous Alarm, the thread loops back up and goes back to sleep. [Implement *[not interrupted] as while(!isInterrupted()).]

Returning back up to the tick() message (Listing 5.2, line 154), sent immediately after the clock() woke up, an_alarm handles the tick by doing two things: First it notifies any objects waiting on the Alarm itself [by calling notifyAll()], then it notifies the listeners by passing either expired (Listing 5.2, line 145) or stopped (Listing 5.2, line 136) to the notifier object that it created when the listener was registered. As I mentioned earlier, these objects implement Runnable in such a way that the run() method sends an actionPerformed() to the observers multicaster. By the way, I've implemented stopped and expired as static-final fields rather than creating them inside tick() because I didn't want the unnecessary overhead of a new on the clock thread. This way the clock thread just uses a preexisting object.

The tick() sends the appropriate Runnable object (either stopped or expired) to the notifier by calling accept(), which causes the notifier object to enqueue the Runnable object onto the requests blocking queue. Note that this enqueue operation is performed on the clock thread: the clock object's run() method calls tick(), which calls accept() which calls enqueue(). The accept() call returns immediately after the Runnable object is queued, long before that object's run() method is executed.

The fact that the request queue has something in it causes the notifier thread to wake up. (Remember, the notifier thread went to sleep when it tried to get an object from the empty requests queue on Listing 5.2, line 128). The dequeue() call now returns the Runnable (expired or stopped) object that the clock thread just enqueued and executes that object's run() method. Note that this activity is occurring on the notifier thread, not the clock thread. The notifier object's run() method calls dequeue(), which returns the expired object, which is in turn passed a run() request. (This last one is the run() call on Listing 5.2, line 124).

I'm effectively using the blocking queue to pass information from one thread to another: the clock thread passes a Runnable object to the notifier thread via the requests queue: The clock thread enqueues the object, and the notifier thread dequeues it.

Returning to the scenario, the notifier thread's run() method now calls the dequeued object's run() method, which asks the observers object (an AWTEventMulticaster) to notify its listeners by sending it an actionPerformed() message. That actionPerformed() message is duly relayed to a_listener, the Runnable object created by the client way up at the start of the scenario.

Whew!

Restarting an *Alarm* (Stopping a Thread)

The foregoing scenario covers the worst of it, but there are a few other things to point out in the code. First of all, how do you restart an Alarm object? The start() method (Listing 5.2, line 46) must kill the existing clock thread (if there is one) and then

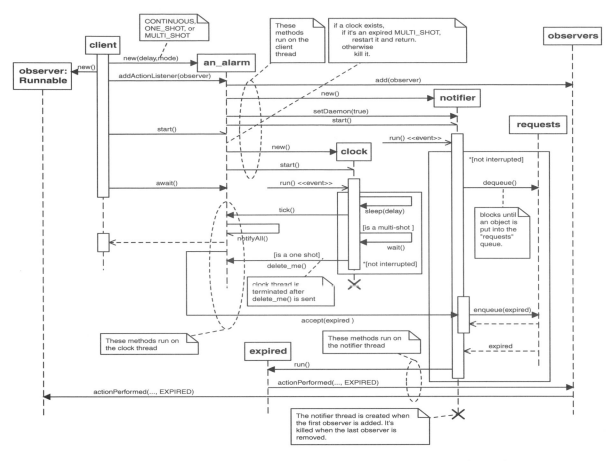

Figure 5.2. Dynamic Model for the Alarm *Class. A worst-case (from the perspective of complexity) scenario. A client object running on the main thread creates an* Alarm, *registers a listener to be notified when the clock ticks, and also waits for the clock to tick.*

create a new Clock. Unfortunately, the stop() method is deprecated, so the Alarm can't just stop() the Clock. Instead, it sends the Clock object a die_silently() message (Listing 5.2, line 221), which resets the notifications_on flag and issues an interrupt(), which breaks out of the Clock's timing loop (line 187). A tick() message (which causes the listeners to be notified) is not sent to the Alarm when notifications_on is false.

This code demonstrates the approved method for terminating a Thread by returning from run(). Sometimes you can do this by setting a simple flag that is tested by run(), but that won't work if the thread is blocked in a wait(). The general strategy is to send an interrupt() to the thread you want to kill, and have that thread test isInterrupted() at appropriate times. The Clock's run() loop (line 187) has to test in several places: in the while loop, of course, but also after sleep() returns [in case the thread was preempted after sleep() returned]. The catch clause down at the bottom of run() handles the normal situation of an interrupt() being received while the thread is blocked in sleep().

The Clock removes all traces of itself as it shuts down by calling delete_me(...) (Listing 5.2, line 165), setting the Alarm's clock reference to null. Meanwhile, several methods of the Alarm itself use or modify clock. All of the relevant Alarm methods, including delete_me(), are synchronized, so there's nothing to worry about there.

There is both a normal and a tricky synchronization issue in this code. First, The Clock cannot hold the monitor lock on the Alarm object while it is suspended on line 206, otherwise it couldn't be restarted. Consequently, it must enter a stand-alone synchronized block *after* sleep() returns. (I used sleep() rather than wait(), which would release the lock, because I'm using wait() for other purposes, discussed later.)

The second synchronization problem is handled by the test on line 166. This test is necessary because of the following scenario:

1. The clock expires, and the thread is preempted just before the delete_me() call.

2. Another thread comes along and stops the clock. This stopping is harmless because the stop() method (Listing 5.2, line 63) just sets the clock reference to null and interrupts the Clock. Neither operation will cause difficulty.

3. Another thread comes along and sends the Clock a start() message (Listing 5.2, line 46), which creates a new clock and starts it up.

4. The original Clock thread now wakes up and executes delete_me(), setting the newly minted Clock reference to null.

The if statement on line 166 solves the delete-an-active-Clock problem by assuring that a given Clock object can remove only a reference to itself.

Suspending the Clock

The fact that suspend() has been deprecated also gives me some grief. When a MULTI_SHOT Alarm expires, I want to keep the clock object around so that I won't have to create another one when the MULTI_SHOT Alarm is restarted. (A ONE_SHOT Alarm does destroy the clock when it expires—that's the only difference between the two modes.) I've used a wait() on line 206, rather than a suspend(), for this purpose. The matching notify() is in restart(), down on line 228. The restart() message is sent to the clock() from line 49 of the the Alarm's start() message.

A wait()/notify() strategy can almost always replace calls to suspend() and resume(), without any of the monitor-related problems caused by the now-deprecated methods. I discussed these back in Chapter 2, but by way of reminder, suspend(), unlike wait() does not give up the monitor's lock when it is called. This was the guy-goes-into-the-bathroom-and-falls-into-a-drug-induced-coma scenario. As a consequence, if you use `suspend()` it's possible to get into deadlock scenarios that you simply can't get into if you use `wait()`, which gives up the monitor's lock before it goes off to wait on the associated condition variable.

Also, note that the lock on the `Clock` object [acquired by the `synchronized(this)` statement on line 195] is released by `wait()` when the thread is suspended on line 206—that's just the way that `wait()` works. Consequently, the fact that `restart()` (Listing 5.2, line 226) is `synchronized` is not relevant. (In fact, it has to be `synchronized` to call `notify()`.)

Notifier Problems

The `addActionListener()` and `removeActionListener ()` methods must be synchronized so that a second thread that calls `addActionListener()` can't interrupt us after the test but before the `Notifier` object is created and started; otherwise we could end up with two `Notifier` threads, one created by each thread.

Also, consider the following scenario:

1. `addActionListener()` is called, and starts up the thread. `run()` is pre-empted just after testing `isInterrupted()` on line 127, but before attempting the `dequeue()`.

2. `removeActionListener()` is called and removes a listener. It is preempted as `AwtEventMulticaster.remove()` is returning, after the listener has been removed but before the control is passed back to the caller. (`AwtEventMulticaster.remove()` is thread safe, so we don't have to worry about it, at least.)

3. `run()` reactivates, and `dequeue()` is called.

The net effect is that we'd have an extra notifier thread hanging out on street corners with nothing to do. This is not a crash-and-burn sort of failure since the existence of an unused `Notifier` is harmless. Nonetheless, I don't like threads to be kicking around unnecessarily. I could solve the problem by synchronizing on the outer-class `Alarm` object inside the `Notifier`'s `run()` method. The restructured version of `run()` (Listing 5.2, line 124) would look like this:

```
private class Notifier extends Thread
{   //...
    public void run()
    {   try
        {   while( true )
```

```
      {   synchronized( Alarm.this )
          {   if( interrupted() || (observers == null) )
                  break;
          }

          ((Runnable)( requests.dequeue() )).run(); //#dequeue
          yield();
      }
    }
    catch(InterruptedException e){/*not an error*/}
  }
}
```

I opted not to do this restructuring because I didn't want to incur the synchronization overhead and I can live with the remote possibility of a dormant, but unnecessary, thread. You can reasonably argue that I've made the wrong choice, however.

Listing 5.2 (/src/com/holub/asynch/Alarm.java): Roll-Your-Own Timer

```
001: package com.holub.asynch;
002:
003: import java.util.*;          // Need Date for testing
004: import java.awt.event.*;     // For ActionListener, etc.
005: import java.awt.*;           // For ActionListener, etc.
006:

    /**
        An interval timer. Once you "start" it, it runs for a pre-
        determined amount of time. The timer runs on it's own,
        relatively high priority, thread while one or more other
        threads block, waiting for the timer to "expire."

        Three sorts of timers are supported:
        A "one-shot" timer
            runs once, then expires. May be started again, but
            generally isn't.
        A "multi-shot" timer
            works like a one-shot timer, but expects to be started
            again, so is more efficient in this situation. Must be
            stopped explicitly by a call to stop().
        A "continuous" (oscillator-style) timer
            runs continuously. Starts up again automatically when
            it expires. Must be stopped explicitly.

        All timers may be restarted (have the time interval set
        back to the original value) while they are running.
```

Warnings:

1. It's easy to forget to stop() a multi-shot or continuous
   timer and create a memory leak as a consequence. (The JVM will
   keep the Thread object alive but suspended, even if there are
   no external references to it.) A finalizer is provided to
   throw an exception in this situation, but since the finalizer
   may not be called, that's not a perfect solution.
2. Calling java.lang.Thread#wait() on a timer is possible, but it
   only works correctly for CONTINUOUS timers. The await() method
   works correctly for all types of timers, and is easier to use
   since you don't have to synchronize first. The only time that
   using a raw wait() makes sense if if you're interested in the
   InterruptedException, which is silently absorbed by await().

@author *Allen I. Holub*

```
        **/
007: public final class Alarm
008: {                                         // A compiler bug (1.1x, 1.2rc1)
009:     private int             delay;        // permit blank finals.
010:     private Alarm.Clock     clock               = null;
011:     private boolean         is_stopped          = false;
012:     private boolean         keeps_process_alive = false;
013:
        /************************************************************
```

Notifiers can be added to an Alarm by addActionListener.
The notifiers are notified on their own thread by enqueueing a notification request on each clock "tick."
If the total time required for notification exceeds the
distance between ticks, these requests will back up in a
queue waiting for service. The REQUEST_LIMIT is the
maximum number of ticks that can be waiting for service
at any given moment. Any additional requests will be
silently ignored when the queue fills.

```
        */
014:     public static final int REQUEST_LIMIT = 8;
015:
        /************************************************************
```

A constrained set of operational modes. Legal values are
CONTINUOUS, ONE_SHOT, and MULTI_SHOT.

```
        */
```

```
016:        public static final class Mode { private Mode(){} }
017:
           /***********************************************************
               CONTINUOUS alarms run continuously (until stopped), sending
               out notification messages and releasing waiting threads
               at a regular interval.
            */
018:        public static final Mode CONTINUOUS  = null;
019:
           /***********************************************************
               ONE_SHOT alarms run once, then stop automatically. [You
               do not have to call stop().] Can be started again manually
               by calling start(), but a new internal thread  must be
               created to do so.
            */
020:        public static final Mode ONE_SHOT     = new Mode();
021:
           /***********************************************************
               MULTI_SHOT alarms work just like ONE_SHOT alarms, but they
               can be restarted more efficiently. (The timer thread for a
               MULTI_SHOT alarm is not destroyed until you stop() the
               alarm.) Use a MULTI_SHOT when you know that the one-shot
               will be restarted at regular intervals and don't mind having
               an extra thread kicking around in a suspended state.
            */
022:        public static final Mode MULTI_SHOT  = new Mode();
023:
024:        private Mode type;
025:
026:        //-----------------------------------------------------------------
027:
028:        private ActionListener  observers   = null;
029:        private Notifier        notifier;
030:
           /***********************************************************
               "Action command" sent to the ActionListeners when the
               timer has been stopped manually.
            */
031:        public static final String STOPPED = "stopped";
032:
           /***********************************************************
               "Action command" sent to the ActionListeners when the
               timer has expired or "ticked."
            */
033:        public static final String EXPIRED = "expired";
034:
035:
           /***********************************************************
               Create a timer that expires after the indicated delay
               in milliseconds.
```

Generally, timers must run at high priority to prevent the waiting threads from starting up immediately on being notified, thereby messing up the timing. If a high-priority thread is waiting on a recurring timer, however, the next "tick" could be delayed by the amount of time the high-priority thread spends doing whatever it does after being notified. Alarms run at the highest priority permitted by the thread group of which they are a member, but spend most of their time sleeping.

@param *delay* Time to expiration (nominal) in milliseconds.

@param *type* One of the following symbolic constants:

Alarm.CONTINUOUS   The timer runs continuously. You must call stop() when you're done with it.

Alarm.ONE_SHOT   The timer runs once, then stops automatically. You do not have to call stop().

Alarm.MULTI_SHOT   Like ONE_SHOT, but can be restarted more efficiently. You must call stop() when you're done with it.

If this argument is null, CONTINUOUS is used.

@param *keeps_process_alive* By default, the Alarm's timing-element thread is a Daemon. This means that the fact that an Alarm is running won't keep the process alive. This behavior can cause problems with some single-threaded applications that sleep, doing every-thing that it does on a clock tick. Specifying a true value will cause a running timer to keep the current process alive; you'll have to stop() the Alarm object [or call system.exit()]to allow the application to shut down. Note that an *expired* ONE_SHOT or MULTI_SHOT never keeps the process alive.

```
               **/
036:    public Alarm( int delay, Mode type, boolean keeps_process_alive  )
037:    {   this.delay               = delay;
038:        this.type                = (type == null) ? CONTINUOUS : type ;
039:        this.keeps_process_alive = keeps_process_alive   ;
040:    }
041:

        /*************************************************************
         Make a continuous timer that won't keep the process alive
         simply because it's running.
        */
042:    public Alarm( int delay )
043:    {   this( delay, CONTINUOUS, false );
044:    }
045:

        /*************************************************************
         Start up a timer or restart an expired timer. If the
         timer is running, it is set back to the original count
         without releasing any of the threads that are waiting for
         it to expire. (For example, if you start up a 10-second
         timer and then restart it after 5 seconds, the waiting
```

threads won't be notified until 10 seconds after the
restart—15 seconds after the original start time.)

Starting a running timer causes a new thread to be created.
```
        **/
046:    public synchronized void start()
047:    {   if( clock != null )
048:        {   if( type == MULTI_SHOT && clock.has_expired() )
049:            {   clock.restart();
050:                return;
051:            }
052:            else
053:            {   clock.die_silently();
054:            }
055:        }
056:
057:        clock = new Clock();
058:        clock.setDaemon( !keeps_process_alive );
059:        clock.start();
060:        is_stopped = false;
061:    }
062:
        /*****************************************************************
            Stops the current timer abruptly, releasing all waiting
            threads. The timer can be restarted by calling start().
            There's no good way for a thread to determine if it was notified
            as the result of a stop() or a normal expiration.
        **/
063:    public synchronized void stop()
064:    {   if( clock != null )
065:            clock.interrupt();
066:
067:        clock      = null;
068:        is_stopped = true;
069:        notifyAll();
070:    }
071:
        /*****************************************************************
            It is a bug not to stop() a CONTINUOUS or MULTI_SHOT timer
            when you're done with it. This finalizer helps you detect the
            bug by printing an error message if the timer that is being
            destroyed is still running, but bear in mind that there's
            absolutely no guarantee in Java that a finalizer will *ever*
            be called, so don't count on this behavior.
        **/
072:    public void finalize()
073:    {   if( clock != null )
074:            System.out.println(
075:                    "Alarm was not stopped before being destroyed");
076:    }
077:
```

```
              /************************************************************
                  A long time (roughly 292,271,023 years) that you can
                  use for the timeout value in await().
               **/
078:          public static final long FOREVER = Long.MAX_VALUE;
079:

              /************************************************************
                  Wait for the timer to expire. Returns immediately in
                  the case of an expired ONE_SHOT or MULTI_SHOT timer.
                  Blocks until the timer expires in all other situations
                  (including any sort of timer that has not yet been
                  started).
                  @return false if the method returned because the timer
                  was stopped, true if the timer simply expired.
                  @see FOREVER
               **/
080:          public synchronized boolean await( long timeout )
081:          {
082:              if( clock == null || !clock.has_expired() )
083:              {   try                            { wait( timeout );  }
084:                  catch( InterruptedException e ) { /*do nothing*/    }
085:              }
086:              return !is_stopped;
087:          }
088:

              /************************************************************
                Same as await(Alarm.FOREVER)
               **/
089:          public boolean await(){ return await( FOREVER ); }
090:
091:

              /************************************************************
                  Add a listener that will be notified the next time
                  that the Alarm goes off. The listeners are notified
                  on a thread that's created just for that purpose,
                  rather than being notified from the timer thread. This
                  way the time spent doing notification doesn't impact
                  the time interval used by the timer. The "action
                  command" in the ActionEvent object will be either the
                  String "stopped" or "expired" (which are also defined in
                  the symbolic constants Alarm.STOPPED and Alarm.EXPIRED),
                  depending on whether this notification occurred because
                  the timer was stopped manually, or because it expired in
                  the normal way.

                  It's your job to make sure that the total time required
                  to notify all listeners does not exceed the time between
                  ticks. Some slop is built into the system, in that up to
                  ticks will be queued up waiting for service, but if the
                  Alarm gets more than 8 ticks behind, then the extra ticks
                  are silently ignored.
               */
```

```
092:    public synchronized void addActionListener(ActionListener observer)
093:    {   observers = AWTEventMulticaster.add(observers, observer);
094:        if( notifier == null )
095:        {   notifier = new Alarm.Notifier();
096:            notifier.start();
097:        }
098:    }
099:
```

```
        /************************************************************
```
        Remove a listener.
```
        */
100:    public synchronized void removeActionListener(ActionListener
101:                                                        observer)
102:    {   observers = AWTEventMulticaster.remove(observers, observer);
103:        if( observers == null )
104:        {   notifier.interrupt();   // kill the notifier thread.
105:            notifier = null;
106:        }
107:    }
108:
```

```
        /************************************************************
```
        The thread that actually notifies other listeners.
        (Notification is done on a separate thread so as to not
        impact the Alarm's timing.)Rather than spawn multiple
        instances of the thread (which can cause problems if the
        actionPerformed() messages takes longer to execute than
        the interval between clock ticks), Runnable objects that
        notify the listeners are queued up in a blocking queue
        which is serviced by the Notifier thread.
```
        */
109:    private final class Notifier extends Thread
110:    {
111:        public Notifier()
112:        {   setDaemon( true );
113:        }
114:
115:        private Blocking_queue requests =
116:                                new Blocking_queue(REQUEST_LIMIT);
117:
```
        /**
            Accept a request for this notifier.
            @throws *Blocking_queue.Full* if more than 8 requests
            are waiting to be serviced.
            @throws *Blocking_queue.Closed* if an internal error occurs.
```
        */
118:        public void accept( Runnable operation )
119:                                        throws Blocking_queue.Full,
120:                                            Blocking_queue.Closed
121:        {   requests.enqueue(operation);
122:        }
123:
124:        public void run()
```

```
125:            {
126:                try
127:                {   while( !interrupted() && (observers != null) )
128:                    {   ((Runnable)( requests.dequeue() )).run();
129:                        yield();
130:                    }
131:                }
132:                catch(InterruptedException e){/*not an error*/}
133:            }
134:        }
135:
```

```
    /**
        Sends an ActionEvent indicating that the timer has stopped.
     */
```

```
136:    private final Runnable stopped =
137:                new Runnable()
138:                {   public void run()
139:                    {   if( observers != null )
140:                            observers.actionPerformed(
141:                                new ActionEvent(Alarm.this,0, STOPPED));
142:                    }
143:                };
144:
```

```
    /**
        Sends an ActionEvent indicating that the timer has expired.
     */
```

```
145:    private final Runnable expired =
146:                new Runnable()
147:                {   public void run()
148:                    {   if( observers != null )
149:                            observers.actionPerformed(
150:                                new ActionEvent(Alarm.this,0, EXPIRED));
151:                    }
152:                };
153:
```

```
    /**
        Sent to us from a Clock on every "tick," queues up a
        request to notify listeners. If too many requests are
        queued, then ticks will be lost.
     */
```

```
154:    synchronized private final void tick()
155:    {   try
156:        {   Alarm.this.notifyAll();
157:            if( notifier != null )
158:                notifier.accept( is_stopped ? stopped : expired );
159:        }
160:        catch( Blocking_queue.Full request_queue_full )
161:        {   // Ignore it.
162:        }
163:    }
164:
```

```
            /**
                Sent to us from a Clock when the clock object wants to remove
                all references to itself.
             */
165:    synchronized private final void delete_me( Clock me )
166:    {   if( clock == me )
167:            clock = null;
168:    }
169:
170:    //===================================================================
171:    // Support classes:
172:    //===================================================================
173:
174:    private final class Clock extends Thread
175:    {
176:        // Note that continuous Alarms don't expire.
177:
178:        private boolean expired          = false;
179:        private boolean notifications_on = true;
180:
181:        Clock()
182:        {   setPriority( getThreadGroup().getMaxPriority() );
183:        }
184:
185:        public void run()
186:        {
187:            while( !isInterrupted() )
188:            {   try
189:                {
190:                    sleep(delay); // The monitor is not released by
191:                                  // sleep() so this call must
192:                                  // be outside the synchronized
193:                                  // block.
194:
195:                    synchronized( this )
196:                    {
197:                        if( isInterrupted() )  // don't notify waiting
198:                            break;             // threads if we've been
199:                                               // stopped by the
200:                                               // Alarm object.
201:                        expired = true;
202:                        if( notifications_on )
203:                            Alarm.this.tick();
204:
205:                        if( type == MULTI_SHOT )
206:                        {   wait();                 // suspend
207:                        }
208:                        else if( type == ONE_SHOT )     // Null out the
209:                        {   Alarm.this.delete_me(this); // outer-class
210:                            break;                      // reference to
211:                                                        // the clock.
212:                        }
```

```
213:                        }
214:                    }
215:                catch(InterruptedException e)// don't notify the waiting
216:                {   break;                  // threads because an
217:                }                           // interrupt is used to
218:            }                               // stop the timer.
219:        }
220:
221:        public void die_silently()
222:        {   notifications_on = false;
223:            interrupt();
224:        }
225:
226:        public synchronized void restart()
227:        {   expired = false;
228:            notify();                       // resume
229:        }
230:
231:        public boolean has_expired()                // CONTINUOUS
232:        {   return (type != CONTINUOUS) && expired; // timers never
233:        }                                           // expire.
234:    };
235:
236:    //================================================================
237:    // Unit test:
238:    //================================================================
239:    static public final class Test
240:    {
241:        public static void main( String[] args ) throws Exception
242:        {
243:            // A recurring timer, runs until it is stoped manually.
244:
245:            Alarm timing_element = new Alarm(1000, Alarm.CONTINUOUS,
246:                                                            false );
247:            timing_element.start();
248:
249:            System.out.println("Print time 3 times, 1-sec. intervals");
250:
251:            for( int i = 3; --i>= 0; )
252:            {
253:                System.out.println( new Date().toString() );
254:                timing_element.await( Alarm.FOREVER );
255:            }
256:
257:            timing_element.stop();  // It is essential to stop the timer
258:                                    // manually, Otherwise, the memory
259:                                    // for it might never be reclaimed.
260:
261:            System.out.println("\nOne-shot:\n");
262:
263:            // A One-shot. Fire it manually. You don't need to stop()
264:            // it explicitly---it automatically frees up all threads
265:            // when it expires.
```

```
266:
267:                timing_element = new Alarm(1000, Alarm.ONE_SHOT, false);
268:                timing_element.start();
269:                for( int i = 3; --i>= 0; )
270:                {
271:                    System.out.println( new Date().toString() + "\r" );
272:                    timing_element.await( Alarm.FOREVER );
273:                    timing_element.start();
274:                }
275:
276:                System.out.println("");
277:                System.out.println("Multi-shot:\n");
278:
279:                // A Multi-shot is much like a one-shot. Fire it manually,
280:                // but you must stop() it explicitly. The main difference
281:                // is that a MULTI_SHOT timer doesn't recreate the timer
282:                // thread when it's restarted. The one-shot timer creates
283:                // the thread anew every time it's started.
284:
285:                timing_element = new Alarm(1000, Alarm.MULTI_SHOT, false);
286:                timing_element.start();
287:                for( int i = 3; --i>= 0; )
288:                {
289:                    System.out.println( new Date().toString() + "\r" );
290:                    timing_element.await( Alarm.FOREVER );
291:                    timing_element.start();
292:                }
293:                timing_element.stop();
294:
295:                System.out.println("");
296:                System.out.println( "Notifier\n" );
297:
298:                timing_element = new Alarm( 1000 ); // 1-second continuous
299:                timing_element.addActionListener
300:                (   new ActionListener()
301:                    {   public void actionPerformed( ActionEvent e )
302:                        {   System.out.println( new Date().toString()
303:                                    + " (" + e.getActionCommand() + ")" );
304:                        }
305:                    }
306:                );
307:                timing_element.start();
308:
309:                System.out.println("Sleeping");
310:                Thread.currentThread().sleep( 3000 );
311:                System.out.println("Waking");
312:
313:                timing_element.stop();
314:                System.exit(0);
315:            }
316:        }
317: }
```

Unit Tests

The final thing to look at in Listing 5.2 is the unit-test class: Test (Listing 5.2, line 239). A "unit" test is piece of code that tests one thing, in this case a class. It's a good idea to associate a unit test with every class you write, and there are several ways to do that. You could pair a test file with every class file, but you'd end up with too many files to maintain. Also, keeping the test routine in phase with the class as it evolves would be difficult, because you could recompile the class without recompiling the test.

Another strategy is to put a main() in every class. I don't do that because I don't want to carry around the baggage of a unit test in every *.class* file that comprises the program. The tests are often bigger than the class I'm testing, and I don't want to inflate the application size with test code.

A third option—putting the test code in a separate class, but in the same file as the class being tested—doesn't work out very well because the package-level name space becomes corrupted with all the names of the test classes. Managing these names can become a problem in its own right.

I eventually hit on the strategy of implementing a test class as an inner class of the class I'm testing. I always call this class Test. This inner class ends up in its own *.class* file, and I don't ship it with the application, so it doesn't increase the application's size. The Test class's name is within the name space of the outer class, so the global name space isn't corrupted with stuff that the user of the class could care less about. Given a set of classes listed in a makefile, I can easily run a whole battery of tests from a makefile by deriving the Test class's name from the source file name using macros. For example, I can test the current class by executing:

```
java Alarm\$Test
```

(You don't need the backslash on Windows machines.) You can't say *java Alarm.Test* because the JVM will think you're trying to run the Test class in the Animator package.

Summing Up

Frankly, I'm not completely convinced that this code will indeed work correctly in all situations. I've stared at the code, made diagrams, and analyzed up the wazoo, but if past experience is any indication, I've still probably missed something. Welcome to the world of thread programming. If you find a flaw in my reasoning (and some of you probably will—sigh), please send me an email (*bugs@holub.com*).

CHAPTER 6

Observers and Multicasters

THIS CHAPTER LOOKS AT the Gang-of-Four Observer design pattern from a multi-threaded perspective. Observer is one of the more useful design patterns if your goal is to loosen coupling relationships between classes. It is essential, really, for building truly reusable components. It turns out that, as usual, problems arise in implementing Observer that wouldn't exist were threads not on the scene, and this chapter examines solutions to those problems.

Implementing Observer in a Multithreaded World

The AWT/Swing listeners (which you should have learned about when learning Java) are an example of a general-purpose design pattern called *Observer*. This design pattern is often called "publisher/subscriber" because publishing is a useful metaphor for describing how it works. Objects interested in finding out about some event "subscribe" to a publication administered by a "publisher." The publisher notifies the "subscribers" that an event occurs by "publishing" it. To complete the metaphor, the event itself—passed as an argument in the notification message—is the "publication." If you're familiar with the Observer pattern, you might want to skip to the next section.

The main intent of Observer is to decouple the generator of some message from the receiver of the message. For example, in the following code, the Sender and Receiver classes are tightly coupled. You couldn't even compile Sender if Receiver didn't exist. Calling tickle() on a Sender object causes a hello() notification to be sent to the Receiver object.

```
class Sender
{   Receiver listener;
    Sender( Receiver listener ){ this.listener = listener };
    //...
    public void tickle(){ listener.hello(); }
}

class Receiver
{   public hello(){ System.out.println("Hello world"); }
}
```

```
//...
    Sender s = new Sender( new Receiver() );
    s.tickle();
```

When the Sender is something as generic as a button, this tight coupling presents a problem. Were a button class to actually use this simple notification strategy, it could only notify one other class that it had been pressed—not a good strategy for reuse.

You can decouple the button from the object to which it is talking by designing the button to talk to objects of an unknown (at least to the button) class through a known *public* interface. The sending class is coupled to the interface, but not to the classes that implement that interface. Here is the previous example reworked to use this interface strategy:

```
interface Observer
{    public void hello();
}

class Sender_2
{    Observer listener;
     Sender_2( Observer listener ){ this.listener = listener };
     //...
     public void tickle(){ listener.hello() };
}

class Receiver implements Observer
{    public hello(){ System.out.println("Hello world"); }
}

//...
    Sender_2 s = new Sender_2( new Receiver() );
    s.tickle();
```

The main thing to notice is how similar the modified code is to the original code; the design pattern imposes almost no inconvenience with respect to coding. Writing in terms of an interface makes Sender_2 much more flexible than the original Sender, since it can now talk to any class that implements the Observer interface.

The current example uses a "unicast" model in which the notifier object can notify only one observer. A more complicated implementation of Observer might use a "multicast" model where several observers would be notified when some event occurs rather than just one. Similarly, you can add some mechanism to dynamically register (and unregister) observers with the notifier object after that object is created. AWT/Swing's "delegation event model," of course, uses the Observer pattern to notify what Sun calls "listeners" (which are just observers) about various UI-related events. (The remainder of this chapter assumes some familiarity with the delegation event model). You can find examples in virtually every Java textbook,

and on the Sun Web site at `http://java.sun.com/products/jdk/1.1/docs/guide/awt/`
`designspec/events.html`.

Observer-side Problems: Inner-class Synchronization

Implementing Observer is simple enough when you're working in a single-threaded
environment. But as usual, adding threads to the mix complicates things considerably. The first thread-related problem with Observer shows up when you implement
a listener as an inner class. This example really drives home the fact that race conditions can appear even in situations where you have written no explicit multithreaded
code at all because several of the Java packages (most notably AWT/Swing) create
threads of their own.

I will demonstrate. The Status class in Listing 6.1 does nothing but monitor a
status that is modified by the (synchronized) `change_status(...)` method (Listing 6.1,
line 26). The Status object's UI is a single button which, when pressed, pops up a
message box that reports the current status. The main() method creates the Status
object, then changes the status a few times, waiting for a few seconds between
each change.

Listing 6.1 (/text/books/threads/ch6/Status.java): Listener-Related Race Conditions

```
01: import javax.swing.*;
02: import java.awt.event.*;
03:
04: class Status extends JFrame
05: {
06:     private String title    = "Status: idle";
07:     private String contents = "Nothing happening";
08:
09:     public Status()
10:     {
11:         JButton pop_it_up = new JButton( "Show status" );
12:         pop_it_up.addActionListener
13:         (   new ActionListener()
14:             {   public void actionPerformed( ActionEvent e )
15:                 {   JOptionPane.showMessageDialog( null,
16:                             contents, title, JOptionPane.INFORMATION_MESSAGE
);
17:                 }
18:             }
19:         );
20:
21:         getContentPane().add( pop_it_up );
22:         pack();
23:         show();
24:     }
25:
```

```
26:     public synchronized void change_status( String status, String explanation )
27:     {   this.title    = "Status: " + status;
28:         this.contents = explanation;
29:     }
30:
31:     public static void main( String[] args )
32:     {
33:         Status myself = new Status();
34:
35:         myself.change_status( "Busy", "I'm busy");
36:         work();
37:         myself.change_status( "Done", "I'm done");
38:         work();
39:         myself.change_status( "Busy", "I'm busy again");
40:         work();
41:         myself.change_status( "Done", "I'm done again");
42:         work();
43:
44:         System.exit( 0 );
45:     }
46:
47:     private static void work()
48:     {   try{ Thread.currentThread().sleep(4000); }catch( Exception e ){}
49:     }
50: }
```

So, what's the problem? Everything is synchronized, isn't it? Well, not really. The problem is that, even though the word Thread appears nowhere in Listing 6.1, this is nonetheless a multithreaded application: There is the main thread (on which main() executes) and there is the AWT/Swing thread that handles GUI events like button presses (as discussed in the previous chapter). These threads are both running in parallel and accessing the same Status object in parallel. Now imagine the following sequence of events:

1. main() executes, popping up the main frame and setting the status message.

2. main() finishes the first piece of work, and sends the message

    ```
    myself.change_status( "Done", "I'm done doing something");
    ```

    to the main-frame object. This method is synchronized, so it appears safe.

3. Halfway through the execution of change_status() (after the title is changed, but before the contents are changed) the user hits the "Show status" button. The main thread is preempted, and the AWT thread wakes up to process the button press.

4. To see what happens next, examine the event-handler setup code on line 13. An anonymous inner-class object handles the button press, and it manufactures the message dialog using the title and contents fields. At this point, however, the title field has been modified, *but the contents have not*, so the displayed title doesn't jibe with the actual message.

A first (incorrect) attempt to solve the problem might be to synchronize the actionPerformed() method:

```
pop_it_up.addActionListener
(   new ActionListener()
    {   public synchronized void actionPerformed( ActionEvent e )
        {   JOptionPane.showMessageDialog( null,
                        contents, title, JOptionPane.INFORMATION_MESSAGE );
        }
    }
);
```

This fix doesn't fix anything, though. Remember, you have two objects and two monitors. Locking the inner-class object does not affect access to the outer-class object, which contains the two fields that are giving us grief. The only solution is to synchronize on the object that actually contains the fields that the two threads are accessing—the outer-class object:

```
pop_it_up.addActionListener
(   new ActionListener()
    {   public void actionPerformed( ActionEvent e )
        {
            synchronized( Status.this )
            {
                JOptionPane.showMessageDialog( null,
                        contents, title, JOptionPane.INFORMATION_MESSAGE );
            }
        }
    }
);
```

To be safe, all inner-class listeners that access outer-class fields should synchronize on the *outer-class* object in this way.

Notifier-side Problems: Notifications in a Multithreaded World

Flipping the perspective over to that of the notifier, various thread-related problems emerge here, too.

1. Observers can be added and removed from the current list while notifications are in progress.

2. Events can occur so fast that several notifications go on at the same time, perhaps using different, but overlapping, observer lists.

3. Observers can be notified after you have already issued the request that an observer be removed from the list.

Let's start by analyzing the modification-while-notifications-are-in-progress problem, which in some ways is the hardest to solve. AWT/Swing listeners can be added or removed at any time, even when notifications are in progress. In fact, a listener can even remove itself from a list of listeners as it services the notification-message passed to it. The following code is perfectly legal:

```
Button some_button;
//...
some_button.addActionListener
(   new ActionListener()
    {   public void actionPerformed( ActionEvent e )
        {   some_button.removeActionListener( this );
            //...
        }
    }
);
```

I'll describe how to get control over this potentially chaotic situation by looking at various examples (which comprise this chapter's entries in the world's-most-complicated-way-to-print-hello-world contest). Listing 6.2 shows an implementation of the world's simplest observer/subscriber. The publication can be any arbitrary Object. (I don't like having to cast it all the time, but it's the price you pay for flexibility—at least until parameterized types are added to Java.) If you're interested receiving notices about something, you implement this interface, providing your own version of receive(), which is called when the event is fired. In a more complex example you might extend Subscriber with another interface that added event-specific methods.

Listing 6.2 (Subscriber.java): A Simple Observer

```
    /** A subscriber in the Observer (or Publisher/Subcriber) pattern.

        Implement this interface to "subscribe" to a publication.
     */
01: public interface Subscriber
02: {   void receive( Object publication );
03: }
04:
```

Listing 6.3 shows a "publisher" implementation that corresponds to the subscriber in Listing 6.2. It provides methods that let you add a new subscriber, remove a subscriber, and publish news of an event to the subscribers. The publish() method (Listing 6.3, line 16) just publishes the string ("Hello world") to the subscribers.

Note that the list is copied by converting it to an array on line 20 of Listing 6.3. You, unfortunately, can't use clone() to copy a generic Collection (because Collection is an interface, and it doesn't require clone() to be implemented by the derived classes). Of the two things you can do to a Collection (make an empty list and explicitly copy the Collection into it or convert the Collection to an array), array conversion seems the most appropriate in the current code: An array is both smaller and easier to assemble than another LinkedList, in any event. I'll come back to this listing in a moment.

Listing 6.3 (Publisher.java): A Simplistic Notifier

```
01: import java.util.*;
02: import Subscriber;
03:
04: public class Publisher
05: {
06:     Collection subscription_list = new LinkedList();
07:
08:     synchronized public void subscribe( Subscriber subscriber )
09:     {   subscription_list.add( subscriber );
10:     }
11:
12:     synchronized public void cancel_subscription( Subscriber subscriber )
13:     {   subscription_list.remove( subscriber );
14:     }
15:     //-----------------------------------------------------------------
16:     public void publish( )           // usually called by other publisher
17:     {                                // methods so would be private
18:         Object[] copy;
19:         synchronized( this )
20:         {   copy = subscription_list.toArray();
21:         }
22:
23:         for( int i = 0; i < copy.length; ++i )
24:             ((Subscriber) copy[i]).receive("Hello world");
25:     }
26:     //-----------------------------------------------------------------
27:     public synchronized void publish_blocking()
28:     {
29:         for(Iterator i = subscription_list.iterator(); i.hasNext();)
30:             ((Subscriber) i.next()).receive("Hello world");
31:     }
32:     //...
33: }
```

The `Hello_world` class in Listing 6.4 shows how the publisher and subscriber classes work together. `main()` manufactures a Publisher on line 5 and a `Subscriber` on line 6. The `Subscriber` implementation is an anonymous inner class whose `receive()` override prints the `String` that is passed in from the publisher as the publication argument (`"Hello world"`). In `main()`, the subscriber is forced to subscribe to the publication (this is not a democracy), and then the publisher is told to publish the event.

Listing 6.4 (Hello_world.java): Publishing to the Subscribers

```
01: import Subscriber;
02:
03: public class Hello_world
04: {
05:     static private Publisher  publisher  = new Publisher();
06:     static private Subscriber subscriber =
07:             new Subscriber()
08:             {   public void receive(Object p)
09:                 {   System.out.println( (String) p );
10:                 }
11:             };
12:
13:     static public void main( String[] args )
14:     {   publisher.subscribe( subscriber );
15:         publisher.publish();                // Publish "Hello world" events
16:     }
17: }
```

Returning to Listing 6.3, you'll note that `subscribe(...)` and `cancel_subscription` (...) are `synchronized`, but `publish()` is not. Also note that `publish()` makes a copy of the `subscription_list` (on line 20) and notifies the subscribers by traversing the copy. This strategy is the one suggested in the JavaBeans specification for handling notifications in a multithreaded environment, the point being that you don't want to lock up all the `synchronized` methods of a publisher class while notifications are in progress.

There is no way to tell how long it will take for a subscriber's `receive()` method to execute, since it is supplied by whoever implements the subscriber. Consequently, `publish()` executes for an indeterminate amount of time. If `publish()` were `synchronized`, then the entire object would be locked until the notifications completed. Any thread that attempted to add or remove a subscriber, or call any other `synchronized` method for that matter, would block. So, `publish()` cannot be `synchronized`.

This lack of synchronization means that publish can't use the `subscription_list` directly, however. Otherwise another thread could come along and add and remove elements while notifications were in progress, perhaps corrupting the `Collection` used for the `subscription_list`. The problem is solved simplistically by synchronizing long enough to make a clean copy, then working from the copy.

In any event, the new *Java 2* Collection classes are deliberately not synchronized, so subscribe() and cancel_subscription() *must* be synchronized in case one thread is trying to add a subscriber while another is removing one (or two threads are adding at the same time, and so on). (Yes, I know about the synchronization wrappers. I'll talk about them in a moment.)

Even though this notify-from-the-copy strategy is recommended by Sun, it is not ideal. First, what if a subscriber is removed from the list after the copy is made but before the notifications begin? It turns out that the subscriber is notified, even though it thinks it has cancelled the subscription. This problem exists in all AWT/ Swing listeners, and there is no easy solution—never assume that you will not be notified simply because you have removed yourself as a listener. To eliminate this problem, I've included a second, synchronized, notification method in the Publisher: publish_blocking() (Listing 6.3, line 27). Since this version is synchronized, nobody can add or remove listeners while notifications are in process. I don't know if this behavior is better than the nonblocking solution, but it is certainly different, and is more appropriate in some scenarios. Note that the publish_blocking() method doesn't have to copy the subscription_list since it synchronizes access to it—it can just use an iterator to traverse the list.

The fact that a simple synchronization strategy is used by publish_blocking causes an additional problem in the blocking notification scenario: the entire Publisher is locked while the subscription_list is being accessed (for the entire period required for notifications), and the notifications could take several years to complete. All threads that try send a message to the Publisher object will block until the notifications complete. The entire object doesn't have to be locked, however. We're synchronizing only to make access to the synchronization_list thread safe. What we really need is two locks, one that guards the subscription_list and another that guards any other fields that we might choose to add to the Publisher. This way you couldn't add or remove subscribers while notifications were in progress, but you *could* call other synchronized methods of the Publisher class without blocking.

Three approaches to introducing a second lock come to mind. First, I could introduce a second lock using the roll-your-own Mutex class discussed in Chapter 3. This solution is implemented in Listing 6.5.

Listing 6.5 (Mutex_publisher.java): Introducing a Second Lock with a Mutex

```
01: import java.util.*;
02: import Subscriber;
03: import com.holub.asynch.Mutex;
04:
05: public class Mutex_publisher
06: {
07:     Collection subscription_list = new LinkedList();
08:     Mutex      guard            = new Mutex();
09:
```

```
10:
11:     public void subscribe( Subscriber subscriber ) throws InterruptedException
12:     {
13:         guard.acquire(1000);
14:         subscription_list.add( subscriber );
15:         guard.release();
16:     }
17:
18:     synchronized public void cancel_subscription( Subscriber subscriber )
19:                                             throws InterruptedException
20:     {
21:         guard.acquire(1000);
22:         subscription_list.remove( subscriber );
23:         guard.release();
24:     }
25:
26:     public void publish( ) throws InterruptedException
27:     {   Object[] copy;
28:         guard.acquire(1000);
29:         copy = subscription_list.toArray();
30:         guard.release();
31:
32:         for( int i = 0; i < copy.length; ++i )
33:             ((Subscriber) copy[i]).receive("Hello world");
34:     }
35:
36:     synchronized public void other_method()
37:     {   //...
38:     }
39: }
```

A Mutex is really overkill in the current situation, however. A second approach encapsulates my original Publisher (from Listing 6.3) into a container class. I've done this in Listing 6.6. Now subscribe and related methods aren't synchronized at all, but chain through to their synchronized cousins in the contained Subscriber object. That is, the lock associated with the contained Publisher object controls access to the subscription_list and the lock associated with the container (Wrapped_publisher) object is used by other synchronized methods. The other_method() method (Listing 6.6, line 19), which is synchronized, locks the *container*, not the Publisher.

Listing 6.6 (Wrapped_publisher.java): Using a Container Strategy

```
01: import Subscriber;
02:
03: class Wrapped_publisher
04: {
05:     Publisher subscribers = new Publisher();
06:
07:     public void subscribe( Subscriber subscriber )
```

```
08:        {    subscribers.subscribe( subscriber );
09:        }
10:
11:        public void cancel_subscription( Subscriber subscriber )
12:        {    subscribers.cancel_subscription( subscriber );
13:        }
14:
15:        public void publish( )
16:        {    subscribers.publish_blocking();
17:        }
18:
19:        synchronized public void other_method()
20:        {                                      // Uses lock associated with "this,"
21:        }                                      // not the one assoicated with
22:                                               // "subscribers."
23: }
```

A third approach is to use the synchronized version of the LinkedList class, and then synchronize on the LinkedList itself. I've done that in Listing 6.7. Rather than creating a simple LinkedList on line 7, I've used Collections.synchronized() to wrap my list in an adapter, all of whose methods are synchronized. Now, I don't have to synchronize subscribe() or cancel_subscription(), and I don't have to synchronize when making the copy in publish(). I do have to explicitly synchronize on line 28 when I iterate across the list, however. This last approach is the most workable in practice, since it is the simplest to implement.

Listing 6.7 (Synchronized_list_publisher.java):
Locking on a Synchronized LinkedList

```
01: import java.util.*;
02: import Subscriber;
03:
04: public class Synchronized_list_publisher
05: {
06:     Collection subscription_list
07:                     = Collections.synchronizedList( new LinkedList() );
08:
09:     public void subscribe( Subscriber subscriber )
010:    {    subscription_list.add( subscriber );
011:    }
012:
013:    public void cancel_subscription( Subscriber subscriber )
014:    {    subscription_list.remove( subscriber );
015:    }
016:
017:    public void publish( )
018:    {
019:        Object[] copy;
020:        copy = subscription_list.toArray();
```

```
021:
022:            for( int i = 0; i < copy.length; ++i )
023:                ((Subscriber) copy[i]).receive("Hello world");
024:        }
025:
026:    public void publish_blocking( )
027:    {
028:        synchronized( subscription_list )
029:        {
030:            for(Iterator i = subscription_list.iterator(); i.hasNext();)
031:                ((Subscriber) i.next()).receive("Hello world");
032:        }
033:    }
034: }
```

Now let's address the problem of the amount of time required to do the notifi-cations, and the fact that the thread that calls either publish() or publish_blocking() is effectively blocked until all the Subscriber's receive() methods have been called. (Don't confuse "locking" with "blocking." A thread can be blocked by attempting to enter a synchronized method that is in use by another thread. Acquiring a lock doesn't cause you to block unless there's contention. A thread is also effectively blocked—in the sense that it can't do anything else—while it is executing a lengthy method, whether or not the object that receives the message is locked.)

The time problem easily solved by wrapping threads around the publication code in Listing 6.7, I've done this in Listing 6.8. Now, the publish() method (Listing 6.8, line 16) creates a new Thread object that notifies the subscribers. The complemen-tary publish_sequentially() method (Listing 6.8, line 32) keeps the list locked while notifications are in progress, so if *N* threads publish simultaneously, you'll effectively go through the list *N* times, one after the other, instead of having *N* noti-fication threads running in parallel. I used a similar strategy to handle the observers of the Alarm class discussed in the previous chapter.

Other, more complex solutions are also possible. It really isn't necessary for publish_sequentially() to create multiple threads when notifications are already in progress when publish_sequentially() is called. The publish_sequentially() method could just ignore any requests that come in while notifications are in progress, for example, or it could remember the fact that the request was made and run through the list a second time when it finished the first traversal.

Listing 6.8 (Background_publisher.java): Publishing from a Thread

```
01: import java.util.*;
02: import Subscriber;
03:
04: public class Background_publisher
```

```
05: {
06:     Collection subscription_list = Collections.synchronizedList( new
LinkedList() );
07:
08:     public void subscribe( Subscriber subscriber )
09:     {   subscription_list.add( subscriber );
10:     }
11:
12:     public void cancel_subscription( Subscriber subscriber )
13:     {   subscription_list.remove( subscriber );
14:     }
15:
16:     public void publish()
17:     {
18:         new Thread()
19:         {   public void run()
20:             {
21:                 Object[] copy;
22:                 synchronized( subscription_list )
23:                 {   copy = subscription_list.toArray();
24:                 }
25:
26:                 for( int i = 0; i < copy.length; ++i )
27:                     ((Subscriber)copy[i]).receive("Hello world");
28:             }
29:         }.start();
30:     }
31:
32:     public void publish_sequentially()
33:     {
34:         new Thread()
35:         {   public void run()
36:             {
37:                 synchronized( subscription_list )
38:                 {   for(Iterator i = subscription_list.iterator(); i.hasNext();)
39:                         ((Subscriber) i.next()).receive("Hello world");
40:                 }
41:             }
42:         }.start();
43:     }
44: }
```

Mysteries of the AWTEventMulticaster

Though the various blocking-publication functions just presented do solve the notification-after-removal problem, they aren't a general solution to the notification problem since any threads which modify the subscriber list are effectively blocked until no notifications are going on (which, again, could be a long time—perhaps several centuries). Though the notify-from-the-copy strategy is perfectly viable when blocking during notification is unacceptable, the dark underbelly of this strategy is the amount of time that it takes, not only to lock the subscription_list, but also to actually make the copy. Remember, you have to make a copy every time you fire off a notification. Fortunately, Sun's John Rose and Amy Fowler came up with an elegant solution to the problem: the AWTEventMulti-caster. The AWTEventMulticaster class implements *all* of the AWT/Swing listener interfaces, so you can literally pass an object of this class any message that can be sent to any listener. The basic idea is that you notify a top-level multicaster, which in turn notifies a whole set of listeners. Moreover, the AWTEventMulticaster does this notification in such a way that no synchronization is required while notifications are in progress (and no copies are made either).

Figure 6.1 shows how an AWTEventMulticaster is used to construct a list of listeners. A static "factory_method" [AWTEventMulticaster.add()] is used to create individual Multicaster instances—you can't create them with new. As you can see in Figure 6.1, this factory method is passed the current head-of-list reference and the listener to add. If either of these is null, it just returns the other, effectively creating a one-element list. If neither argument is null, then an AWTEventMulticaster object, which is effectively a binary-tree node, is created, initialized so that one child points at the existing list and the other to newly added listener. A reference to the newly minted node is returned from add(), and the calling method then overwrites the old head-of-list reference with the newly returned reference. The example continues in this way, building a binary tree whose interior nodes are all AWTEventMulticasters and whose leaf notes are standard AWT or Swing listener objects.

Notification is done with a simple, recursive tree-traversal. (This can be a problem. You'll note in Figure 6.1 that the "tree" will most likely degrade into a linked list, and recursive traversal of a linked list can use up a lot of runtime stack. Typically, there aren't enough listeners for stack overflow to be a problem, but be careful with large lists.)

As I mentioned earlier the AWTEventMulticaster implements *all* of the standard listener interfaces [(actionPerformed(), mouseClicked(), and so on)], so it can masquerade as any of them. The multicaster overrides do nothing but pass the message to their children, using instanceof in the case of the leaf nodes to assure that the message can be received by the actual object.

Immutable Objects and Blank Finals

The most important feature of the AWTEventMulticaster is not actually evident in Figure 6.1. The multicaster is an "immutable" object—all of its fields are declared static final, but are initialized as follows in the constructor (rather than the declaration):

```
public class AWTEventMulticaster implements ComponentListener, ...
{   protected final EventListener a, b;

    protected AWTEventMulticaster(EventListener a, EventListener b)
    {   this.a = a; this.b = b;
    }
    //...
}
```

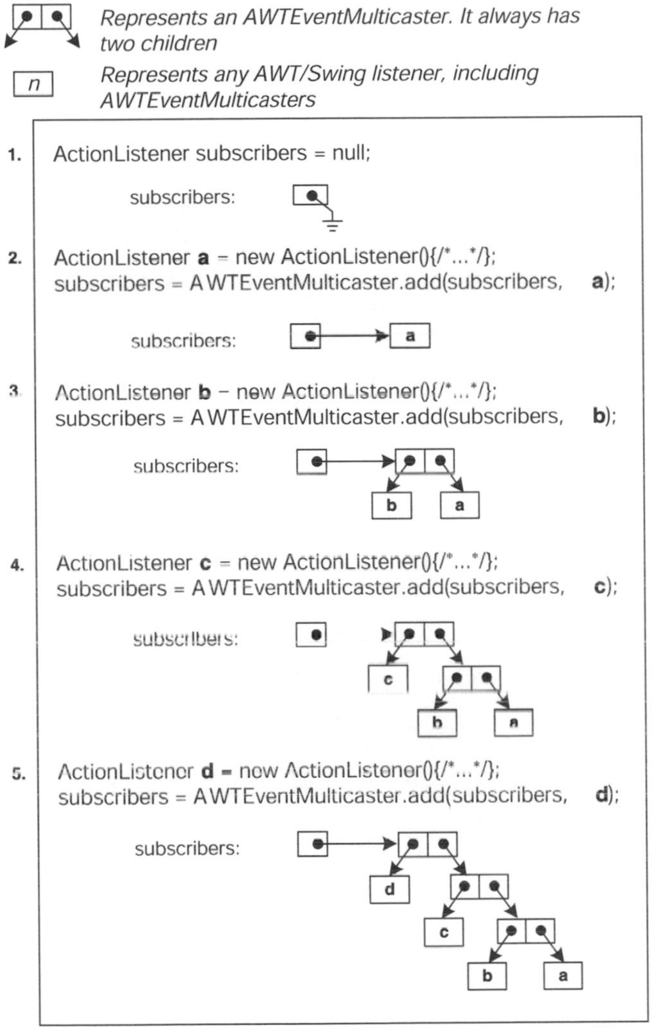

Figure 6.1. Building a Subscription List with a Multicaster

Since everything is final, the object's state can't change once the object is created. A Java `String` is "immutable," for example. Immutable objects, have a significant advantage over normal objects in multithreaded environments: you never have to synchronize access to them, because they can't change state. Consequently, replacing the `Collection` in the earlier listings with a multicaster eliminates the synchronization overhead entirely.

A `final` field that is initialized in the constructor rather than the declaration is called a *blank final*. You should use them whenever you can, which is unfortunately not as often as you'd like. In general, if you intend for an object to be used in a multithreaded situation, and the object is accessed more often than it is changed you should make the object immutable. (In other words, if the overhead of making an occasional copy to make a change is less then the overhead of synchronizing on every access to the object, make the object immutable.) The only downside of using immutable objects is a compiler bug that has been around for a couple of years now—and which Sun deems too unimportant to fix—sometimes prevents you from declaring a blank final in a class that contains inner classes. (The compiler sometimes spits out the hard-error: "Blank final may not have been initialized," even when the field in question has been initialized.) Though you can just comment out the `final`, I don't like the fact that I lose a valuable compile-time check for immutability. You could move the inner class out to the global level, but I *really* hate to corrupt the global- or package-level namespace with class names that the user could care less about.

Using the Multicaster

The multicaster exhibits a lot of very desirable behavior. For example, you can safely add listeners to the list while traversals are in progress because the tree is constructed from the bottom up and the part of the tree that exists when notifications commence will not change—it is immutable. The new listeners are not notified by any of the in-progress notification threads, but adding a listener doesn't damage the list either.

Listener removal is also interesting. How do you remove nodes from a tree whose nodes can't be modified? The flip answer is that you build another tree. Figure 6.2 shows the easy scenario. To effectively delete node C, you create a new root node and make its child pointers reference node D and node C's right subtree. If you overwrite subscribers with `new_list`—the normal case—there will be no more references to the gray-colored nodes, and they will eventually be garbage collected. (The multicaster is a good example of why garbage collection is so cool—you couldn't do this in C++.)

Figure 6.3 shows the more difficult deletion of a node that is further down in the tree (C again). Here, you effectively have to build a second tree that looks exactly like that part of the original tree that is above the deleted node. As before,

```
AWTEventMulticaster new_list =
        AWTEventMulticaster.remove(subscribers, C);
```

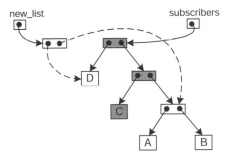

Figure 6.2. Deleting a Node from a Multicaster: The Easy Case

the gray colored nodes are subject to garbage collection once `subscribers` is over-written (and any traversals positioned in that part of the tree complete). This rebuilding of the supertree is, of course, a copy operation of sorts, but note that (1) you don't need to build the entire tree, and (2) you only make the copy when you delete a node, not every time the listeners are notified. If you delete nodes in the opposite order that you add them, you'll minimize the copy overhead as well; the most-recently added nodes are closest to the top of the tree.

```
AWTEventMulticaster new_list =
        AWTEventMulticaster.remove(subscribers, C);
```

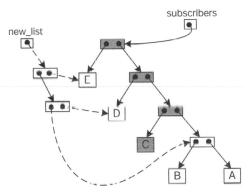

Figure 6.3. Deleting a Node from a Multicaster: The Hard Case

Building a Multicaster

The first time I looked at the `AWTEventMulticaster` sources, I thought it was weird, unnecessarily complex code. On reflection, though, there is a lot of neat stuff here. The more I looked at it, the more I liked it. Multiple threads can happily add and remove nodes without conflicting either with each other or with threads that are traversing the tree, and multiple threads can traverse the tree simultaneously. Moreover, absolutely no synchronization is required to do any of this. The data structure that is used is no larger than the doubly-linked list that I used earlier, and the overhead of copying part of the tree when you do deletions is a lot less than the overhead of copying the entire subscriber list every time you publish an event.

So, not being one to look a gift algorithm in the mouth, I wrote up my own general-purpose version of the multicaster, based on the AWTEventMulticaster. It is in Listing 6.9 and Listing 6.10. It is remarkable how little code there is here. (Ahh, the miracle of recursion!) All the complexity, in fact, is in the removal. (I'll leave it as an "exercise to the reader" to puzzle through how it works—opacity is the downside of most recursive algorithms—but in essence, the algorithm traverses down to the node you want to delete and then builds the copy it returns back up to the root.) This implementation is very general purpose in that it can publish any Object to any class that implements the generic Command interface (from Listing 6.9). (I opted to introduce Command, rather than continue to use Subscriber, because Command is a more-generic interface that suitable for outer purposes as well as the current one—I can use it to implement the Gang-of-Four Command pattern, for example). There is a test class Test at the bottom of the listing (Listing 6.10, line 49) that demonstrates how to use the Multicaster.

Listing 6.9 (/src/com/holub/tools/Command.java):
The Multicaster's version of `Subscriber`

```
001: package com.holub.tools;
002:
     /**
        A generic interface for implementing the Command pattern with
        a single-argument method. Use Runnable for no-argument methods.
        This interface is also implemented by subscribers to a "multi-
        caster." In the Multicaster model, a "publisher" can also be a
        "subscriber," so the Subscriber interface extends EventListener
        to give you some flexibility. This way the top-level publisher
        can choose to "be" a Subscriber (e.g., implement Subscriber) or to
        "use" a Subscriber (e.g., contain a reference to a Multicaster,
        which is a Subscriber).
        @see Multicaster
     */
003: public interface Command
004: {   void execute( Object argument );
005: }
006:
```

Listing 6.10 (/src/com/holub/tools/Multicaster.java): A Roll-Your-Own Multicaster

```
001: package com.holub.tools;
002:
003: import java.util.EventObject;
004: import com.holub.tools.Command;
005:
```

```
    /**
```
The `Multicaster` class (modeled after the `AWTEventMulticaster`)
provides an efficient way to manage relatively short lists of
"subscribers." Each `Multicaster` object can reference two
`Subscriber` objects, one or both of which can be another -
`Multicaster`. The top-level `Multicaster` is passed a "publish"
message, which it broadcasts (recursively) to both of the (`Command`-
class) subscribers that it references.

The `Multicaster` is an "immutable" object, so you can't modify it.
The "`add()`" method, for example, is passed two `Multicaster`s and
returns a third one that effectively references all the subcri-
bers referenced by the original two. Any notifications that are in
progress when the `add()` is executed will not be affected by the
operation, however. It is perfectly acceptable for notifications
to be performed on one thread while a second thread is adding or
removing members from the `Multicaster`. The order in which `Subscri-`
bers are notified is undefined. (It is NOT necessarily the order
of insertion.)
@see *java.awt.AWTEventMulticaster*
@see *Command*
```
    */
006: public class Multicaster implements Command
007: {
008:     private final Command a, b;
009:
010:     private Multicaster(Command a, Command b)
011:     {   this.a = a;
012:         this.b = b;
013:     }
014:
```

```
    /****************************************************************
```
Ask the subscribers of this multicaster to receive the
`publication`. This is the "publish" operation, as seen from
the perspective of a subscriber. (Remember, a multicaster
is a list of subscribers. Note that the order of traversal
should generally be considered undefined. However, if you
really need to notify listeners in a known order, and you
consistently add nodes as follows:
```
    subscription_list = Multicaster.add( subscription_list, new_node );
```
(Where `subscription_list` is the head-of-list reference and
`new_node` is the node you're adding), subscribers will be
notified in the order they were added. Removing nodes does not
affect the order of notification. If you transpose the two

arguments in the foregoing code:
```
        subscription_list = Multicaster.add( new_node, subscription_list );
```
subscribers will be notified in reverse order.
```
         */
015:    public void execute( Object publication )
016:    {   a.execute( publication );
017:        b.execute( publication );
018:    }
019:

        /****************************************************************
```
Add a new subscriber to the list. The way this call is used
can impact the order in which subscribers are notified.
(See *execute*.) Note that you must use proper synchronization
around the call to add() to prevent preemption after add()
returns, but before its return value is assigned to the head-
of-list reference.
@param *a* Typically the head-of-list pointer.
@param *b* Typically the subscriber you're adding to the list.
```
         */
020:    public static Command add(Command a, Command b)
021:    {   return  (a == null) ? b :
022:                    (b == null)  ? a : new Multicaster(a, b);
023:    }
024:

        /****************************************************************
```
Remove the indicated subscriber from the list. As with add(),
you must use proper synchronization around the call to
remove() to prevent preemption after remove returns, but
before its return value is assigned to the head-of-list reference.
```
         */
025:    public static Command remove(Command list, Command remove_me)
026:    {
027:        if( list == remove_me || list == null  )
028:            return null;
029:        else if( !(list instanceof Multicaster) )
030:            return list;
031:        else
032:            return ((Multicaster)list).remove( remove_me );
033:    }
034:
035:    private Command remove(Command remove_me)
036:    {
037:        if (remove_me == a)   return b;
038:        if (remove_me == b)   return a;
039:
040:        Command a2 = remove( a, remove_me );
041:        Command b2 = remove( b, remove_me );
042:
043:        return (a2 == a && b2 == b ) // it's not here
044:                    ? this
045:                    : add(a2, b2)
046:                    ;
047:    }
```

```
048:        //===================================================================
049:        public static class Test
050:        {   private static class Leaf implements Command
051:            {   String s;
052:                public Leaf(String s){ this.s = s; }
053:                public void execute( Object publication )
054:                {   System.out.print(s);
055:                }
056:            }
057:
058:            public static void main( String[] args )
059:            {   Leaf a = new Leaf("A");
060:                Leaf b = new Leaf("B");
061:                Leaf c = new Leaf("C");
062:                Leaf d = new Leaf("D");
063:                Leaf e = new Leaf("E");
064:
065:                Command subscription_list = null;
066:                subscription_list = Multicaster.add( subscription_list, a );
067:                subscription_list = Multicaster.add( subscription_list, b );
068:                subscription_list = Multicaster.add( subscription_list, c );
069:                subscription_list = Multicaster.add( subscription_list, d );
070:                subscription_list = Multicaster.add( subscription_list, e );
071:
072:                System.out.print("List is: ");
073:                subscription_list.execute( null );
074:
075:                System.out.print("\nRemoving c: ");
076:                subscription_list = Multicaster.remove( subscription_list, c );
077:                subscription_list.execute( null );
078:
079:                System.out.print("\nRemoving a: ");
080:                subscription_list = Multicaster.remove( subscription_list, a );
081:                subscription_list.execute( null );
082:
083:                System.out.print("\nRemoving d: ");
084:                subscription_list = Multicaster.remove( subscription_list, d );
085:                subscription_list.execute( null );
086:
087:                System.out.print("\nRemoving b: ");
088:                subscription_list = Multicaster.remove( subscription_list, b );
089:                subscription_list.execute( null );
090:
091:                System.out.print("\nRemoving e: ");
092:                subscription_list = Multicaster.remove( subscription_list, e );
093:
094:                if( subscription_list != null )
095:                    System.out.println("Couldn't remove last node");
096:
097:                subscription_list = Multicaster.add( a, subscription_list );
098:                subscription_list = Multicaster.add( b, subscription_list );
099:                subscription_list = Multicaster.add( c, subscription_list );
```

```
100:                    subscription_list = Multicaster.add( d, subscription_list );
101:                    subscription_list = Multicaster.add( e, subscription_list );
102:
103:                    System.out.print("\nShould be: EDCBA: " );
104:                    subscription_list.execute( null );
105:
106:                    System.out.println();
107:            }
108:        }
109: }
```

The final task is to modify our publisher to use a Multicaster object. I've done that in Listing 6.11 (for this month's final entry in the world's-most-complicated-way-to-print-hello-world contest). This version is built on the one-thread-per-publication model discussed earlier.

Listing 6.11 (Multicast_publisher.java): Using the Multicaster in a Publisher

```
01: import java.util.*;
02: import com.holub.tools.Command;
03: import com.holub.tools.Multicaster;
04:
05: public class Multicast_publisher
06: {
07:     Command subscription_list; // = null
08:
09:     public synchronized void subscribe( Command subscriber )
10:     {   subscription_list =
11:                         Multicaster.add(subscription_list,subscriber);
12:     }
13:
14:     public synchronized void cancel_subscription( Command subscriber )
15:     {   subscription_list =
16:                         Multicaster.remove(subscription_list, subscriber);
17:     }
18:
19:     public void publish()
20:     {
21:         new Thread()
22:         {   public void run()
23:             {   if( subscription_list != null )
24:                     subscription_list.execute( "Hello world" );
25:             }
26:         }.start();
27:     }
28:
29:     public void publish_sequentially()
30:     {
31:         new Thread()
32:         {   public void run()
```

```
33:                { synchronized( subscription_list )
34:                    { if( subscription_list != null )
35:                        subscription_list.execute( "Hello world" );
36:                    }
37:                }
38:            }.start();
39:        }
40:        //=================================================================
41:        public static class Test
42:        {
43:            static private Multicast_publisher publisher  =
44:                                        new Multicast_publisher();
45:
46:            static private Command subscriber =
47:                                new Command()
48:                                { public void execute(Object p)
49:                                    { System.out.println((String)p);
50:                                    }
51:                                };
52:
53:            static public void main( String[] args )
54:            { publisher.subscribe( subscriber );
55:                publisher.publish();    // Publish "Hello world" events
56:            }
57:        }
58: }
```

I'll finish up with one final warning. Though nothing in the `Multicaster` class itself needs to be synchronized, you *do* have to synchronize the methods that call `add()` or `remove()`. Consider this code:

```
Multicaster publisher - null;
//...
public void add_listener(Object listener)
{   publisher - Multicaster.add(publisher,listener);
}
```

The difficulty is that you may be preempted after the `add()` method returns but before the `publisher` is overwritten, thereby (perhaps) ending up with the wrong head-of-list pointer and effectively losing a listener. You can, of course, use a roll-your-own lock if you don't want to synchronize the method itself.

CHAPTER 7

Singletons, Critical Sections, and Reader/Writer Locks

THIS CHAPTER ADDS a few more tools to your mutithreading arsenal: I'll discuss *Singletons* (one-of-a kind objects) and *critical sections* (blocks of code that can be executed by only one thread at a time). Singletons in particular, are surprisingly difficult to implement efficiently in a multithreaded environment, but are essential in most programs (java.awt.Toolkit is an example of a Singleton).

I'll finish up with a seemingly unrelated topic: *reader/writer locks* (locks that give you efficient thread-safe access to read/write resources such as data structures and files). Reader/writer locks are simple enough to implement that I didn't want to devote an entire chapter to them, but they're essential in any multithreaded program that performs I/O operations or accesses global resources from multiple threads. I've put reader/writer locks into the current chapter because you often need them to control access to Singletons.

The reader/writer lock combined with the various semaphores and locks I've presented in previous chapters comprise a reasonably complete toolkit for solving threading-related synchronization problems.

Critical Sections, Singletons, and the "Class Object"

So far in this book I've been concentrating on the monitor—a means of blocking access to an object while a message is being processed by that object. The other essential sort of lock that you should be aware of is the critical section. Critical sections are essential in implementing one-time initialization code when that code can be accessed from multiple threads.

A critical section is a chunk of code that can be executed only by one thread at a time. Compare this notion with a normal synchronized code block—a *monitor*— which is effectively an exclusion semaphore that guards a single object, but not the code itself. For example, several threads can simultaneously execute a synchronized method, but only if the objects that receive the associated messages (the objects to the left of the dot in the call are different). In a critical section, the code itself is locked, not the object. Only one thread can be in the critical section at a time, even if the receiving objects are different.

Consider a simple queue implementation: If you use a monitor to guard queue objects, then two threads could both access different queues simultaneously, but the two threads couldn't access the same queue object at the same time. On the other hand, if you use a critical section rather than a monitor to guard the enqueue operation, for example, then no two enqueue operations could occur simultaneously, even if two threads were enqueueing to different queues.

The mutex that guards a monitor is an object-level mutex; the mutex that guards a critical section is effectively a class-level mutex. Think of it this way: the code is defined in the class, not the object, so when you're locking the code itself, you're locking the entire class of objects.

Static Members

In Java, the notion of a critical section is closely tied to that of a `static` class member, so let's start there. Java, like all OO languages, supports two categories of fields and methods:

class variables: Variables that control the state of all objects within a class.

instance variables: Variables that control the state of a single object within a class.

You implement a class variable in Java by putting the `static` keyword at the head of the definition. To best explain how the two types of variables are used in practice, an example seems in order: Back in the dark ages (the early 1990s) somebody had the bright idea that every window on the screen should use a different color scheme, even within a single application. Magenta backgrounds with yellow borders, turquoise backgrounds with chartreuse borders—it made your eyes hurt. The reasoning was that the users would somehow remember the color combinations and thereby identify the windows. Nice theory, but the human mind just doesn't work that way. In this system, however, a window's color scheme is an "instance variable"—every instance, or every window, potentially has a different value for its color scheme.

Eventually, people came to their senses and made all the windows the same color. Now the color scheme is a "class variable." The entire class of window objects uses the same color scheme. If the scheme changes, then all the windows should change their appearance.

You can model the class-level behavior like this:

```
class Window                      // not the AWT window
    {
        private static Color foreground = SystemColor.windowText;
        private static Color background = SystemColor.window;
```

```
synchronized static public change_color_scheme( Color foreground, Color background )
{
    this.foreground = foreground;
    this.background = background;

    // code goes here that tells all the extant Window objects to
    // redraw themselves in the new color scheme.
    }
}
```

but there are several problems with this simplistic approach, the first being threading.

Java creates a Class class object for every class in your system, loaded by the JVM typically when the class is first used. The Class object is an object in a very real sense. It exists on the heap, is subject to garbage collection in some situations, has a constructor (the "static-initializer block"), and can be referenced in the same way as a reference to any object would be referenced. A Class object has methods (declared static in the class definition) and state (defined by the static fields; that is, the static fields of a class are effectively fields of the Class object.)

The Class object also has its own monitor. When you call a synchronized static method, you enter the monitor associated with the Class object. This means that no two synchronized static methods can access the static fields of the Class at the same time. You can also lock the Class object explicitly, like this:

```
synchronized( Window.class )
{   // modify static fields here
}
```

Unfortunately, the Class-level monitor is in no way connected to the monitors of the various instances of the object, and a synchronized, but non-static, method can also access the static fields. Entering the synchronized non-static method does not lock the Class object. Why is this a problem? Well, in the previous example, it would appear to be harmless to omit the static (but not the synchronized) from the definition of change_color_scheme() since the static fields will be modified, even if the modifying method isn't static. Appearances are deceiving, though. If two threads simultaneously send change_color_scheme() messages to two *different* objects of class Window, a race condition results, and the color scheme will be in an unknown state. In other words, the individual Window objects are locked, but locking a Window object does not lock the corresponding Class object (which contains the class variables), and the static fields are unguarded. Consequently, we have two threads modifying two variables at the same time.

As another example, consider the code in Listing 7.1. The Longish class (Listing 7.1, line 1) simulates the non-atomic nature of a long by representing the value as two int fields. The value method (Listing 7.1, line 9) returns the high and low words, merged into a single long. The Class_monitor() class defines two methods of interest The clear() method (Listing 7.1, line 11) sets a Longish number to zero, but it forces preemption by sleeping for half a second when the clear operation is only half complete. Remember from Chapter 2 that assignment to a `long` is not atomic in Java, so if `value` were defined as `long`, a simple `value=0` could conceivably work the same way. Preemption could occur after only half of the value had been cleared. The `set()` method (Listing 7.1, line 21) is more straightforward. It just sets `value` to an arbitrary value. Note that `clear()` is both `synchronized` and `static`, but `set()` is `synchronized`, but not `static`.

The interesting code is in `main(...)` (Listing 7.1, line 28). A thread is created to call `clear()` (which will be preempted halfway through clearing the object). The main thread is still running though, and it calls `set()` (on line 40) after giving the clearing thread a chance to start up. The resulting value printed by the program is `123456700000000`. That is, even though the first thread is inside `clear()` (which *is* `synchronized`), entering the class-level monitor, which you do when you enter a `synchronized static` method, does not prevent a second thread from entering the object-level monitor, which you do by entering a `synchronized` non-`static` method. Consequently, the partially modified `Longish` value is corrupted.

Listing 7.1: Class_monitor.java

```
01: class Longish
02: {    public int high;
03:      public int low;
04:      public long value(){ return ((long)high << 32) | (long)low; }
05: }
06:
07: public class Class_monitor
08: {
09:      private static Longish value =  new Longish();
10:
11:      public synchronized static void clear()
12:      {   try
13:          {
14:              value.high = 0;
15:              Thread.currentThread().sleep( 500 ); // simulate preemption
16:              value.low = 0;
17:          }
18:          catch( Exception e ){}
19:      };
20:
21:      public synchronized void set()
22:      {
23:          value.low  = 0x89abcdef;
24:          value.high = 0x01234567;
25:      };
26:
27:
28:      public static void main(String[] args) throws Exception
29:      {
30:          final Class_monitor object = new Class_monitor();
```

```
31:
32:            Thread t = new Thread()
33:            {   public void run()
34:                {   Class_monitor.clear();
35:                }
36:            };
37:            t.start();
38:
39:            Thread.currentThread().sleep( 100 );
40:            object.set();
41:
42:            t.join();
43:            System.out.println( "value is " +
44:                    Long.toHexString(Class_monitor.value.value()) );
45:        }
46: }
```

Returning to the window-color problem, the second difficulty with the naive implementation is that there is no way to guarantee that all the existing objects stay in sync with changes to the class variables. A sloppy programmer can add an instance method (one that is not static) to the Window class, and that instance method *can* change the foreground or background fields without notifying the other windows (or even updating its own color). I think this behavior is a flaw in the Java language, but there it is.

You can fix both the race-condition and lack-of-update problems by encapsulating the two static fields in a class of their own:

```
/*package*/ class Color_scheme
{
    private Color foreground = SystemColor.windowText;
    private Color background = SystemColor.window;

    /*package*/ synchronized change_color_scheme(
                                Color foreground, Color background )
    {
        this.foreground = foreground;
        this.background = background;

        // code goes here that tells all the extant Window objects to
        // redraw themselves with the new color scheme.
    }
}

public class My_window
{
    static Scheme color_scheme = new Color_scheme();

    static change_color_scheme( Color foreground, Color background )
    {   scheme.change_color_scheme( foreground, background );
    }
}
```

Now there is no way to modify the foreground or background color without notifying the other windows.

Two style notes: (1) Encapsulating static fields to prevent access is one of the few cases in which you must use package access rather than an inner class. Had `Color_scheme` been an inner class of `Window`, direct access to `foreground` and `background` fields would still be possible from methods of `Window`. This approach also has the advantage of making the monitor that controls the `Color_scheme` more visible—it is obviously the one associated with the explicit `Color_scheme` object, not the one associated with the `Window`. (2) Also note that I've commented the package access with an explicit `/*package*/`. The fact that there is a default access privilege at all is another flaw in the language. There are no other defaults, and I see no reason why there should be one here. (Defaults are generally a bad thing—it is too easy to forget something like an access privilege and then have it default to an undesirable value.) That the access default is "package" rather than `private` adds insult to injury. I always comment package access, as I've done here, to remind myself that I'm doing it on purpose rather than simply forgetting to specify an access privilege.

Singletons

There is yet another problem with the earlier window-color code. You really want only one `Color_scheme` to exist, ever. In the earlier code, I've guaranteed uniqueness accidentally by making the reference `static` and only calling `new` once, but I'd really like to guarantee that only one instance of the object can exist. The Gang-of-Four Singleton pattern describes exactly this situation. Two excerpts from the Gang-of-Four book are relevant. The "Intent" section in the Gang-of-Four book's chapter on Singleton states:

> Ensure a class only has one instance, and provide a global point of access to it.

and the "Consequences" section says:

> [Singleton] permits a variable number of instances. The pattern makes it easy to change your mind and allow more than one instance of the Singleton class. Moreover, you can use the same approach to control the number of instances that the application uses. Only the [class] operation that grants access to the Singleton instance needs to change.

That excerpt from the Consequences section is interesting because it allows a `Class` object to be considered a Singleton, even though there is more than one instance of the `Class` class in the program. There is guaranteed to be only a single instance of `Class` for a given class, so it's a Singleton: both `Some_class.class` and `some_object.getClass()` (the "operation[s] that grant access") always evaluates to references to the *same* `Class` object for a given class of objects. The `static` fields and methods, since they are members of the `Class` object, define the state and methods of the Singleton object as well. Exploiting this reasoning, I can ensure that only one instance of the `Color_scheme` exists by moving everything into the `Class` object (making everything `static`).

```
class Color_scheme
{
    private static Color foreground = SystemColor.windowText;
    private static Color background = SystemColor.window;

    private Color_scheme(){}

    /*package*/ synchronized static change_color_scheme(
                                    Color foreground, Color background )
    {
        this.foreground = foreground;
        this.background = background;

        // code goes here that tells all the extant Window objects to
        // redraw themselves with the new color scheme.
    }
}
```

Note that I've also added a `private` constructor. A class, all of whose constructors are `private`, can be created only by a `new` that is invoked in a method that legitimately has access to the class's other `private` components. There are no such methods here, so no instances of `Color_scheme` can actually be created. This guarantees that only one object can exist—the `Class` object, a Singleton.

I also have to change the `Window` to use the `Class` object rather than a specific instance:

```
class Window                    // not the AWT window
{
    // Note that there is no field here, now.

    change color scheme( Color foreground, Color background )
    {   Color_scheme.change_color_scheme( foreground, background );
    }

}
```

I've eliminated the `static` field in the `Window` class and have invoked `change_color_scheme()` directly through the class.

This sort of Singleton—a class all of whose methods are `static`—is called a "Booch Utility" (after Grady Booch, who identified the pattern in one of his early books.) Java's `Math` class is a good example of a Utility-style Singleton.

The problem with the make-everything-`static` approach to Singleton creation is that all the information needed to create the object must be known at class-load time, and that isn't always possible. Java's `Toolkit` is a good example. An application must load a different `Toolkit` than an applet, but a given chunk of code doesn't know whether it is running in an application or an applet until run time. The actual instance of the `Toolkit` is brought into existence by calling the `static` method `Toolkit.getDefaultToolkit()`. The object itself doesn't exist until the method is called the first time. Subsequent calls return a reference to the object that is created by the first call.

Critical Sections, Doubled-checked Locking, and Cache-related Problems in Multiple-CPU Machines

Bringing a Singleton into existence at run time (rather than load-time) is fraught with peril in a multithreaded environment. You can implement the creation function naively as follows:

```
public static synchronized Singleton get_instance()
{   if( instance == null )
        instance =  new Singleton();
    return instance;
}
```

The `static synchronized` method forms a *critical section*—a block of code that can be executed by only one thread at a time. If `get_instance()` weren't `synchronized`, a thread could be preempted after the `if` statement was processed, but before the `instance=new Singleton()` was executed. The preempting thread could then call `get_instance()`, create an instance, and then yield (temporarily give up control to another thread). The preempted thread would then wake up, think that there were no instances (because it has already performed the test), and create a second instance of the object. The critical section eliminates the multiple-creation problem by preventing any thread from entering `get_instance()` if another thread is already inside the method. Any Singleton object can be used to implement a critical section. Here, the `Class` object whose monitor we're using is itself a Singleton, so by locking this object implicitly when we enter the `static` method, we prevent other threads from executing the the method in parallel. (All `synchronized static` methods are effectively critical sections when you look that them that way.)

This strategy of using the `Class` object's monitor as the critical-section lock doesn't always work out because you lock all the `static` methods of the class, not just the Singleton-creation method. You can do the same thing with an explicitly declared Singleton lock as follows:

```
private static Object lock = new Object();

public static Singleton get_instance()  // not synchronized
{   synchronized( lock )
    {   if( instance == null )
            instance =  new Singleton();
        return instance;
    }
}
```

This version still assures that only one instance of the Singleton will be created, but it won't interfere with the execution of other `static` methods.

The main problem with this naive approach is efficiency. We acquire the lock every time we call `get_instance()`, even though the code only needs to be locked the first time the method is called. As we saw back in Chapter 1, the synchronization overhead imposed by Sun's HotSpot JVM isn't extreme provided that there is no contention. Unfortunately, Singleton access is often a high-contention situation. One less-than-ideal solution to the efficiency problem is Doug Schmidt's "Double-Checked Locking" strategy. Here's the general pattern:

```
class Singleton
{
    private Singleton instance;
    //...

    public static Singleton get_instance()  // not synchronized
    {   if( instance == null )
        {   synchronized( Singleton.class )
            {   if( instance == null )
                    instance = new Singleton();
            }
        }
        return instance;
    }
}
```

Most of the time, the object will exist when `get_instance()` is called, so we won't do any synchronization at all. On the first call, however, `instance` is `null`, so we enter the `if` statement and synchronize explicitly on the `Class` object to enter a critical section. Now we have to test for `instance==null` again, because we might have been preempted just after the first `if` was processed, but before the `synchronized` statement was executed. If `instance` is *still* `null`, then no other thread will be creating the Singleton, and we can create the object safely.

The main problem with the double-checked locking strategy is that it won't always work. The Java Language Specification (JLS) says that changes made by one thread are guaranteed to be visible to another thread only if the writing thread releases a lock that is subsequently acquired by the reading thread. This behavior is particularly a problem when your box has multiple CPUs in it, since each CPU might cache the same chunk of memory and be working with the cached version of an object rather than the "real" version in shared memory. The CPU that releases a lock is required to flush its cache to the main memory store as part of the release, but main memory is not necessarily updated until that release occurs.

The `volatile` keyword causes a similar cache flush to main memory (immediately after the `volatile` field is modified). That is one of the reasons why it is essential to declare fields that are accessed by two threads without the benefit of synchronization as `volatile`. On the other hand, modification of a `volatile` field can be more expensive than you think since it will force a cache flush (and a reload on all the other CPUs that have cached the `volatile` memory). If the `volatile` field is modified extensively, it may end up being cheaper (in terms of execution speed) to just synchronize the access. By the same token, it is risky for a constructor to create a thread if that thread can access the partially constructed object, since constructors cannot be declared as `synchronized`. Note that cache memory is also flushed as a side effect of a thread terminating.

Since the initial test in the double-checked-locking idiom occurs outside of a `synchronized` block, changes to instance made by one thread might not be visible to another. It's possible, then, for two CPUs to simultaneously load the `get_instance()` method, but if the timing is wrong, end up with different values of `instance`. In other words, one CPU might think that `instance` is `null`, and another might think that it has been initialized. You can solve this problem by synchronizing `get_instance()`, but then you're back to having unnecessary synchronization overhead in single-CPU boxes. I know of no good platform-independent solution to this problem.

The Std Class: An Example of Singleton

Listing 7.2 shows you a real-world application of Singleton that compensates for a problem in the design of the `System` class. A proper OO design *never* uses public fields except for symbolic constants, and I really mean "constant" here—the exposed field must be immutable, not just `final`. (An object accessed via a `final` reference can be modified—an "immutable" object (like a `String`) can't be modified at all.) This rule applies to both "class" and "instance" variables, and there are no exceptions to this rule. Ever. Period. Strong encapsulation of an object's implementation is so central to what "Object Orientation" means, that this point is simply not negotiable. If you use public fields, your program just isn't object-oriented—it is some sort of part-OO/part-procedural polyglot, and you will reap virtually none of the real benefits of OO, such as improved maintenance. The only legitimate public members of a class are those methods that handle messages defined in your design's dynamic model.

The forgoing notwithstanding, there is one place in the Java packages where instance variables are exposed: `System.in`, `System.out`, and `System.err`. To my mind, this exposure is a serious design flaw: These fields are not `Reader` or `Writer` derivatives, so are not Internationalizable. Consequently, you can't use these variables without wrapping them in a `Reader` or `Writer`. If `System.in`, `System.out`, and `System.err` had been accessed through "accessor" methods rather than directly, this wrapping could have been done transparently by the (missing) method that returned the I/O stream. This (missing) method could have easily been modified to return a `Print-Writer` rather than a `PrintStream` without impacting hardly any of the code that used it. As it is, there is a lot of incorrect code out there that uses the three streams directly. The solution, though, isn't pretty. The "correct" way to print a UNICODE string is:

```
new PrintWriter( System.out ).println("the string");
```

Ugh! Not only is the code ungainly, but you're creating `PrintWriter` objects all over the place. [As an aside, it is reasonable to argue that the real flaw is that the design of the I/O system is inverted: That you should print a string by saying `some_string.print_to(some_stream)` rather than `some_stream.println(some_string)`.] Listing 7.2 solves the exposed-field problem (or at least hides it) by using the Singleton pattern. You write to standard output, for example, like this:

```
Std.out().println("Hello world");
```

The `out()` method (Listing 7.2, line 40) creates a Singleton `PrintWriter` wrapper around `System.out` and returns it. Subsequent calls to `Std.out()` return the same wrapper object, so you don't have to create a new one every time you need to write a string.

Other methods in the class work the same way: `Std.err()` returns a Singleton `PrintWriter` that wraps `System.err`, and `Std.in()` returns a `BufferedReader` that wraps `System.in`. I've also provided a `Std.bit_bucket()` that returns an implementation of `PrintWriter` that does nothing. This is occasionally useful for throwing away otherwise undesirable output. For example, you might pass a method a `Writer` onto which it prints error or status messages. Passing this method `Std.bit_bucket()` effectively causes the messages to not be printed.

Listing 7.2 (/src/com/holub/io/Std.java): An I/O Singleton

```
01: package com.holub.io;
02: import java.io.*;
03: import com.holub.asynch.JDK_11_unloading_bug_fix;
04: import com.holub.io.Bit_bucket;
05:


    /**
        Convenience wrappers that hide the complexity of creating Readers and
        Writers simply to access standard input and output. For example, a call to
            Std.out().println("hello world");
        is identical in function to:
            new PrintWriter(System.out, true).println("hello world");
        and
            String line = Std.in().readLine();
        is identical in function to:
            String line;
              try
```

```
       {   line = new BufferedReader(new InputStreamReader(System.in)).readLine();
       }
        catch( Exception e )
       {    throw new Error( e.getMessage() );
       }
```

Equivalent methods provide access to standard error and a "bit bucket" that just absorbs output without printing it.

All of these methods create Singleton objects. For example, the same PrintWriter object that is created the first time you call Std.out() is returned by all subsequent calls. This way you don't incur the overhead of a new with each I/O request.

@see *com.holub.tools.P*
@see *com.holub.tools.R*
@see *com.holub.tools.E*
@author *Allen I. Holub*

```
    */

06: public final class Std
07: {
08:     static{ new JDK_11_unloading_bug_fix(Std.class); }
09:
10:     private static BufferedReader input;         //= null
11:     private static PrintWriter    output;        //= null
12:     private static PrintWriter    error;         //= null
13:     private static PrintWriter    bit_bucket;    //= null
14:
15:     // These are static because they're used to implement
16:     // critical sections.
17:
18:     private static final Object input_lock      = new Object();
19:     private static final Object output_lock     = new Object();
20:     private static final Object error_lock      = new Object();
21:     private static final Object bit_bucket_lock = new Object();
22:

    /*****************************************************************
        A private constructor prevents anyone from manufacturing an instance.
    */
```

```
23:     private Std(){}
24:


        /******************************************************************
           Get a BufferedReader that wraps System.in.
         */

25:     public static BufferedReader in()
26:     {   synchronized( input_lock )
27:         {   if( input == null )
28:             {   try
29:                 {   input = new BufferedReader(
30:                                     new InputStreamReader(System.in));
31:                 }
32:                 catch( Exception e )
33:                 {   throw new Error( e.getMessage() );
34:                 }
35:             }
36:             return input;
37:         }
38:     }
39:


        /******************************************************************
           Get a PrintWriter that wraps System.out.
         */

40:     public static PrintWriter out()
41:     {   synchronized( output_lock )
42:         {   if( output == null )
43:                 output = new PrintWriter( System.out, true );
44:             return output;
45:         }
46:     }
47:


        /******************************************************************
           Get a PrintWriter that wraps System.err.
         */

48:     public static PrintWriter err()
49:     {   synchronized( error_lock )
50:         {   if( error == null )
51:                 error = new PrintWriter( System.err, true );
52:             return error;
53:         }
54:     }
55:
```

```
      /*****************************************************************
          Get an output stream that just discards the characters that are sent to it.
          This convenience class makes it easy to write methods that are passed a
          "Writer" to which error messages or status information is logged.
          You could log output to standard output like this:
            x.method( Std.out() );  // pass in the stream to which messages are logged
          But you could cause the logged messages to simply disappear by calling:
            x.method( Std.bit_bucket() );   // discard normal logging messages
      */
```

```
56:     public static PrintWriter bit_bucket()
57:     {   synchronized( bit_bucket_lock )
58:         {   if( bit_bucket == null )
59:                 bit_bucket = new Bit_bucket();
60:             return bit_bucket;
61:         }
62:     }
63:
```

```
      /**
          A small test class. This class reads a line from standard input and
          echoes it to standard output and standard error. Run it with:
                java com.holub.tools.Std\$Test
          (Don't type in the \ when using a Microsoft-style shell.)
      */
```

```
64:     static public class Test
65:     {
66:         static public void main( String[] args ) throws IOException
67:         {   String s;
68:             while( (s = Std.in().readLine()) != null )
69:             {   Std.out().println( s );
70:                 Std.err().println( s );
71:                 Std.bit_bucket().println( s );
72:             }
73:         }
74:     }
75: }
```

The final thread-related subtlety is the static initializer block (Listing 7.2, line 8):

```
static{ new JDK_11_unloading_bug_fix(Std.class); }
```

The JDK_11_unloading_bug_fix class in Listing 7.3 gets around a bug in the JVM released with all versions of JDK 1.1. The JVM in those releases was much too aggressive about unloading (and garbage collecting) Class objects: If the only reference to an object of a given class was a self-referential static member of the Class object, then the JVM would unload the class from memory, thereby destroying our only copy of the Singleton. The next time someone tried to get an instance, the class would be reloaded and a second instance of the Singleton would be created.

Sometimes this behavior did nothing but make the program a little slower. But if the act of creating the Singleton object has side effects (like creating temporary files or opening database connections), this second creation can be a problem.

The fix in Listing 7.3 is a kludge, but it works. I'm counting on the fact that the JVM itself keeps around references to potentially active threads. If the current program is not running under a 1.1 version of the JDK (System.getProperty ("java.version").startsWith("1.1")) is false), nothing at all happens. If version 1.1 is active, the JDK_11_unloading_bug_fix's constructor creates a Thread derivative whose run() method contains a local variable that holds a reference to the Class object passed in as an argument. The thread's run() method immediately suspends itself by calling wait(). Since there never will be a notify(), the thread doesn't use up any machine cycles, but since the Thread object isn't garbage collected and run() is officially running (albeit inactive), a reference to the Class object for the Singleton is guaranteed to exist on a runtime stack, preventing the associated class from being unloaded. The created thread is given "daemon" status so that its existence won't stop the program from terminating when the non-daemon threads shut down.

Listing 7.3 (/src/com/holub/asynch/JDK_11_unloading_bug_fix.java):
Fixing the 1.1 JDK's Unloading Problem

```
01: package com.holub.asynch;
02:

    /**

        This class provides a workaround for a bug in the JDK 1.1 JVM that unloads
        classes too aggressively. The problem is that if the only reference to an
        object is held in a static member of the object, the class is subject to
        unloading and the static member will be discarded. This behavior causes a
        lot of grief when you're implementing a Singleton. Use it like this:
            class Singleton
            {   private Singleton()
                {   new JDK_11_unloading_bug_fix(Singleton.class);
                }
                // ...
            }

        In either event, once the "JDK_11_unloading_bug_fix" object is created, the
        class (and its static fields) won't be unloaded for the life of the program.
```

@author Allen I. Holub

```
    */
```

```
03: public class JDK_11_unloading_bug_fix
04: {
05:     public JDK_11_unloading_bug_fix( final Class the_class )
06:     {
07:         if( System.getProperty("java.version").startsWith("1.1") )
08:         {
09:             Thread t =
10:                 new Thread()
11:                 {   public void run()
12:                     {   Class singleton_class = the_class;
13:
14:                         synchronized(this)
15:                         {   try                         { wait();  }
16:                             catch(InterruptedException e){         }
17:                         }
18:                     }
19:                 };
20:
21:             // I'm not exactly sure why synchronization is necessary,
22:             // below, but without it, some JVMs complain of an
23:             // illegal-monitor state. The effect is to stop the wait()
24:             // from executing until the thread is fully started.
25:
26:             synchronized( t )
27:             {   t.setDaemon(true);  // so program can shut down
28:                 t.start();
29:             }
30:         }
31:     }
32: }
```

If you have a lot of Singletons in your system and don't want to create a thread to keep each one alive, you can create a "Singleton registry" that uses a single JDK_11_unloading_bug_fix object to keep several Singletons alive. The Singleton_registry class in Listing 7.4 is a simple class that does nothing but keep active references to the Class objects for Singletons in a local Vector. It uses a JDK_11_unloading_bug_fix object to keep itself alive, and it contains a Vector of references to the other Singletons's class objects. The Singletons you create should register themselves with the Singleton_registry in their static-initializer blocks to keep themselves alive. Do it like this:

```
class Singleton
{
    static{ Singleton_registry.register( Singleton.class ); }

    //...
}
```

Note that the `Singleton_registry` implements an (empty) `private` constructor to prevent someone from instantiating an instance of one.

Listing 7.4 (/src/com/holub/tools/Singleton_registry.java): A Singleton Registry

```
01: package com.holub.tools;
02: import com.holub.asynch.JDK_11_unloading_bug_fix;
03: import java.util.*;
04:
```

```
/**
```
Use this class to keep a body of Singletons alive. Each Singleton should pass its class object to "register" from its static initializer block. For example:
```
    class Singleton
            {   static{ Singleton_registry.register( Singleton.class ); }
                //...
            }
```

@author *Allen I. Holub*
```
    */
```
```
05: class Singleton_registry
06: {    static
07:     {   new JDK_11_unloading_bug_fix(Singleton_registry.class);
08:     }
09:
10:     private Singleton_registry(){}
11:
12:     static Collection singletons = new LinkedList();
13:
14:     public synchronized static void register( Object singleton )
15:     {   singletons.add( singleton );
16:     }
17: }
```

Closing Singletons

There is an serious impediment to the correct implementation of Singleton: How do you get rid of the thing? The Singleton object is created on first use, but what if global resources like temporary files or database connections are created by the Singleton's constructor? How do you get rid of the temporary file or close the database connection in an orderly way? C++ lets you destroy Singletons using global-level destructors, but Java has no equivalent mechanism.

Let's consider the possibilities. Putting clean-up code in a Singleton's `finalize()` method doesn't work because there is absolutely no guarantee that `finalize()` will ever be called. (The JDK 1.1 `System.runFinalizersOnExit()` method has been deprecated.) You can add a `release_instance()` method to the Singleton implementation that releases global resources, but not only is it easy to forget to call such a method, there might not be an obvious place in the code where such a method can be called. In any event, I don't want to run all the finalizers; I just want to finalize the Singletons. The `Runtime` class doesn't let you register a shut-down listener, so there is no way to find out when the system is shutting down. The `ThreadGroup` class doesn't support `join()`, so you can't put the user threads into a group, wait for the threads in the group to terminate, then finalize the Singletons.

One possibility, I suppose, is to create a low-priority thread that sits in a loop calling `Thread.activeCount()` repetitively, as I've done in Listing 7.5. The main problem with this strategy (other than the ugliness of the polling loop) is that it is difficult to figure out what the correct minimum thread count will be. AWT/Swing creates threads that you don't know about, for example, and these system-engendered threads must be considered in the count. Another possibility, useful only if the application exposes a UI, is to clean up the Singletons in the main frame's `windowClosing()` handler.

Listing 7.5: Thread_monitor.java

```
/**
    A thread monitor. Calls the run() method of a user-supplied Runnable object
    when the active-thread count goes to 1. Create a monitor as follows:
      new Thread_monitor
          (   new Runnable()
              {   public void run()
                  {   System.out.println("Goodbye world");
                      // CLEAN UP SINGLETONS HERE
                  }
              }
          ).start();

    */

01: public class Thread_monitor extends Thread
02: {   Runnable exit_routine;
```

```
03:
04:        Thread_monitor( Runnable call_on_exit )
05:        {    exit_routine = call_on_exit;
06:             setDaemon( true );
07:             setPriority( Thread.MIN_PRIORITY );
08:        }
09:
10:        public void run()
11:        {
12:             int count;
13:             while( (count = Thread.activeCount()) > 1 )
14:             {
15:                 System.out.println( "Count = " + count );
16:                 try
17:                 {    Thread.currentThread().sleep( 100 );
18:                 }
19:                 catch( InterruptedException e )
20:                 {    /*ignore*/
21:                 }
22:             }
23:             exit_routine.run();
24:        }
25: }
```

Another strategy is to explicitly close a Singleton by implementing a `close()` method that nulled out the instance reference, cleaned up any side effects like temporary files created by the constructor, and then set a flag to indicate that the Singleton can no longer be used. You'd then test for the "closed" state in the `get_instance()` method and throw an exception if anyone tried to access the closed Singleton. Though this approach doesn't solve the closing problem, it at least lets you detect any unwanted access.

Though I hate to end this section on a pessimistic note, I don't have an ideal solution to this problem. If you do, please write to me (*aih@holub.com*).

Reader/Writer Locks

And now for something completely different...

Controlling access to a shared resource like a Singleton, file, or data structure in a multithreaded environment is a commonplace problem: Typically, you'd like to allow any number of threads to simultaneously read from or otherwise access a resource, but you want only one thread at a time to be able to write to or otherwise modify the resource. That is, read operations can go on in parallel, but write operations must be serialized, and reads and writes can't go on simultaneously. Moreover, it is nice if the write requests are guaranteed to be processed in the order that they are received so that sequential writes to a file, for example, are indeed sequential.

The simplest solution to this problem is to just lock the entire data structure by synchronizing everything. This approach is just too simplistic to be workable in the real world, though. With most resources (such as data structures and file systems), there is absolutely no problem with multiple threads all accessing a shared resource simultaneously, provided that the resource isn't modified while its being accessed. If the read operations were all `synchronized` methods, though, no thread could read while another was in the process of reading—you'd effectively serialize the read operations.

This problem is effectively solved using a "reader/writer lock." An attempt to acquire the lock for reading will block only if any write operations are in progress, so simultaneous read operations are the norm. An attempt to acquire the lock for writing will block while either another write operation or any of the current batch of read operations are in progress, and the requesting thread will be released when either the current write completes or all of the current read operations complete. Write operations are effectively serialized (on a first-come first-served basis in the current implementation), so that no two writing threads will be permitted to write simultaneously. Readers who are waiting when a writer thread completes are permitted to execute (in parallel) before subsequent write operations are permitted.

Listing 7.6 implements a reader/writer lock that behaves as I've just described. Generally, you'll use it like this:

```
public class Data_structure_or_resource
{
    Reader_writer lock = new Reader_writer();

    public void access( ) throws InterruptedException
    {
        lock.request_read();
        try
        {
            // do the read/access operation here.
        }
        finally
        {   lock.read_accomplished();
        }
    }

    public void modify( ) throws InterruptedException
    {
        lock.request_write();
        try
        {
            // do the write/modify operation here.
        }
        finally
        {   lock.write_accomplished();
        }
    }
}
```

Note that `request_read()` and `request_write()` both throw an `InterruptedException` object if the waiting thread is interrupted while blocked. In the previous example, I chose to propagate this exception out to the caller, but if an interrupt is impossible ("famous last words" if I ever heard them), you might consider eating the interrupt by catching it. You will not have acquired the resource in this case, so the results of any read or write operation on the resource will be undefined. Perhaps, it would be best to simply return an error code in the case of an interrupt.

I've also provided nonblocking versions of `request_write()` [`request_immediate_write()`, Listing 7.6, line 71] and `request_read()` [`request_immediate_read()`, Listing 7.6, line 26] which return error flags (`false`) if they can't get the resource, but these are not used as often as the blocking forms.

The implementation logic is straightforward, and requires a surprisingly small amount of code. (Most of Listing 7.6 is comments and a test routine.) I keep a count of the number of active readers—readers that are in the process of reading [`active_readers` (Listing 7.6, line 6)]. This count is incremented when a reader requests the lock, and decremented when the reader releases the lock. If a writer thread comes along and requests access to the resource while reads are in progress, it has to wait for the active readers to finish before the writer can be let loose. A lock is created (on line 51) and the requesting thread is made to `wait()` on that lock. These locks are queued up in the `writer_locks` linked list (Listing 7.6, line 10). If any additional reader threads come along while a writer is waiting, they are blocked (by a `wait()` on line 18) until the current batch of readers and the waiting writer have finished. (The `waiting_readers` field [Listing 7.6, line 7] keeps track of how many readers are blocked, waiting for access.) The same goes with additional writers that come along at this point; they're just added to the queue of waiting writers, blocked on a roll-your-own lock.

As the readers finish up, they call `read_accomplished()` (Listing 7.6, line 34) which decrements the the `active_readers` count. When that count goes to zero, the first writer in the queue is released. That thread goes off and does its thing, then calls `write_accomplished()` (Listing 7.6, line 80). If any readers have been patiently waiting while all this is going on, they're released all at once at this point (they're all waiting on the current `Reader_writer` object's internal condition variable). When that batch of readers finishes reading, the process just described is repeated, and the next batch of readers is released. If no readers are waiting when a writer completes, then the next writer in line is released.

One behavior worth considering is a call to `write_accomplished()` when both a reader and a writer are waiting. The current implementation of the lock gives priority to the read operation, so the readers are notified. But why does that `else` statement prevent the writers from being notified? Well, we want the writers to continue blocking while read operations are in progress, so notifying them now is definitely not the correct behavior, but how do they get notified? The answer lies in `read_accomplished()`, which is called when the reader that we just released finishes up. (If any readers have come along while the current read is in progress, they will have been permitted to go ahead and read and the `active_readers` count will have been incremented accordingly.) As the readers finish up, they call `read_accomplished()`, which decrements the count. When the last of these readers calls `read_accomplished()` our patient writer is then notified by `read_accomplished()`. Note that if readers and multiple writers are all waiting, the read and write operations will alternate, so starvation will not occur.

Listing 7.6 (/src/com/holub/asynch/Reader_writer.java): A Reader/Writer Lock

```
001: package com.holub.asynch;
002: import java.util.LinkedList;
003:

    /**
        This reader/writer lock prevents reads from occurring while writes are in
        progress and vice versa, and also prevents multiple writes from happening
        simultaneously. Multiple read operations can run in parallel, however.
        Reads take priority over writes, so any read operations that are pending
        while a write is in progress will execute before any subsequent writes
        execute.
        Writes are guaranteed to execute in the order that they were requested—
        the oldest request is processed first.

        You should use the lock as follows:
            public class Data_structure_or_resource
            {
                Reader_writer lock = new Reader_writer();

                public void access( ) throws InterruptedException
                {   lock.request_read();
                    try
                    {
                            // do the read/access operation here.
                    }
                    finally
                    {   lock.read_accomplished();
                    }
                }

                public void modify( ) throws InterruptedException
                {   lock.request_write();
                    try
                    {
                            // do the write/modify operation here.
                    }
                    finally
                    {   lock.write_accomplished();
                    }
                }
            }
```

The current implementation of Reader_writer doesn't support timeouts.

This implementation is based on the one in Doug Lea's *Concurrent Programming in Java* (Reading: Addison Wesley, 1997, pp. 300–303), I've simplified the code (and cleaned it up) and added the nonblocking acquisition methods. I've also made the lock a stand-alone class rather than a base class from which you have to derive. You might also want to look at the very different implementation of the reader/writer lock in Scott Oaks and Henry Wong's *Java Threads* Sebastopol [Calif.]: O'Reilly, 1997, pp. 180–187).

@author *Allen I. Holub*
```
        */
```

```
004: public final class Reader_writer
005: {
006:     private int active_readers;      // = 0
007:     private int waiting_readers;     // = 0
008:     private int active_writers;      // = 0
009:

        /*****************************************************************
```
I keep a linked list of writers waiting for access so that I can release them in the order that the requests were received. The size of this list is effectively the "waiting writers" count. Note that the monitor of the Reader_writer object itself is used to lock out readers while writes are in progress, thus there's no need for a separate "reader_lock."
```
        */

010:     private final LinkedList writer_locks = new LinkedList();
011:

        /*****************************************************************
```
Request the read lock. Block until a read operation can be performed safely.

This call must be followed by a call to read_accomplished() when the read operation completes.
```
        */
```

```
012:        public synchronized void request_read() throws InterruptedException
013:        {
014:            if( active_writers==0 && writer_locks.size()==0 )
015:                ++active_readers;
016:            else
017:            {   ++waiting_readers;
018:                wait();
019:
020:                // The waiting_readers count is decremented in
021:                // notify_readers() when the waiting reader is
022:                // reactivated.
023:            }
024:        }
025:
```

```
        /****************************************************************
```

This version of read() requests read access, returns true if you get it.
If it returns false, you may not safely read from the guarded resource.
If it returns true, you should do the read, then call read_accomplished()
in the normal way. Here's an example:

```
            public void read()
            {   if( lock.request_immediate_read() )
                {   try
                    {
                        // do the read operation here
                    }
                    finally
                    {   lock.read_accomplished();
                    }
                }
                else
                    // couldn't read safely.
            }

        */
```

```
026:        public synchronized boolean request_immediate_read()
027:        {
028:            if( active_writers==0 && writer_locks.size()==0 )
029:            {   ++active_readers;
030:                return true;
031:            }
032:            return false;
033:        }
```

```
        /****************************************************************
```

Release the lock. You must call this method when you're done with the
read operation.

```
        */
```

```
034:    public synchronized void read_accomplished()
035:    {   if( --active_readers == 0 )
036:            notify_writers();
037:    }
```

```
/****************************************************************
```
Request the write lock. Block until a write operation can be performed safely. Write requests are guaranteed to be executed in the order received. Pending read requests take precedence over all write requests. This call must be followed by a call to write_accomplished()when the write operation completes.
```
*/
```

```
038:    public void request_write() throws InterruptedException
039:    {
040:        // If this method was synchronized, there'd be a nested-monitor
041:        // lockout problem: We have to acquire the lock for "this" in
042:        // order to modify the fields, but that lock must be released
043:        // before we start waiting for a safe time to do the writing.
044:        // If request_write() were synchronized, we'd be holding
045:        // the monitor on the Reader_writer lock object while we were
046:        // waiting. Since the only way to be released from the wait is
047:        // for someone to call either read_accomplished()
048:        // or write_accomplished() (both of which are synchronized),
049:        // there would be no way for the wait to terminate.
050:
051:        Object lock = new Object();
052:        synchronized( lock )
053:        {   synchronized( this )
054:            {   boolean okay_to_write = writer_locks.size()==0
055:                                    && active_readers==0
056:                                    && active_writers==0;
057:                if( okay_to_write )
058:                {   ++active_writers;
059:                    return; // the "return" jumps over the "wait" call
060:                }
061:
062:                writer_locks.addLast(lock); // Note that the
063:                                            // active_writers count
064:                                            // is incremented in
065:                                            // notify_writers() when
066:                                            // this writer gets control
067:            }
068:            lock.wait();
069:        }
070:    }
```

```
/****************************************************************
```
This version of the write request returns false immediately (without blocking) if any read or write operations are in progress and a write isn't safe; otherwise it returns true and acquires the resource. Use it like this:

```
             public void write()
             {   if( lock.request_immediate_write() )
                 {   try
                     {
                         // do the write operation here
                     }
                     finally
                     {   lock.write_accomplished();
                     }
                 }
                 else
                     // couldn't write safely.
             }
         */

071:    synchronized public boolean request_immediate_write()
072:    {
073:        if( writer_locks.size()==0  && active_readers==0
074:                                    && active_writers==0 )
075:        {   ++active_writers;
076:            return true;
077:        }
078:        return false;
079:    }
```

```
    /****************************************************************
        Release the lock. You must call this method when you're done with
        the read operation.
        */
```

```
080:    public synchronized void write_accomplished()
081:    {
082:        // The logic here is more complicated than it appears.
083:        // If readers have priority, you'll  notify them. As they
084:        // finish up, they'll call read_accomplished(), one at
085:        // a time. When they're all done, read_accomplished() will
086:        // notify the next writer. If no readers are waiting, then
087:        // just notify the writer directly.
088:
089:        --active_writers;
090:        if( waiting_readers > 0 )   // priority to waiting readers
091:            notify_readers();
092:        else
093:            notify_writers();
094:    }
```

```
    /****************************************************************
        Notify all the threads that have been waiting to read.
        */
```

```
095:    private void notify_readers()        // must be accessed from a
096:    {                                    //   synchronized method
```

```
097:            active_readers  += waiting_readers;
098:            waiting_readers = 0;
099:            notifyAll();
100:        }

        /*****************************************************************
            Notify the writing thread that has been waiting the longest.
        */

101:        private void notify_writers()        // must be accessed from a
102:        {                                    //   synchronized method
103:            if( writer_locks.size() > 0 )
104:            {
105:                Object oldest = writer_locks.removeFirst();
106:                ++active_writers;
107:                synchronized( oldest ){ oldest.notify(); }
108:            }
109:        }
110:
```

```
        /*****************************************************************
            The Test class is a unit test for the other code in the current file.
            Run the test with:

                java com.holub.asynch.Reader_writer\$Test
```

(the backslash isn't required with Windows boxes), and don't include this class file in your final distribution. Though the output could vary in trivial ways depending on system timing. The read/write order should be exactly the same as in the following sample:

```
        Starting w/0
                            w/0 writing
        Starting r/1
        Starting w/1
        Starting w/2
        Starting r/2
        Starting r/3
                            w/0 done
        Stopping w/0
                            r/1 reading
                            r/2 reading
                            r/3 reading
                            r/1 done
        Stopping r/1
                            r/2 done
                            r/3 done
        Stopping r/2
        Stopping r/3
                            w/1 writing
                            w/1 done
```

```
                    Stopping w/1
                              w/2 writing
                              w/2 done
                    Stopping w/2

          */

111:    public static class Test
112:    {
113:        Resource resource = new Resource();
114:

          /**
          The Resource class simulates a simple locked resource. The read
          operation simply pauses for .1 seconds. The write operation
          (which is typically higher overhead) pauses for .5 seconds.  Note
          that the use of try...finally is not critical in the current  test, but
          it's good style to always release the lock in a finally block in
          real code.
          */

115:        static class Resource
116:        {   Reader_writer lock = new Reader_writer();
117:
118:            public void read( String reader )
119:            {   try
120:                {   lock.request_read();
121:                    System.out.println( "\t\t" + reader + " reading" );
122:                    try{ Thread.currentThread().sleep( 100 ); }
123:                    catch(InterruptedException e){}
124:                    System.out.println( "\t\t" + reader + " done" );
125:                }
126:                catch( InterruptedException exception )
127:                {   System.out.println("Unexpected interrupt");
128:                }
129:                finally
130:                {   lock.read_accomplished();
131:                }
132:            }
133:
134:            public void write( String writer )
135:            {   try
136:                {   lock.request_write();
137:                    System.out.println( "\t\t" + writer + " writing" );
138:                    try{ Thread.currentThread().sleep( 500 ); }
139:                    catch(InterruptedException e){}
140:                    System.out.println( "\t\t" + writer + " done" );
141:                }
142:                catch( InterruptedException exception )
143:                {   System.out.println("Unexpected interrupt");
144:                }
```

```
145:                finally
146:                {   lock.write_accomplished();
147:                }
148:            }
149:
150:        public boolean read_if_possible()
151:        {   if( lock.request_immediate_read() )
152:            {
153:                // in the real world, you'd do the read here
154:                lock.read_accomplished();
155:                return true;
156:            }
157:            return false;
158:        }
159:
160:        public boolean write_if_possible()
161:        {   if( lock.request_immediate_write() )
162:            {
163:                // in the real world, you'd do the write here
164:                lock.write_accomplished();
165:                return true;
166:            }
167:            return false;
168:        }
169:    }
```

```
       /**
           A simple reader thread. Just reads from the resource, passing it a
           unique string ID.
        */
```

```
170:    class Reader extends Thread
171:    {   private String name;
172:        Reader( String name ){ this.name = name; }
173:        public void run( )
174:        {
175:            System.out.println("Starting " + name );
176:            resource.read( name );
177:            System.out.println("Stopping " + name );
178:        }
179:    }
```

```
       /**
           A simple writer thread. Just writes to the resource, passing it a unique
           string ID.
        */
```

```
180:    class Writer extends Thread
181:    {   private String name;
182:        Writer( String name ){ this.name = name; }
183:        public void run()
```

```
184:                {
185:                    System.out.println("Starting " + name );
186:                    resource.write( name );
187:                    System.out.println("Stopping " + name );
188:                }
189:        }
190:

            /**
            Test by creating several readers and writers. The initial write
            operation (w/0) should complete before the first read (r/1) runs.
            Since readers have priority, r/2 and r/3 should run before w/1,
            and r/1, r/2, and r/3 should all run in parallel. When all three
            reads complete, w/1 and w/2 should  execute sequentially
            in that order.
            */

191:        public Test()
192:        {
193:            if( !resource.read_if_possible() )
194:                System.out.println("Immediate read request failed");
195:            if( !resource.write_if_possible() )
196:                System.out.println("Immediate write request failed");
197:
198:            new Writer( "w/0" ).start();
199:            new Reader( "r/1" ).start();
200:            new Writer( "w/1" ).start();
201:            new Writer( "w/2" ).start();
202:            new Reader( "r/2" ).start();
203:            new Reader( "r/3" ).start();
204:        }
205:
206:        static public void main( String[] args )
207:        {   Test t = new Test();
208:        }
209:    }
210: }
```

It's a Wrap

So, that is it for the part of this book that discusses what I think of as the "low-level" thread-related problems. The toolkit I've developed over the past few chapters should put you well on the way to solving many thorny issues that crop up in every multithreaded program. But we're not done yet. You're probably asking yourself why you ever thought that programming with threads was a good idea: There is just so much complexity, and the bugs are so hard to find. Fortunately, there is a general solution to both problems: good architecture. It's possible to design a program for multithreading in such a way that many of the synchronization issues I've been discussing become immaterial. (Which is not to say that synchronization-related problems don't pop up regularly, even when the overall system is well-designed. I regularly use all those semaphores and locks we've been looking at. With the proper architecture, though, synchronization issues do tend to move to the background). In the next chapter I'll start looking at architectural solutions to threading problems with a discussion of thread pools and synchronous dispatching.

CHAPTER 8

Threads in an Object-Oriented World

IN THE PREVIOUS CHAPTERS, I've looked at low-level solutions to threading problems: locks of various sorts, timers, and so forth. This chapter moves on to discuss architectural solutions to threading problems. We'll look at threads from the perspective of an OO designer, and at how to implement threads in an OO environment, focusing on the implementation of asynchronous methods. Along the way, I'll look at another design pattern: *Command*—a means of implementing function pointers in an object-oriented way. I'll also look at an architectural-level solution to the threading-complexity problem: namely the thread pool, which is useful for minimizing thread-creation overhead. Finally, I'll demonstrate the practical application of a thread pool by showing you how to implement a server-side socket's "accept" loop efficiently.

One of the biggest problems associated with using threads in an OO environment is a conceptual one: Though procedural programmers naturally think about the flow of control from function to function as the system works, OO designers focus on the message flow within an individual scenario or use case. The traditional view of threading, however, concerns itself entirely with flow of control. As a consequence, OO designers typically don't think about threads—at least not until they get down to the very low-level implementation part of the design. Rather, they think about two categories of messages: *synchronous messages* that don't return until they're done doing whatever they do, and *asynchronous messages*, which initiate some background operation and return immediately. That is, there is a fundamental clash of metaphor, here: control flow versus message type. Unfortunately, Java's threading model is not in the least object oriented. It is built around the procedural control-flow metaphor. This chapter (along with Chapter 9) addresses these issues by showing you how to reconcile these two points of view and implement OO-style threading using Java's essentially procedural implementation of threads.

Modeling Threads in Object-Oriented Systems

Java's threading system is built on the notion of extending the Thread class and overriding run(). The run() override, and any methods called directly or indirectly from run(), comprise the behavior of the thread. I've found, in teaching this stuff, that Java's threading structure is fundamentally misleading to people. The fact that you create a thread by deriving from Thread leads many a novice Java programmer to the erroneous belief that all the methods of the Thread derivative will run on that thread. In fact, a method of a Thread derivative is just like any other method—it runs on a thread only if called directly or indirectly from that thread's run() method. Objects do not run on threads, methods do.

The situation is made worse by the way that OO systems are organized. In a procedural system, one procedure just calls another, starting at a single starting point. Even when there are many threads and many paths through the code, each path starts at a known place, and the control flow through a given thread is predictable (though sometimes not easily). OO systems are another matter. OO systems are not controlled from the top by a "God" class that encapsulates main(); rather, they are a network of cooperating objects communicating with one another via a well-defined messaging system. In many OO systems, main() does nothing but create a bunch of objects, hook them up to each other, and then terminate. Because of this network structure, it is sometimes difficult to predict any control flow in an OO system.

Synchronous vs. Asynchronous Messages

An OO designer looks at the world in terms of objects and messages. Objects pass messages to each other, and the receipt of some message causes an appropriate message-handler—a Java method—to be executed. Most of these messages are synchronous—their handlers don't return until they're finished doing whatever they do. Other messages are asynchronous—the handler returns immediately, before the requested operation completes; meanwhile, work is going on in the background to satisfy the original request. A good example of an asynchronous message in Java is Toolkit.getImage(), which initiates the process of fetching an image and then returns immediately, long before the actual image arrives.

The broad categories of messages (synchronous and asynchronous) can themselves be subdivided in various ways. For example, a *balking* message is one that can't even be initiated. Imagine that you could only open a limited number of database connections at a given moment, and that all the connections were in use. A message that required access to the database could *balk* if it couldn't get the connection. It is not that it tried to do the operation and failed; rather, it couldn't even initiate the operation to give it a chance to fail.

Another variant on synchronous messages is a *time-out message*. Rather than balking immediately, the method decides to wait for a predetermined amount of time for the resource to become available. The request fails if that time expires. (The operation probably never started, but if the operation had indeed started, it certainly didn't complete successfully.) In Java, a read from a socket can timeout in this way. Designing asynchronous systems in an object-oriented way isn't particularly difficult. OO-design notations such as UML (Booch, Rumbaugh, and Jacobson's "Universal Modeling Language") can easily capture notions like synchronous and asynchronous messages. Implementing these notions in the essentially procedural system mandated by the the Java threading model is another matter.

Implementing Asynchronous Messages Using Thread-per-Method

Given an OO design perspective—a network of objects communicating via messages—what is the best way to implement an asynchronous message? The most naive way, which is workable in simple situations, is for each asynchronous-message handler to spawn off its own thread.

Consider the following synchronous method, which flushes an internal buffer out to a file. (The Reader_writer lock was discussed in the previous chapter.)

```
// Flush a stream as follows:
//
//   outputStream stream;
//   Synchronous_flush flusher = new Synchronous_flush(stream);
//   flusher.flush();
//

import com.holub.asynch.Reader_writer;
import java.io.*;

class Synchronous_flush
{
    private final OutputStream  out;
    private Reader_writer        lock = new Reader_writer();
    private byte[]               buffer;
    private int                  length;

    public Synchronous_flush( OutputStream out )
    {   this.out = out;
    }
    //...
    synchronized void flush( ) throws IOException
    {   lock.request_write();
        try
        {   out.write( buffer, 0, length );
            length - 0;
        }
        finally
        {   lock.write_accomplished();
        }
    }
}
```

This blocking version of flush() presents several problems. First of all, flush() can block indefinitely while waiting to acquire the Reader_writer lock. Moreover, if the OutputStream was a socket connection rather than a file, the write operation itself could take a long time to do. Finally, because flush() is synchronized, the entire object is locked while the flush is in progress, so any thread that tries to call any other synchronized method of Synchronous_flush will block until the flush() completes.

This wait could turn into a nested-monitor-lockout situation should the lock not be released.

These problems can be solved by making flush() asynchronous; the flush() method should initiate the flush operation and then return immediately. Here's an initial (not very successful) attempt:

```
import com.holub.asynch.Reader_writer;
import java.io.*;

class Asynchronous_flush
{
    private OutputStream    out;
    private Reader_writer    lock = new Reader_writer();
    private byte[]          buffer;
    private int            length;
    //...
    synchronized void flush( )
    {   new Thread()
        {   public void run()
            {   try
                {   lock.request_write();
                    out.write( buffer, 0, length );
                    length = 0;
                }
                catch( IOException e )
                {   // ignore it.
                }
                finally
                {   lock.write_accomplished();
                }
            }
        }.start();
    }

    public synchronized write( byte[] stuff )
    {   lock.request_write();
        try
        {
            // add stuff to buffer here
        }
        finally
        {   lock.write_accomplished();
        }
    }
}
```

I've wrapped the former contents of the flush() method inside the run() method of an anonymous inner class that extends Thread. The flush() method currently does nothing but fire off the thread and return. In the current implementation, we're hoping that operations execute in the correct sequence because of the way that the Reader_writer lock is written: All in-progress read operations should finish before the flush happens, and the flush must finish before any additional reads are permitted. This simple asynchronous-methods-create-their-own-thread strategy can work for simple situations, but unfortunately, it doesn't work here. Let's analyze the problems one at a time.

First, the write() operation is no longer thread safe. Simply synchronizing the flush() method locks the object only while we're in the flush() method, which isn't for very long. The actual write() operation is performed on its own thread long after flush() has returned, and the buffer may have been modified several times in the interim (even worse, may be modified while the write is in progress). That is, the thread created by flush() may be preempted by other threads that write to the buffer, and this preemption may occur before the flushing thread requests the reader/writer lock. A possible solution to the synchronization problem is to make a copy of the buffer while we're synchronized, and then work from the copy when inside the (non-synchronized) auxiliary thread. Synchronization is necessary only while we're actually making the copy.

Because it is so easy, it would be nice if we could implement this strategy like this:

```
synchronized void flush( )
{
    final byte[] copy = buffer.clone(); // must be final so that
                                        // it can be accessed by
                                        // the inner-class Thread
                                        // derivative.
    length = 0;

    new Thread()
    {   public void run()
        {   try
            {   lock.request_write();
                out.write( copy, 0, length );
            }
            catch( IOException e )
            {   // ignore it.
            }
            finally
            {   lock.write_accomplished();
            }
        }
    }.start();
}
```

but that doesn't work particularly well either because it is always flushing a stale buffer. Moreover, I've made the copy field final so that it can be accessed from the inner-class object. [Remember, a normal local variable—which exists on the method's stack frame—cannot be used directly by an inner-class object simply because the lifetime of the inner-class object can be longer than that of the method. The flush() method will probably have returned long before run() is executed.

You have to make locals and arguments that are used by inner-class objects final, in which case a *copy* of the local variable or argument is implicitly stored in a (hidden) field of the inner class.] It is not always convenient to make local variables final, however. A larger problem is the nonexistent exception handling. Simply eating the exception is not a great strategy, but what else is there to do? Listing 8.1 solves most of these problems by using the copy strategy I just discussed. The strange-looking thing on line 24 is an *instance initializer* for the inner class. Think of it syntactically as a static initializer that isn't static—a sort-of meta constructor. The code in the instance initializer is effectively copied into all constructors—including the compiler-generated "default" constructor—above any code specified in the constructor itself. If you have both an instance initializer and a constructor, the code in the instance initializer executes first. (The one exception to this rule is that the instance initializer is not copied into any constructor that calls another constructor using the this(optional_args) syntax. This way, the code in the instance initializer is executed only once). The syntax is pretty ugly, but there it is.

As an alternative to the instance initializer, you could encapsulate the code from the instance initializer in a non-static method, and then call that method when initializing the field:

```
new Thread()
{   int     length;
    byte[]  copy = init();

    private void init()
    {   length       = Flush_example.this.length;
        byte[] copy  = new byte[length];
        System.arraycopy(Flush_example.this.buffer, 0, copy, 0, length);
        Flush_example.this.length = 0;
        return copy;
    }
    //...

    synchronized void flush( final Flush_error_handler handler )
    {
        new Thread()
        {   //...
            byte[]  copy = init();;
            //...
        }
    }
}
```

This is not much of an improvement over the instance initializer in clarity, and zeroing length as a side effect of the init() call is particularly hideous. I've used arraycopy() rather than clone() because I didn't want to mess with the CloneNotSupportedException. Exceptions are not allowed to propagate out of instance initializers.

Whatever method we use for initialization, the inner-class's construction happens in the new() on line 20 of *Flush_example.java* while the outer-class object is locked, so the copy operation is thread safe. Because flush() is synchronized, we are in the monitor when the inner-class constructor executes, and we won't give up the monitor until flush() exits after start() returns. The newly-created thread acquires the Reader_writer lock and writes to the file in its own good time, using the copy for this purpose.

Listing 8.1: /text/books/threads/ch8/Flush_example.java

```
01: import com.holub.asynch.Reader_writer;
02: import java.io.*;
03:
04: class Flush_example
05: {
06:     public interface Flush_error_handler
07:     {   void error( IOException e );
08:     }
09:
10:     private final OutputStream   out;
11:     private Reader_writer        lock = new Reader_writer();
12:     private byte[]               buffer;
13:     private int                  length;
14:
15:     public Flush_example( OutputStream out )
16:     {   this.out = out;
17:     }
18:     //...
19:     synchronized void flush( final Flush_error_handler handler )
20:     {   new Thread()
21:         {   int     length;
22:             byte[]  copy;
23:
24:             {   length = Flush_example.this.length;
25:                 copy   = new byte[length];
26:               System.arraycopy(Flush_example.this.buffer, 0, copy, 0, length);
27:                 Flush_example.this.length = 0;
28:             }
29:
30:             public void run()
31:             {   try
32:                 {   lock.request_write();
33:                     out.write( copy, 0, length );
34:                 }
35:                 catch( IOException e )
36:                 {   handler.error(e);
37:                 }
38:                 finally
39:                 {   lock.write_accomplished();
```

```
40:                         }
41:                     }
42:                 }.start();
43:         }
44: }
```

An Exceptional Problem

The next perplexing issue solved in Listing 8.1 is what to do with the IOException. Back in the original version of the code; the exception propagated out of the flush() method to whomever called flush(). We can't do that here, because there is nobody to propagate it *to*. If you start backtracking down the call stack, you'll end up back in run(), but you didn't call run(); the system did when it fired up the thread. Simply ignoring the write error, as I've been doing, isn't a good strategy for obvious reasons.

One solution to this problem is the Observer pattern discussed a couple of chapters back. (AWT's listeners are examples of Observer.) The method that finally catches the IOException must be a method that calls flush(), either directly or indirectly, so this method could simply register a listener and be notified when something goes wrong. In the current situation, a full-blown observer is something of an overkill. There will only be one observer for a given I/O operation after all.

A better solution to the error-notification problem is a different, though related, design pattern, namely *Command*. To quote the Gang-of-Four book's Applicability section, "Commands are an object-oriented replacement for callbacks." In a procedural language, for example, a method like flush() could be passed a pointer to a function to call when something goes wrong—a callback. The basic notion in the Command patterns is to encapsulate that callback method into an object. That is, don't pass a pointer to a function that performs some operation; rather, pass an object that performs the same operation.

This strategy is used for the error handler in the flush() method in Listing 8.1 (above). The Flush_error_handler interface (Listing 8.1, line 6) defines a method to call when an IOException is encountered on line 36. The caller of flush defines what to do on an error as follows:

```
flush(  new Flush_error_handler()
        {   public void error( IOException e )
            {   // the code that would normally handle the exception goes here.
                System.err.println("Flush error: " + e );
                System.exit(1);
            }
        }
    );
```

The error() method contains whatever code would normally be found in the exception handler. Note that error() is executed on the thread that detects the error, not on the thread that creates the error handler. Be careful of synchronization problems if error() accesses any fields outside its own class.

Thread Pools and Blocking Queues

Perhaps the biggest problem with the one-thread-per-method problem is that we're creating an awful lot of threads on the fly as the program executes. Both the Thread constructor and the start() method take up an awful lot of time. Creating a thread is not a low-overhead operation. Many system calls are often involved. (In NT for example, there is a 600-machine-cycle penalty imposed every time you enter the kernel.) Listing 8.2 demonstrates the problem. The program creates 10,000 strings (as a reference point), then creates 10,000 threads, then creates and starts 10,000 threads, printing the time required to perform these operations. The slightly reformatted output (running on a 600MHz Wintel box running NT 4.0/SP6) shows just how much overhead there is:

```
Creating               10000 Strings took 0.0040 milliseconds per operation.
Creating               10000 Threads took 0.0491 milliseconds per operation.
Creating and starting 10000 Threads took 0.8021 milliseconds per operation.
```

That .80 milliseconds-per-thread create-and-start time is the killer. In a busy server application in which several threads can be created per connection, this overhead can noticeably affect throughput.

Listing 8.2: Thread_creation_overhead.java

```
01: class Thread_creation_overhead
02: {
03:     final int trys = 10000;
04:
05:     public Thread_creation_overhead()
06:     {
07:         time( "Creating " + trys + " Strings",
08:                 new Runnable(){ public void run()
09:                 {
10:                     String s;
11:                     for( int i = trys; --i >= 0 ; )
12:                         s = new String("abc");
13:                 }}
14:             );
15:
16:         time( "Creating " + trys + " Threads",
17:                 new Runnable(){ public void run()
18:                 {
19:                     Thread t;
20:                     for( int i = trys; --i >= 0 ; )
21:                         t = new My_thread();
22:                 }}
23:             );
24:
```

```
25:            time( "Creating and starting " + trys + " Threads",
26:                new Runnable(){ public void run()
27:                    {
28:                        Thread t;
29:                        for( int i = trys; --i >= 0 ; )
30:                        {
31:                            t = new My_thread();
32:                            t.start();
33:                        }
34:                    }}
35:                );
36:    }
37:
38:    private void time( String description, Runnable operation )
39:    {
40:        long start = System.currentTimeMillis();
41:        operation.run();
42:        long end   = System.currentTimeMillis();
43:
44:        System.out.println( description
45:                            + " took "
46:                            + ( ((double)end-start)/trys )
47:                            + " milliseconds per operation." );
48:    }
49:
50:    private static class My_thread extends Thread
51:    {   public void run(){}
52:    }
53:
54:    public static void main( String[] arguments )
55:    {   new Thread_creation_overhead();
56:    }
57: }
```

A better strategy is to precreate a bunch of threads, and have them sitting around waiting for something to do. When it's time to do something, wake up one of these existing threads rather than creating one from scratch. There is also no reason why the same thread cannot be recycled many times to perform the same (or different) operations. This strategy for thread management is called a thread pool.

Blocking Queues

The first step in building a thread pool is coming up with a realistic implementation of the Notifying_queue discussed in previous chapters. I've done that in Listing 8.3. The basic notion is that a thread that tries to dequeue from an empty queue will block until an object is enqueued by a second thread.

I've implemented the queue itself as a (Java 2) LinkedList object, declared on line 7 of Listing 8.3. The enqueue (Listing 8.3, line 83) operation just adds an Object to the end of the queue. The dequeue(...) operation removes whatever happens to be at the front. If the queue is empty, the dequeue(...) (Listing 8.3, line 94) method waits (on line 116) until enqueue() notifies it that an element has been added (line 47).

You must use a spin lock for the wait in dequeue(...) because one thread (call it the entering thread) could call dequeue() just as a thread that was waiting for an element to be enqueued (call it the waiting thread) was notified. (I went over this earlier, but it can't hurt to do it again.) It is possible for the entering thread to sneak in just after the waiting thread has been released from the internal condition variable, but before it has reentered the monitor. Both the entering and waiting thread will be contending for the same mutex, and there is no way to determine which thread will actually get it. There is no problem if the waiting thread gets the mutex. If the entering thread gets the mutex, however, it will also get the item that was just enqueued, and the waiting thread will return from wait() with the queue empty. Consequently, we have to spin back up to make sure that there really is something to dequeue.

Another important wait-related issue is that it's convenient to know how many threads are blocked, waiting for something to be enqueued. (The waiting_threads() method (Listing 8.3, line 156) returns this number.) I keep track of the number of waiting threads by incrementing the a waiting_threads count on line 114 and decrementing it on line 130. In order for this count not to jitter (rapidly go up and down) while inside the spin lock, I've surrounded the spin lock with a separate test statement, so that the modification can occur external to the while loop that comprises the lock [as compared to bracketing the wait() call itself].

Adding a timeout to the dequeue() method is hard; wait() doesn't tell us whether it has returned because it was notified or because it timed out. In the first case, you might have to spin back up and wait again if a second thread steals the enqueued item, as I just described. In the timeout case the dequeue() method should return. there is no easy way to determine the correct action to take, however. I've solved the problem as I suggested in Chapter 1, by getting the current system time in milliseconds, computing the time at which the wait will expire, and then waiting in the spin lock either for that expiration time to occur or for the queue to be nonempty.

I've also added an optional timeout to the enqueue operation, implemented by the version of enqueue() on line 51. This version calls the standard enqueue() operation, then creates a thread that waits for a time specified as a method argument. When that time arrives, the enqueued object is removed from the queue (if it is still there), and a Runnable Command object (also passed in as an argument) is notified. For example, the following code enqueues a string in such a way that an error message is printed if the string hasn't been dequeued within one second. The string is removed from the queue in this case:

```
some_queue.enqueue
(    "Enqueue this String",
     1000,                      // wait one second for dequeue operation.
     new Runnable()
     {    public void run()
          {    System.out.println("String not dequeued within one second");
          }
     }
);
```

The current implementation of this version of enqueue() is probably suboptimal in that it creates a thread to handle every timeout. Not only can the thread creation take upwards of half a millisecond, there can be lots of threads hanging around. An alternative (though more complex) solution would maintain a priority queue of association objects that contain an expiration time and a reference to the object to remove. The queue would be ordered by expiration time, and a single thread would wait until the next association object's time comes up, handle that one timeout, then go back to sleep. I'll leave this implementation as an exercise for the reader.

Unlike the various notifying-queue variants I've used for examples in earlier chapters, its possible to close a Blocking_queue by calling close() (Listing 8.3, line 161). This method does two things: First, it sets the closed flag, which causes enqueue() to start throwing exceptions when its called. Then close() releases all threads that are blocked on the current queue by issuing a notifyAll(). All these threads will then return from the wait() on line 116, and because closed will be true, the previously waiting threads will return from dequeue() with an exception toss.

A soft close is also available. If you call enqueue_final_item(...) (Listing 8.3, line 88) to enqueue the last item to the queue, then subsequent calls to enqueue() will fail with an exception toss, but calls to dequeue() will work normally until the queue is empty, at which time the queue is closed automatically (thereby preventing subsequent dequeue operations).

Listing 8.3: /src/com/holub/asynch/Blocking_queue.java

```
001: package com.holub.asynch;
002:
003: import java.util.*;
004:

     /**********************************************************************
          This is a thread-safe queue that blocks automatically if you
          try to dequeue from an empty queue. It's based on a linked
          list, so will never fill. (You'll never block on a queue-full
          condition because there isn't one.)

          This class uses the LinkedList class, introduced into the JDK at
          version 1.2. It will not work with earlier releases.
```

@author *Allen I. Holub*
```
     */
```

```
005: public final class Blocking_queue
006: {
007:     private LinkedList elements                = new LinkedList();
008:     private boolean    closed                  = false;
009:     private boolean    reject_enqueue_requests = false;
010:     private int        waiting_threads         = 0;
011:     private int        maximum_size            = 0; // no limit
012:

         /*****************************************************************
             The Blocking_queue.Exception class is the base class of
             the other exception classes, provided so that you can catch
             any queue-related error with a single catch statement.
          */

013:     public class Exception extends RuntimeException
014:     {   public Exception(String s){ super(s); }
015:     }
016:

         /*****************************************************************
             The Closed exception is thrown if you try to used an
             explicitly closed queue. See close().
          */

017:     public class Closed extends Exception
018:     {   private Closed()
019:         {   super("Tried to access closed Blocking_queue");
020:         }
021:     }
022:

         /*****************************************************************
             The full exception is thrown if you try to enqueue an item
             in  a size-limited queue that's full.
          */
```

```
023:      public class Full extends Exception
024:      {   private Full()
025:          {   super("Attempt to enqueue item to full Blocking_queue.");
026:          }
027:      }
028:

          /*****************************************************************
              Convenience constructor, creates a queue with no upper
              limit on the size.
           */

029:      public Blocking_queue(){}
030:

          /*****************************************************************
              Convenience constructor, creates a queue with no upper
              limit on the size.
           */

031:      public Blocking_queue( int maximum_size )
032:      {   this.maximum_size = maximum_size;
033:      }
034:

          /*****************************************************************
              Enqueue an object that will remain in the queue until it is
              dequeued.
           **/

035:      public synchronized final void enqueue( Object new_element )
036:                                                  throws Closed, Full
037:      {   if( closed || reject_enqueue_requests )
038:              throw new Closed();
039:
040:          // Detect a full queue. Queues of size 0 are allowed to grow
041:          // indefinitely.
042:
043:          if( (maximum_size != 0) && (elements.size() >= maximum_size) )
044:              throw new Full();
045:
046:          elements.addLast( new_element );
047:          notify();
048:      }
049:

          /*****************************************************************
              Enqueue an object that will remain in the queue for at
              most "timeout" milliseconds. The run() method of the
              on_removal object is called if the object is removed in.
              This way, if a given object is in the queue more than once,
              then the first occurrence of the object is removed.
```

@param *new_element* The object to enqueue
@param *timeout* The maximum time that the object will
spend in the queue (subject to the usual variations
that can occur if a higher priority thread happens to be
running when the timeout occurs).
@param *on_removal* If non-null, the run() method is
called if the object is removed due to a timeout. If null,
nothing in particular is done when the object is removed.
```
        */
```

```
050:
051:    public synchronized final void enqueue( final Object    new_element,
052:                                             final long      timeout,
053:                                             final Runnable  on_removal )
054:    {
055:        enqueue( new_element );
056:
057:        new Thread()
058:        {   { setDaemon(true); }     // instance initializer, effectively
059:                                      // a constructor for this object.
060:            public void run()
061:            {   try
062:                {   boolean found;
063:
064:                    sleep( timeout );
065:                    synchronized( Blocking_queue.this )
066:                    {   found = elements.remove( new_element );
067:
068:                        if( found && (elements.size()==0)
069:                                  && reject_enqueue_requests )
070:                        {
071:                            close(); // Have just removed final item,
072:                        }
073:                    }
074:
075:                    if( found && on_removal != null )
076:                        on_removal.run();
077:                }
078:                catch( InterruptedException e ){ /* can't happen */ }
079:            }
080:        }.start();
081:    }
082:
```

```
    /******************************************************************
        Convenience method, calls enqueue(Object,long,Runnable)
        with a null on_removal reference.
        */
```

```
083:    public synchronized final void enqueue( final Object new_element,
084:                                             final long    timeout )
085:    {   enqueue( new_element, timeout, null );
```

```
086:      }
087:


          /******************************************************************
              Enqueue an item, and thereafter, reject any requests to
              enqueue additional items. The queue is closed auto-
              matically when the final item is dequeued.
           */

088:     public synchronized final void enqueue_final_item( Object last )
089:                                                        throws Closed
090:     {   enqueue( last );
091:         reject_enqueue_requests = true;
092:     }
093:


          /******************************************************************
              Dequeues an element; blocks if the queue is empty (until
              something is enqueued). Be careful of nested-monitor lock-
              out if you call this function. You must ensure that there's
              a way to get something into the queue that does not involve
              calling a synchronized method of whatever class is blocked,
              waiting to dequeue something. A timeout is not supported
              because of a potential race condition (see text). You can
              interrupt the dequeueing thread to  break it out of a blocked
              dequeue operation, however.
              @param timeout  Timeout value in milliseconds. An
              ArithmeticException is thrown if this value is greater than a
              million years or so. Use Semaphore#FOREVER to wait forever.
              @see #enqueue
              @see #drain
              @see #nonblocking_dequeue
              @return the  dequeued object or null if the wait timed out and
              nothing was dequeued.
              @throws InterruptedException  if interrupted while blocked
              @throws Semaphore.Timed_out  if timed out while blocked
              @throws Blocking_queue.Closed  on attempt to dequeue from
              a closed queue.
           */

094:     public synchronized final Object dequeue( long timeout )
095:                                    throws InterruptedException,
096:                                           Closed,
097:                                           Semaphore.Timed_out
098:     {
099:         long expiration = (timeout == Semaphore.FOREVER)
100:                              ? Semaphore.FOREVER
101:                              : System.currentTimeMillis() + timeout;
102:                              ;
103:         if( closed )
104:             throw new Closed();
105:         try
```

```
106:         {
107:             // If the queue is empty, wait. I've put the spin lock
108:             // inside an "if" so that the waiting_threads count doesn't
109:             // jitter while inside the spin lock. A thread is not
110:             // considered to be done waiting until it's actually
111:             // acquired an element or the timeout is exceeded.
112:
113:             if( elements.size() <= 0 )
114:             {   ++waiting_threads;
115:                 while( elements.size() <= 0 )
116:                 {   wait( timeout );
117:
118:                     if( System.currentTimeMillis() > expiration )
119:                     {   --waiting_threads;
120:                         throw new Semaphore.Timed_out(
121:                                 "Timed out waiting to dequeue " +
122:                                 "from Blocking_queue" );
123:                     }
124:
125:                     if( closed )
126:                     {   --waiting_threads;
127:                         throw new Closed();
128:                     }
129:                 }
130:                 --waiting_threads;
131:             }
132:
133:             Object head = elements.removeFirst();
134:
135:             if( elements.size() == 0 && reject_enqueue_requests )
136:                 close(); // just removed final item, close the queue.
137:
138:             return head;
139:         }
140:         catch( NoSuchElementException e )    // Shouldn't happen
141:         {   throw new Error(
142:                 "Internal error (com.holub.asynch.Blocking_queue)");
143:         }
144:     }

    /**********************************************************************
       Convenience method, calls dequeue(long) with a timeout of
       Semaphore.FOREVER.
     */

145:     public synchronized final Object dequeue()
146:                                         throws InterruptedException,
147:                                                Closed,
148:                                                Semaphore.Timed_out
149:     {   return dequeue( Semaphore.FOREVER );
150:     }
151:
```

217

```
/*****************************************************************
```

The `is_empty()` method is inherently unreliable in a multi-threaded situation. In code like the following, it's possible for a thread to sneak in after the test but before the dequeue operation and steal the element you thought you were dequeueing.

```
Blocking_queue queue = new Blocking_queue();
//...
if( !some_queue.is_empty() )
    some_queue.dequeue();
```

To do the foregoing reliably, you must synchronize on the queue as follows:

```
Blocking_queue queue = new Blocking_queue();
//...
synchronized( queue )
{   if( !some_queue.is_empty() )
        some queue.dequeue();
}
```

The same effect can be achieved if the test/dequeue operation is done inside a `synchronized` method, and the only way to add or remove queue elements is from other `synchronized` methods.

```
*/
```

```
152:    public final boolean is_empty()
153:    {   return elements.size() <= 0;
154:    }
155:
```

```
/*****************************************************************
```

Return the number of threads waiting for a message on the current queue. See `is_empty` for warnings about synchronization.

```
 */
```

```
156:    public final int waiting_threads()
157:    {   return waiting_threads;
158:    }
159:
160:
```

```
/*****************************************************************
```

Close the blocking queue. All threads that are blocked [waiting in `dequeue()` for items to be enqueued] are released. The `dequeue()` call will throw a `Blocking_queue.Closed` runtime exception instead of returning normally in this case. Once a a queue is closed, any attempt to `enqueue()` an item will also result in a `Blocking_queue.Closed` exception toss. The queue is emptied when it's closed, so if the only references to a given

object are those stored on the queue, the object will become
garbage collectible.
```
         */

161:     public synchronized void close()
162:     {   closed    = true;
163:         elements = null;
164:         notifyAll();
165:     }
166:


         /******************************************************************
            Unit test for the Blocking_queue class.
         */

167:     public static final class Test
168:     {
169:         private static  Blocking_queue queue = new Blocking_queue();
170:         private boolean timed_out = false;
171:
172:         public static void main( String[] args )
173:                                             throws InterruptedException
174:         {   new Test();
175:         }
176:
177:         public Test() throws InterruptedException
178:         {
179:             // Test the enqueue timeout. Wait two seconds for a
180:             // dequeue operation that will never happen.
181:             queue.enqueue
182:             (   "Enqueue this String",
183:                 2000,                     // two seconds
184:                 new Runnable()
185:                 {   public void run()
186:                     {   System.out.println("Enqueue timeout worked.");
187:                         timed_out = true;
188:                     }
189:                 }
190:             );
191:             Thread.currentThread().sleep( 2500 );
192:             if( !timed_out )
193:                 System.out.println( "Enqueue timeout failed." );
194:
195:
196:             // Create a thread that enqueues numbers and another
197:             // that dequeues them
198:             Thread enqueueing =
199:                     new Thread()
200:                     {   public void run()
201:                         {   for( int i = 10; --i >= 0; )
202:                                 queue.enqueue( "" + i );
203:
```

```
204:                              queue.enqueue_final_item(null);
205:                          }
206:                      };
207:
208:             Thread dequeueing =
209:                 new Thread()
210:                 {   public void run()
211:                     {   try
212:                         {   String s;
213:                             while( (s=(String)queue.dequeue()) != null )
214:                                 System.out.println(s);
215:                         }
216:                         catch(InterruptedException e)
217:                         {   System.out.println(
218:                                     "Unexpected InterruptedException");
219:                         }
220:
221:                         boolean close_handled_correctly = false;
222:                         try
223:                         {   queue.enqueue(null);
224:                         }
225:                         catch(Blocking_queue.Closed e)
226:                         {   close_handled_correctly = true;
227:                         }
228:
229:                         if( close_handled_correctly )
230:                             System.out.println("Close handled");
231:                         else
232:                             System.out.println("Error: Close failed");
233:                     }
234:                 };
235:
236:         dequeueing.start();
237:         enqueueing.start();
238:     }
239:   }
240: }
```

Pooling Threads

Armed with our blocking queue, we can now implement the Thread_pool class
(Listing 8.7, line 5). A Thread_pool is an extension of ThreadGroup whose threads execute arbitrary actions. That is, you ask the pool to execute some action for you on
one of its threads. The request returns immediately; the action goes on in the background. You create a thread pool like this:

```
Thread_pool pool = new Thread_pool(
                        initial_thread_count, maximum_thread_count);
```

The pool initially has `initial_thread_count` threads in it, poised with bated breath, ready to leap into action at a moment's notice. If all of the threads in the pool are busy when you ask the pool to do something for you, additional threads are created (up to a maximum of `maximum_thread_count`). If you don't want to keep these additional threads around permanently, the thread pool does implement the notion of deflation. If you send the pool a `deflate(true)` request, then the pool size is reduced to the original size. Thereafter, any extra threads (above the `initial_thread_count`) that are created are discarded immediately after they do whatever they do. To revert to the original behavior—in which the extra threads hang around indefinitely—send a `deflate(false)` request to the `Thread_pool` object.

A convenience no-argument constructor creates an initially empty thread pool that grows indefinitely as threads are requested—think of it as a recyclable-thread factory.

You tell the pool to do something on one of its threads by calling `execute()` and passing a `Runnable` object that encapsulates the operation to perform on the pooled thread:

```
pool.execute(   new Runnable()          // print on another thread
            {   public void run()
                {   System.out.println("Hello World");
                }
            }
        );
```

The `run()` method then executes on a thread in the pool (if one is available). When you're done with the pool, you can send it a `close()` message (Listing 8.7, line 154) to destroy all the threads in the pool. You can also wait for all the threads in the pool to be idle by calling `join()` (Listing 8.7, line 159) or by issuing a `wait()` request on the `Thread_pool` object. This last capability solves a problem in Java's implementation of `ThreadGroup`, which does not support a `join()` operation.

Note that the join capability solves the Singleton-destruction problem discussed earlier. You can create a thread pool with the default constructor (having a zero initial size and no maximum count), and then create all the threads within your program by sending `Runnable` objects to the `Thread_pool`. [That is, create all threads by implementing `Runnable`, then call `some_pool.execute(run_object)` rather than `new Thread(run_object).start()`]. The `main()` function can then `join()` on the thread pool to find out when all the threads complete, and clean up the Singletons at that juncture.

Passing Arguments to the Operation

One obvious problem with using a Runnable object as the vehicle for passing an operation to a pooled thread is that you can't pass arguments to it very easily. [The run() method, after all, takes no arguments.] The main problem is that the arguments are used long after the request is submitted to the thread pool, so they have to be cached away for later use inside another object. For the sake of an easy example, let's rewrite the earlier "hello world" example with an argument.

The easiest way to pass an argument to the run() method is to encapsulate the call in a method with final arguments, like this:

```
Thread_pool pool = new Thread_pool(2,5);
//...

void asynchronous( final String argument )
{   pool.execute
    (   new Runnable()
        {   public void run()
            {   System.out.println( argument );
            }
        }
    );
}
```

The final arguments to (and fields of) a method that creates inner-class objects are effectively stored in compiler-generated fields of those inner-class objects, which can be used by the inner-class object even if the creating method has returned in the interim. In the earlier example, the final String argument in the method definition effectively causes a field called argument of type String to be created in the anonymous inner class, and that field is initialized from the method's local version when the inner-class object is created. It is the copy that's accessed by the run() method when it executes [long after asynchronous_method() has returned].

A second variant of execute builds the wrapper method for you, and lets you pass an argument explicitly without making a wrapper function.. This version is handy when you can't make the argument final for some reason:

```
pool.execute
(   new Command()
    {   public void execute( Object argument )
        {   System.out.println( argument );
        }
    },
    "Hello world."  // Argument passed to Command object when it is
);                  // executed on a thread in the pool.
```

The first argument to this version of execute() is a Command object that specifies what to do. The second argument to execute() is the argument to pass to the

Command object when its version of execute() runs. The Command interface is defined in Listing 8.4.

Listing 8.4: /src/com/holub/tools/Command.java

```
01: package com.holub.tools;
02:

    /**
        A generic interface for implementing the Command pattern with a
        single-argument method. Use Runnable for no-argument methods.
        This interface is also implemented by subscribers to a "multicaster."
        In the Multicaster model, a "publisher" can also be a "subscriber,"
        so the Subscriber interface extends EventListener to give you some
        flexibility. This way the top-level publisher can choose to "be" a
        Subscriber (e.g., implement Subscriber) or to "use" a Subscriber
        (e.g., contain a reference to a Multicaster, which is a Subscriber).
        @see Multicaster
        @author Allen I. Holub
    */

03: public interface Command
04: {   void execute( Object argument );
05: }
06:
```

Using Introspection for Runnable Objects that Pass Arguments

There is one additional solution to the calling-a-method-with-arguments problem that's either hideous overkill or way-cool, depending on your perspective. It is slow, but can declutter the code, so I've included it in the book in case you want to use it. Listing 8.5 shows a generic-command object that implements Runnable in such a way that any arbitrary method, with any number of arguments, is executed when the run() method is called.

```
private f( String first, String second )    // arbitrary method
{   System.out.println( first + " " + second );
}

pool.execute
(   new Generic_command(this, "f", new Object[]{"hello", "world"}));
);
```

This particular generic-command object passes the f("hello","world") message to this from a thread on the thread pool. (The arguments are, in order, a reference to the receiving object, the message to send to that object (which must be declared in the object's class), and an array of Object references, one for each argument. You can pass numeric arguments by wrapping them in the appropriate *java.lang* wrappers (such as Integer, Long, and Short).

Looking at Listing 8.5, I'm using Java's "reflection" APIs to get the method called. Most of the work is going on in the constructor (Listing 8.5, line 51). In order to get the correct overload of the specified method, I first have to make an array of Class objects that tell the system the types of each argument by calling classes(...) (Listing 8.5, line 84). The subsequent call to getMethod gets a Method object that represents the method that we're calling. The remainder of the constructor just builds a reasonable error message if we can't find the method—I'm creating a string that shows a function prototype for the method that the system couldn't find.

After all that work, actually calling the required method is something of a letdown. The invoke() call in run() (Listing 8.5, line 93) invokes the indicated method. There is one design issue of importance. I'm creating the Method object in the constructor primarily because that's the best place to do error recovery. Creating the Method takes some time, however, and you could reasonably argue that this operation should be done on the thread [e.g., in run()], not in the constructor. The only problem with moving the code is that the exception toss will most likely terminate the thread. It seemed better to not fire off the thread at all if the requested method doesn't exist. I can imagine situations where this code, quite reasonably, will move into run(), however.

Listing 8.5: /src/com/holub/tools/Generic_command.java

```
001: package com.holub.tools;
002:
003: import com.holub.io.E;
004: import java.lang.reflect.*;
005:
    */
    This class is a generic Runnable object that allows you to set
    up a listener at run time rather  than compile time. Instead of
    doing this:
006:
007:    class My_class
008:    {
009:        private f( Object argument ){ ... }
010:
011:        private class My_action implements Runnable
012:        {   Object argument;
013:            My_action( Object argument )
014:            {   this.argument = argument;
015:            }
016:            public static void Run()
017:            {   f( argument );
018:            }
019:        }
020:
021:        void set_up_a_listener
022:        {   a_notifier.add_listener( new My_action("hello"); );
```

```
023:        }
024:    }
025:
```

you can say:

```
026:
027:    class My_class
028:    {
029:        private f( Object argument ){ ... }
030:
031:        void set_up_a_listener
032:        {   a_notifier.add_listener(
033:                    new Generic_command( this, "f", new Object[]{ "hello" } ));
034:        }
035:    }
036:
037:
038:
039:
```

@author *Allen I. Holub*

```
040:
041:
042:
043:    */
044:
045:    public class Generic_command implements Runnable
046:    {
047:        Object      receiver;
048:        Method      message;
049:        Object[]    arguments;
050:
```

```
        /**
```

Create a Command object—a Runnable object that runs an arbitrary Java method. Calling run invokes the method with the arguments passed to the Generic_command-object's constructor.
@param *receiver* The receiver of the message: x in x.f(a,b). This argument can be this if you want to call a local method.
@param *method* A string holding the name of a public method of the class of the receiver object: "f" for x.f(a,b).
@param *arguments* An array of Objects, one for each argument. Primitive-type objects should be wrapped in the standard *java.lang* wrappers. Given:

```
        int a    = 10;
        String b = "hello world";
        x.f(a,b);
```

use

```
    new Object[]{ new Integer(a), b };
```

or

```
    new Object[]{ new Integer(10), "hello world" };
```

@throws *NoSuchMethodException* if a function with the given name, whose argument types match the types specified in the arguments array, doesn't exist.
@throws *SecurityException* if the current application isn't allowed to use the Introspection APIs—an untrusted applet, for example.

```
    */

051:    public Generic_command( Object receiver,
052:                                    String method, Object[] arguments )
053:                    throws NoSuchMethodException, SecurityException
054:    {
055:        this.receiver = receiver;
056:        this.arguments  = (arguments==null) ? new Object[0]
057:                                            : arguments;
058:
059:        Class[] types  = (arguments==null) ? new Class[0]
060:                                            : classes(arguments);
061:        try
062:        {   message = receiver.getClass().getMethod( method, types );
063:        }
064:        catch( NoSuchMethodException e)
065:        {   StringBuffer message = new StringBuffer();
066:
067:            message.append( "\n\tMethod not found: "        );
068:            message.append( receiver.getClass().getName()   );
069:            message.append( "$"                             );
070:            message.append( method                          );
071:            message.append( "("                             );
072:
073:            for( int i = 0; i < types.length; ++i )
074:            {   message.append( types[i].getName() );
075:                if( i < types.length-1  )
076:                    message.append(", ");
077:            }
078:            message.append( ")\n" );
079:
080:            throw new NoSuchMethodException( message.toString() );
081:        }
082:    }
083:
```

```
            /**
                Create an array of Class objects, one for each element of
                arguments, that represents the class of each argument.
             */

084:        private Class[] classes( Object[] arguments )
085:        {   Class[] classes = new Class[ arguments.length ];
086:
087:            for( int i = 0; i < arguments.length; ++i )
088:                classes[i] = arguments[i].getClass();
089:
090:            return classes;
091:        }
092:


            /**
                Execute the method specified in the constructor, passing
                it the arguments specified in the constructor.
             */

093:        public void run()
094:        {   try
095:            {   message.invoke( receiver, arguments );
096:            }
097:            catch(IllegalAccessException e    )
098:            {   E.rror("Internal Access Error: Generic_command$run()");
099:            }
100:            catch(InvocationTargetException e)
101:            {   E.rror("Internal Target Error: Generic_command$run()");
102:            }
103:        }
104:
105:        static class Test
106:        {
107:            public void print(String first, String second) // must be public
108:            {   System.out.println( first + " " + second );
109:            }
110:
111:            public Test()    throws Exception
112:            {   Runnable command =
113:                    new Generic_command( this,
114:                            "print", new Object[]{"hello", "world"} );
115:                command.run();
116:            }
117:
118:            public static void main( String[] args ) throws Exception
119:            {   new Test();
120:            }
121:        }
122: }
```

Listing 8.6: /src/com/holub/io/E.java

```
001: package com.holub.io;
002:

    /**
        A convenience wrapper around Std.err(). All of the following do the
        same thing:
            Std.err().println("hello world");
            P.rintln_err("hello world");
            E.rror("hello world");

        @see Std
        @see P
    */

003: public class E
004: {   public static final void rror( String s ){ Std.err().println( s ); }
005: }
```

Implementing the **Thread_pool**

Looking at the implementation, the Thread_pool constructor (Listing 8.7, line 79) simply creates a bunch of Pooled_thread objects (each of which extends Thread) and starts the associated threads up. Skipping up to the Pooled_thread definition (Listing 8.7 line 19), these thread's run() methods enter their main execution loop, and then block on a Blocking_queue (pool, defined on line 7). The implementation of execute(Runnable) (Listing 8.7, line 105) just passes the Runnable objects to the threads in the pool by enqueueing the Runnable object on the Blocking_queue. The enqueue operation causes one of the waiting Pooled_thread objects to wake up, dequeue the Runnable object, execute its run() method, and then go back to sleep.

The complexity of this method is all concerned with making the pool grow in size (up to, but not to exceed, the maximum size specified in the original constructor call). I don't want to synchronize on the pool unnecessarily, so I first test to see if the pool has to grow, then synchronize, then test again in case some previously busy Pooled_thread sneaked in between lines 124 and 125 and added itself back to the pool.

This use of the Runnable object is another example of the Command pattern. The Runnable Command object defines a method [run()] that's executed on some thread in the pool.

The version of execute() with a Command argument (Listing 8.7, line 138) is much like the version with a Runnable argument, but the (final) arguments to execute() are stored inside the anonymous inner-class object (in compiler-generated fields that you don't see) until they're needed. When run() executes, it calls the execute() method of the Command object, passing it the argument that was passed into Thread_pool's execute() method.

Listing 8.7: /src/com/holub/asynch/Thread_pool.java

```
001: package com.holub.asynch;
002: import  com.holub.asynch.Blocking_queue;
003: import  com.holub.tools.Command;
004:
```

```
/**
     A generic implementation of a thread pool. Use it like this:
         Thread_pool pool = new Thread_pool();
         pool.execute
         (   new Runnable()
             {   public void run()
                 {   // execute this function on an existing
                     // thread from the pool.
                 }
             }
         );
```

The size of the thread pool can expand automatically to accommodate requests for execution. That is, if a thread is available in the pool, it's used to execute the Runnable object, otherwise a new thread can be created (and added to the pool) to execute the request. A maximum count can be specified to limit the number of threads in the pool, however.

Each thread pool also forms a thread group (all threads in the pool are in the group). In practice this means that the security manager controls whether a thread in the pool can access threads in other groups, but it also gives you an easy mechanism to make the entire group a Daemon. Unlike a ThreadGroup, it's possible to do the equivalent of a join()operations simply by calling wait() on the thread pool itself. The following code blocks until all the threads in the thread pool are idle:

```
         Thread_pool pool = new Thread_pool();
         //...
         try
         {   synchronized(pool){ pool.wait(); }
         }
         catch( InterruptedException exception )
         {   // error action goes here
         }
```

For convenience, the foregoing code is implemented as a join() method. You can remove a thread from the pool by interrupting it. Often the easiest way to do this is to enqueue a request that issues the interrupt:

```
         some_pool.execute
         (   new Runnable()
             {   public void run()
                 {   interrupt();    // Remove this thread from the pool
                 }
             }
         );
```

The deflate() method removes all threads that were created over and above the initial size, and is usually a better choice than an explicit interrupt, however.

....

....

@author *Allen I. Holub*

```
      */
005: public final class Thread_pool extends ThreadGroup
006: {
007:     private final Blocking_queue pool          = new Blocking_queue();
008:     private /*final*/ int        initial_size = 0;
009:     private /*final*/ int        maximum_size = 0;
010:     private volatile  int        idle_threads = 0;
011:     private          int         pool_size    = 0;
012:     private          boolean     has_closed   = false;
013:     private          boolean     deflate      = false;
014:     private          int         joiners      = 0;
015:
016:     private static int  group_number = 0;
017:     private static int  thread_id    = 0;
018:
```

```
      /*****************************************************************
```
These are the objects that wait to be activated. They are typically blocked on an empty queue. You post a Runnable object to the queue to release a thread, which will execute the run() method from that object. All Pooled_thread objects will be members of the thread group the comprises the thread pool.
```
      */
019:     private final class Pooled_thread extends Thread
020:     {
021:         public Pooled_thread()
022:         {   super( Thread_pool.this, "T" + thread_id );
023:         }
024:
025:         public void run()
026:         {   try
027:             {
```

```
028:            // The Thread_pool constructor synchronizes on the
029:            // Thread_pool object that's being constructed until
030:            // that Thread-pool object is fully constructed. The
031:            // Pooled_thread objects are both created and started
032:            // from within that constructor. The following
033:            // "synchronized" statement forces the pooled threads
034:            // to block until initialization is complete and the
035:            // constructor gives up the lock. This synchronization
036:            // is essential on a multiple-CPU machine to make sure
037:            // that the various CPU caches are in synch with each
038:            // other.
039:
040:            synchronized( Thread_pool.this )
041:            {   ++idle_threads;
042:            }
043:
044:            while( !isInterrupted() && !has_closed )
045:            {   try
046:                {
047:                    synchronized(Thread_pool.this){ --idle_threads;}
048:                    ((Runnable)( pool.dequeue() )).run();
049:                }
050:                finally
051:                {
052:                    synchronized( Thread_pool.this )
053:                    {
054:                        ++idle_threads;
055:
056:                        // If none of the threads in the pool are
057:                        // doing anything, and some thread has
058:                        // join()ed the current thread pool,
059:                        // notify the joined threads.
060:
061:                        if( !has_closed && joiners > 0 )
062:                        {   if( idle_threads == pool_size )
063:                                Thread_pool.this.notify();
064:                        }
065:                    }
066:                }
067:            }
068:
069:            synchronized( Thread_pool.this )
070:            {   --idle_threads;
071:                --pool_size;
072:            }
073:        }
074:        catch(InterruptedException  e){/* ignore it, stop thread */}
075:        catch(Blocking_queue.Closed e){/* ignore it, stop thread */}
076:    }
077: }
078:
```

```
                /**************************************************************
                    Create a thread pool with initial_thread_count threads in it.
                    The pool can expand to contain additional threads if they are
                    needed.
                    @param initial_thread_count The initial thread count. If the
                    initial count is greater than the maximum, it is silently
                    truncated to the maximum.
                    @param maximum_thread_count Specifies the maximum number
                    of threads that can be in the pool. A maximum of 0 indicates
                    that the  pool will be permitted to grow indefinitely.
                 */

079:      public Thread_pool(int initial_thread_count,
080:                                                int maximum_thread_count)
081:      {   super( "Thread_pool" + group_number++ );
082:
083:          // I'm synchronizing, here, to prevent the Pooled_thread objects
084:          // that are created below from being able to access the current
085:          // object until it's fully initialized.
086:
087:          synchronized( this )
088:          {
089:              initial_size = initial_thread_count;
090:              maximum_size = (maximum_thread_count > 0)
091:                                  ? maximum_thread_count: Integer.MAX_VALUE;
092:              pool_size = Math.min(initial_thread_count, maximum_size);
093:
094:              for(int i = pool_size; --i >= 0 ;)
095:                  new Pooled_thread().start();
096:          }
097:      }
098:


                /**************************************************************
                    Create a dynamic Thread_pool as if you had used
                    Thread_pool(0, true).
                 **/

099:      public Thread_pool()
100:      {
101:          super( "Thread_pool" + group_number++ );
102:          this.maximum_size = 0;
103:      }
104:


                /**************************************************************
                    Execute the run() method of the Runnable object on a thread
                    in the pool. A new thread is created if the pool is empty
                    and the number of threads in the pool is not at the maximum.
                    @throws Thread_pool.Closed if you try to execute an action
                    on a pool to which a close() request has been sent.
                 */
```

```
105:      public synchronized void execute( Runnable action ) throws Closed
106:      {
107:          // You must synchronize on the pool because the Pooled_thread's
108:          // run method is asynchronously dequeueing elements. If we
109:          // didn't synchronize, it would be possible for the is_empty()
110:          // query to return false, and then have a Pooled_thread sneak
111:          // in and put a thread on the queue (by doing a blocking dequeue).
112:          // In this scenario, the number of threads in the pool could
113:          // exceed the maximum specified in the constructor. The
114:          // test for pool_size < maximum_size is outside the synchronized
115:          // block because I didn't want to incur the overhead of
116:          // synchronization unnecessarily. This means that I could
117:          // occasionally create an extra thread unnecessarily, but
118:          // the pool size will never exceed the maximum.
119:
120:
121:          if( has_closed )
122:              throw new Closed();
123:
124:          if( pool_size < maximum_size && pool.waiting_threads() == 0 )
125:          {   synchronized( pool )
126:              {   if( pool_size < maximum_size && pool.waiting_threads()==0 )
127:                  {   ++pool_size;
128:                      new Pooled_thread().start(); // Add thread to pool
129:                  }
130:              }
131:          }
132:
133:          pool.enqueue( (Object)action );   // Attach action to the thread
134:
135:      }
136:

          /**********************************************************************
              Execute the execute() method of the Command object on a
              thread in the pool. A new thread is created if the pool is
              empty and the number of threads in the pool is not at the
              maximum. Note that the argument's value at the point of
              execution is what's used. It can change between the time
              that execute() is called and the time whin the action is
              actually executed.
              @throws Thread_pool.Closed if you try to execute an action
              on a pool to which a close() request has been sent.
          */

137:      final synchronized
138:      public void execute( final Command action, final Object  argument)
139:                                                          throws Closed
140:      {   execute(    new Runnable()
141:                      {   public void run()
142:                          {   action.execute( argument );
143:                          }
```

```
144:                          }
145:                      );
146:      }
147:
```

```
       /****************************************************************
           Objects of class Thread_pool.Closed are thrown if you try
           to execute an action on a closed Thread_pool.
        */
```

```
148:      public final class Closed extends RuntimeException
149:      {   Closed()
150:          {   super("Tried to execute operation on a closed Thread_pool");
151:          }
152:      }
153:
```

```
       /****************************************************************
           Kill all the threads waiting in the thread pool, and arrange
           for all threads that came out of the pool, but which are
           working, to die natural deaths when they're finished with
           whatever they're doing. Actions that have been passed to
           execute() but which have not been assigned to a thread for
           execution are discarded.

           No further operations are permitted on a closed pool,
           though closing a closed pool is a harmless no-op.
        */
```

```
154:      public synchronized void close()
155:      {   has_closed = true;
156:          pool.close();                       // release all waiting threads
157:      }
158:
```

```
       /****************************************************************
           Wait for the pool to become idle. This method is a conve-
           nience wrapper for the following code:
               Thread_pool pool = new Thread_pool();
               //...
               try
               {   synchronized(pool){ pool.wait(); }
               }
               catch( InterruptedException exception )
               {   // eat it.
               }

        */
```

```
159:      public synchronized void join()
160:      {   try
```

```
161:        {    ++joiners;
162:             wait();
163:             --joiners;
164:        }
165:        catch( InterruptedException exception )
166:        {   // eat it
167:        }
168:    }
169:
```

```
    /****************************************************************
        If the argument is true, discard threads as they finish
        their operations until the  number of threads in the pool
        equals the initial thread count (passed to the constructor).
        That is, the number of threads in the pool will not go
        below the initial count, but if the number of threads
        in the pool expanded, then the pool size will shrink to
        the initial size as these extra threads finish whatever
        they're doing. It's generally best to set this flag before
        any threads in the pool are activated. If the argument
        is false (the default behavior of the thread pool), then
        threads created above the initial count remain in the
        pool indefinitely.
    */
```

```
170:    public synchronized void deflate( boolean do_deflate )
171:    {
172:        if( deflate = do_deflate )
173:        {   while( idle_threads > initial_size )
174:            {
175:                // Terminate the pooled thread by having
176:                // run (which runs on the pooled thread)
177:                // issue an interrupt. You could also terminate
178:                // the thread with some sort of "sentinel"
179:                // strategy. For example, you could enqueue
180:                // "null," and then rewrite the pooled_thread's
181:                // run() method to recognize that as a terminate
182:                // request. It seemed like interrupting the
183:                // thread was a more generic solution, however,
184:                // since this option is open to users of the
185:                // thread pool as well.
186:
187:                pool.enqueue( new Runnable()
188:                            { public void run()
189:                                { Thread.currentThread().interrupt();
190:                                }
191:                            }
192:                        );
193:            }
194:        }
195:    }
196:
```

```
197:     /* ============================================================= */
198:
199:     public static final class Test
200:     {
201:         private static Thread_pool pool = new Thread_pool( 10, 10 );
202:
203:         public static void main( String[] args )
204:         {
205:             Test test_bed = new Test();
206:             test_bed.fire_runnable( "hello" );
207:
208:             pool.execute
209:             (   new Command()
210:                 {   public void execute( Object argument )
211:                     {   System.out.println("Starting " + argument );
212:
213:                         try{    Thread.currentThread().sleep(250); }
214:                         catch(InterruptedException e){}
215:
216:                         System.out.println("Stoping " + argument );
217:                     }
218:                 },
219:                 "world"
220:             );
221:
222:             // Wait for the pool to become idle, then close it:
223:
224:             System.out.println("Waiting for idle pool");
225:             pool.join();
226:             pool.close();
227:             System.out.println("Pool closed");
228:         }
229:
230:         // The argument must be final in order for it to be accessed
231:         // from the inner class.
232:
233:         private void fire_runnable( final String id )
234:         {   pool.execute
235:             (   new Runnable()
236:                 {   public void run()
237:                     {   System.out.println("Starting " + id );
238:
239:                         try{    Thread.currentThread().sleep(250); }
240:                         catch(InterruptedException e){}
241:
242:                         System.out.println("Stoping " + id );
243:                     }
244:                 }
245:             );
246:         }
247:     }
248: }
```

Putting the Pool to Work

Now let's return to the earlier flush() example and add a Thread_pool. I've done that in Listing 8.8. The changes are minimal (and are all boldfaced). Rather than creating a Thread and starting it up, I create a Runnable object and pass it to the pool's execute() method. Note that, since the operation is defined by the Runnable object, not by the pooled thread itself, single thread pool can be shared by many asynchronous methods that would pass in different Runnable command objects.

Listing 8.8: /text/books/threads/ch8/Thread_pool_flush.java

```
01: import com.holub.asynch.Reader_writer;
02: import com.holub.asynch.Thread_pool;
03: import java.io.*;
04:
05: class Thread_pool_flush
06: {
07:     Thread_pool pool = new Thread_pool( 3, 10 );
08:
09:     public interface Flush_error_handler
10:     {   void error( IOException e );
11:     }
12:
13:     private final OutputStream  out;
14:     private Reader_writer       lock = new Reader_writer();
15:     private byte[]              buffer;
16:     private int                 length;
17:
18:     public Thread_pool_flush( OutputStream out )
19:     {   this.out - out;
20:     }
21:     //...
22:     synchronized void flush( final Flush_error_handler handler )
23:     {
24:         pool.execute
25:         (   new Runnable()
26:             {   int     length;
27:                 byte[]  copy;
28:
29:                 {   length = Thread_pool_flush.this.length;
30:                     copy   = new byte[length];
31:                     System.arraycopy(Thread_pool_flush.this.buffer, 0,
32:                                                     copy, 0, length);
33:                     Thread_pool_flush.this.length = 0;
34:                 }
35:
36:                 public void run()
37:                 {   try
```

```
38:                              {   lock.request_write();
39:                                  out.write( copy, 0, length );
40:                              }
41:                              catch( IOException e )
42:                              {   handler.error(e);
43:                              }
44:                              finally
45:                              {   lock.write_accomplished();
46:                              }
47:                          }
48:                      }
49:                  );
50:          }
51: }
```

Sockets and Thread Pools

Another good application for thread pools is in Socket programming. (If you've never used Java Sockets, you should read about them before proceeding.)

The main difficulty in programming a socket is on the server side, where you need an "accept" loop like the following one to pick up client connections:

```
ServerSocket main = new ServerSocket( port_number );
while( true )
{   new Thread()
    {   Socket client_connection = main.accept();
        public void run()
        {
            // Communicate with the client over the client_connection
            // socket.
        }
    }.start();
}
```

The accept loop spends most of its time blocked [in the accept() call], waiting for clients to connect. Each time through the loop, the server creates a new anonymous Thread derivative whose purpose is to communicate with the client. In this implementation, the connection with the client is established in the anonymous Thread derivative's implicit constructor. That is, main.accept() is called as part of the implicit construction process; start() is called after accept() returns and the object is fully constructed. Then run() executes (on its own thread), performing any necessary communication with the client.

The problem with this approach centers around limitations in the socket system itself. Only a limited number of clients can wait to be connected to the server at any given moment (sometimes as few as five). If the clients-waiting-to-be-connected queue fills, then the server will refuse requests for connections. This means that the accept loop has to be as tight as possible. That's why a thread was created in the foregoing example, so that the server could go right back to waiting once a connection was established. Nonetheless, the foregoing accept loop spends a not inconsiderable amount of time creating threads and starting them up. (Most of the examples you find in books do the same thing.) It is easily possible for the waiting-for-connection queue to fill while all this thread-creation activity is going on.

You can shorten the time spent in the body of the accept loop considerably by using a thread pool. I've demonstrated the process with the Socket_server class in Listing 8.9. To create one of these beasts, you first need to extend the Client class (Listing 8.9, line 10) to define two things: (1) the action to perform once you've been connected to the socket, and (2) the mechanics for creating new client-connection objects when necessary. Here's one that implements a simple echo server (it just echoes back to the client whatever strings the client sends it).

```
class Action extends Socket_server.Client
{
    // The communicate() method defines the client-server
    // interaction. It is called when a socket connection
    // is established with the client, and should perform
    // any necessary communication.

    public void communicate( Socket socket )
    {   try
        {
            BufferedReader in =
                new BufferedReader(
                    new InputStreamReader(socket.getInputStream()));
            OutputStreamWriter out =
                    new OutputStreamWriter(socket.getOutputStream());

            String line;
            while( (line = in.readLine()) != null )
            {   out.write( line, 0, line.length() );
                out.write( "\n", 0, 1           );
                out.flush();
            }
            socket.close();
        }
        catch( Exception e )
        {   System.out.println(e.toString());
        }
    }

    public Client replicate()   // Called by the Socket_server
    {   return new Action();     // to create new objects to service
    }                            // client connections.
};
```

(Most of the complexity is in setting up the Unicode-compliant readers and writers needed to talk to the client.)

You set things up for client communication as follows:

```
Socket_server echo_server = new Socket_server
                            (   port_number,
                                expected_connection_count,
                                new Action(),                  // prototype client
                                new Socket_server.Death()
                                {   public void action( Exception e )
                                    { // performed when server aborts or
                                      // is killed
                                    }
                                }
                            );
echo_server.start();
//...
echo_server.kill();
```

The first two arguments are to the `Socket_server`'s constructor, the port number for the main socket, and the number of client connections that you're expecting (used as the initial size of the thread pool). If more than `expected_connection_count` clients connect, then the threads for the additional clients will be created, but they are created inside the accept loop, thereby slowing the loop down a bit.

The third argument is a prototype `Client` derivative (Listing 8.9, line 10) that encapsulates all communication between the server and client. The `Socket_server` dynamically creates copies of this object on a one-instance-per-connection basis. Initially, it creates `expected_connection_count` copies, but as with threads, it can create more if it needs to. This cloning of a prototype is another example of a Gang-of-Four design pattern, in this case *Prototype* (surprise!). The essential motivation behind Prototype is the creation of objects whose state is unknown: The `Socket_server` doesn't really know what the initial state of the client-service objects should be. To behave correctly, the client-service object might have been put into some unknown state by the program before it is passed to the `Socket_server`. Consequently, the `Socket_server` couldn't create these objects using `new` or equivalent, because the default state might not be the correct one. The `Socket_server` solves the problem by cloning an object that's in an unknown, but valid, state. [Note that I've put an abstract `replicate()` method in the `Client` class (Listing 8.9, line 33) to handle the replication—`clone()`—because it is `protected`, turns out to be awkward to use, and I don't expect anyone to derive classes from the `Client` derivative.]

These client-communication objects are never destroyed. They're cached internally and, when a client connects to the server, the `Socket_server` pulls a `Client` object out of the cache, causes its `communicate()` method to execute on an independent thread, and then puts the object back into the cache. Since a given `Client` object is dedicated to talking to an individual thread, it can contain client-specific state information (e.g., the class can have fields in it). Since the objects are recycled, however, `communicate()` should reinitialize this state information at the top of the `communicate()` method. (The constructor in the `Client` derivative is not called at all by the Socket_server object.) Similarly communicate() should make any memory that's used by the communicate() method reclaimable by assigning null to all accessible references just before communicate() returns.

The final argument to the Socket_server constructor is another Command object—an instance of class Socket_server.Death whose on_exit() method is called when the Socket_server itself shuts down. If the shutdown occurred because of an exception toss, the exception object is passed into the action as an argument; null is passed for a normal shut down. This way an exception that's not caught by the Client derivative's communicate() override can be handled by a user-defined default.

The Socket_server is implemented in Listing 8.9. The Client class (Listing 8.9, line 10) defines the Runnable object that's passed to the Thread_pool's execute() method. Each Client encapsulates a Client_connection. The main accept loop (on line 85) either pulls a Client out of an internal cache or makes a new one if the cache is empty. It then blocks waiting for a client to connect, finishes initializing the Client by setting its socket field to reference the socket just returned from accept(), and then passes the Client object off to the Thread_pool for execution.

I suppose I could have made Client implement Runnable and then used it directly, rather than wrapping the Runnable object in the Client, but that's actually a more-complex solution from the perspective of the user of a Socket_server. For one thing, simply implementing Runnable is not sufficient because there would be no well-defined way to get the socket argument into the object—run() doesn't take arguments. I figured that, because I'd need the user to implement an interface, that extended Runnable by adding a set_socket() method, I might as well make the user's life as simple as possible and dispense with the extra method entirely. Also, I didn't want to expose the mechanisms that Socket_server uses for thread management to the end user. That's just bad design. The current architecture makes it easy to handle clients any way I wish, without having to modify any code that uses Socket_server. This statement wouldn't hold if I forced my users to implement Runnable along with whatever methods would be necessary to get the socket argument passed into run().

Finally this implementation could be sped up a bit more by implementing the thread pool locally rather than using the generic Thread_pool class. This way you'd never have to create a Client object in the accept loop. On the other hand, if you have specified a reasonable expected_connections argument to the Socket_server constructor, Clients won't be created very often, and the current implementation will work just fine, even in the most demanding scenarios.

Listing 8.9: /src/com/holub/net/Socket_server.java

```
001: package com.holub.net;
002:
003: import java.net.*;
004: import java.util.*;
005: import java.io.*;
006: import com.holub.asynch.Thread_pool;
007:
```

```
/**
```

A generic server-side socket that efficiently executes client
-related actions on their own threads. Use it like this:

```
    class Connection_strategy implements Socket_server.Client
    {
        protected void communicate( Socket socket )
        {
            // Called every time a connection is made to
            // a client, encapsulates whatever communication
            // needs to occur. This method runs on its own
            // thread, but Client object are recycled for
            // subsequent connections, so should reinitialize
            // themselves at the top of the communicate() method.
        }

        public Object replicate()
        {   return new Connection_strategy();
        }

    };

    Socket_server echo_server = new Socket_server
                                (   port_number,
                                    expected_connection_count,
                                    new Connection_strategy(),
                                    new Socket_server.Death()
                                    {   public void on_exit( Exception e )
                                        { // performed when server aborts or
                                            // is killed
                                        }
                                    }
                                );
echo_server.start();
//...
echo_server.kill();
```

The Client derivative encapsulates whatever action must be
performed when a client connects to the current server. The
communicate() method runs on its own thread, and is passed
the socket that is connected to the client. Client objects are
manufactured by the Socket_server, and a minimal number
of objects are created and recycled as necessary. Consequently, the socket argument should not be cached. Moreover,
the Client object should reinitialize itself every time the
communicate() method is called; it's only called once per connection. (This is *not* the same architecture as a Servlet. One
instance of the Client will exist for *each* connection, so the
object can maintain a unique state in local fields if it wishes.
Once the action completes, however, the object might be used
again for another connection, so it should reinitialize itself at
the top of the action() method.)

@author *Allen I. Holub*

```
        */

008: public class Socket_server extends Thread
009: {

     /**********************************************************************
         Extend this class and override the communicate() method to
         provide an object to service an individual client connection.
         Objects of this class are recycled, so you should reinitialize
         the object, if necessary, at the top of the call to communicate()
         This class is very tightly coupled to the Socket_server, which
         accesses a few of its fields directly.
     */

010:     public abstract static class Client implements Runnable
011:     {
012:         private LinkedList  client_handlers;    // initialized on creation.
013:         private Socket      socket;             // Reinitialized by the
014:                                                 // Socket_server on
015:                                                 // each use.
016:

         /**
             Must be public, but do not override this method.
         */
017:         public void run()
018:         {
019:             try
020:             {   communicate(socket);
021:                 socket.close();
022:             }
023:             catch( Exception e ){ /* ignore */ }
024:
025:             synchronized( client_handlers )
026:             {   client_handlers.addLast( this ); // Put self back into queue to
027:             }                                    // be used again
028:         }
029:
030:
```

243

```
       /**
               A Gang-of-Four "Template Method." Override this
               method to provide an operation to perform when
               connected to a client. The client socket is already
               hooked up to the client, and is closed automatically
               after communicate() returns. The communicate()
               operation executes on its own thread.

               Client objects are not released to the garbage collector
               after they are used; rather, they are recycled for subse-
               quent connections. A well-behaved communicate()
               method will initialize the Client object before doing
               anything else, and will null out all references to which
               it has access just before terminating (so that the
               associated memory can be garbage collected between
               client connections).

               Any exceptions thrown out of this message handler are
               ignored, which is probably not a great strategy, but
               given the generic nature of an "action," I don't have
               much choice. Consequently, you should catch all
               exceptions within communicate().
        */
031:       protected abstract void communicate( Socket client );
032:

       /**
               Return a pre-initialized copy of the current object.
               This method is something like clone, but there's no
               requirement that the returned object be an exact
               replica of the prototype. In any event, clone() is
               protected, so it's rather awkward to use.
        */
033:       public abstract Client replicate();
034:   }
035:


   /*********************************************************************
           The Socket_server.Death object is passed into the server to
           specify a shut-down action. Its on_exit() method is called
           when the server thread shuts down.
           @param culprit This argument is null for a normal shutdown,
           otherwise it's the exception object that caused the
           shutdown.
        */
036:   public interface Death
037:   {   void on_exit( Exception culprit );
038:   }
039:
040:
```

```
041:       //-------------------------------------------------------------------
042:       // All of the following should be final. A compiler bug (that's
043:       // in all compiler versions up to and including 1.2) won't permit it.
044:
045:       private /*final*/ ServerSocket            main;
046:       private /*final*/ Thread_pool             threads;
047:       private /*final*/ Socket_server.Client  prototype_client;
048:       private /*final*/ Socket_server.Death   shutdown_operation;
049:       private   final   LinkedList             client_handlers = new LinkedList();
050:
```

```
          /**********************************************************************
              Thrown by the Socket_server constructor if it can't be
              created for some reason.
           */
```

```
051:       public class Not_created extends RuntimeException
052:       {   public Not_created( Exception e )
053:           {    super("Couldn't create socket: " + e.getMessage() );
054:           }
055:       }
056:
```

```
          /**********************************************************************
              Create a socket-server thread that creates and maintains a
              server-side socket, dispatching client actions on individual
              threads when clients connect.
              @param port_number The port number to use for the
              main socket.
              @param expected_connections The number of simulta-
              neous connections that you expect. More connections are
              supported, but the threads that service them may need to be
              created dynamically when the client connects.
              @param action A Socket_server.Client derivative that
              encapsulates the action performed on each client connec-
              tion. This object is cloned on an as-needed basis to service
              clients. This cloning is an example of the Gang-of-Four
              Prototype pattern: The action object is a prototype that's
              used to create the objects that are actually used.
              @param shutdown_strategy Socket_server.Death object that
              encapsulates the action to take when the server thread shuts
              down (either by being passed a kill message, or by some
              internal error).
              @throws Not_created If the object can't be created success-
              fully for one of various reasons (such as the socket can't be
              opened or client actions can't be manufactured).
           */
```

```
057:       public Socket_server( int port_number,  int expected_connections,
058:                                         Socket_server.Client connection_strategy,
059:                                         Socket_server.Death  shutdown_strategy)
060:                                                          throws  Not_created
```

```
061:      {   try
062:          {
063:              main                  = new ServerSocket(port_number);
064:              threads               = new Thread_pool( expected_connections, 0 );
065:              prototype_client      = connection_strategy;
066:              shutdown_operation    = shutdown_strategy;
067:
068:              for( int i = expected_connections; --i >= 0 ; )
069:                  client_handlers.addLast( create_client_from_prototype() );
070:
071:              setDaemon( true );        // Don't keep the process alive
072:          }
073:          catch( Exception e ){ throw new Not_created(e); }
074:      }
075:
```

```
        /****************************************************************
            Create a copy of the Client prototype and initialize any
            relevant fields. We can't do this particularly easily since
            we're replicating a class whose name is not known to us
            (a derived class of the Client).
         */
```

```
076:      private Client create_client_from_prototype()
077:      {   Client replica = prototype_client.replicate();
078:          replica.client_handlers = this.client_handlers;
079:          return replica;
080:      }
081:
```

```
        /****************************************************************
            Implements the accept loop, waits for clients to connect,
            and when a client does connect, executes the communicate()
            method on a clone of the Client prototype passed into the
            constructor. This method is executed on its own thread.
            If the accept() fails catastrophically, the thread shuts
            down, and the shut_down object passed to the constructor
            is notified (with a null argument).
         */
```

```
082:      public void run()
083:      {   try
084:          {   Client client;
085:              while( !isInterrupted() )
086:              {   synchronized( client_handlers )
087:                  {   client = client_handlers.size() > 0
088:                                  ? (Client) client_handlers.removeLast()
089:                                  : create_client_from_prototype()
090:                                  ;
091:                  }
```

```
092:                    client.socket = main.accept();  // Reach into the client-handler
093:                                                    // object and modify its socket
094:                                                    // handle.
095:                        if( isInterrupted() )
096:                        {   client.socket.close();
097:                            break;
098:                        }
099:
100:                        threads.execute( client );
101:                    }
102:                }
103:            catch(Exception e)
104:            {   if( shutdown_operation != null )
105:                    shutdown_operation.on_exit(e);
106:            }
107:            finally
108:            {   threads.close();
109:                if( shutdown_operation != null )
110:                    shutdown_operation.on_exit(null);
111:            }
112:        }
113:
```

```
     /*****************************************************************
         Shut down the Socket_server thread gracefully. All assoc-
         iated threads are terminated (but those that are working
         on serving a client will remain active until the service is
         complete). The main socket is closed as well.
      */
```

```
114:    public void kill()
115:    {   try
116:        {   threads.close();
117:            interrupt();
118:            main.close();
119:        }
120:        catch( IOException e ){ /*ignore*/ }
121:    }
122:
```

```
     /*****************************************************************
         A small test class. Creates a Socket_server that implements
         an echo server, then opens two connections to it and runs
         a string through each connection.
      */
```

```
123:    static public class Test
124:    {
125:        static class Connection_strategy extends Socket_server.Client
126:        {   protected void communicate( Socket socket )
127:            {   try
```

```
128:                  { BufferedReader in =
129:                      new BufferedReader(
130:                          new InputStreamReader(
131:                              socket.getInputStream() ));
132:
133:                      OutputStreamWriter out =
134:                          new OutputStreamWriter(
135:                              socket.getOutputStream() );
136:
137:                      String line;
138:                      while( (line = in.readLine()) != null )
139:                      {   out.write( line, 0, line.length() );
140:                          out.write( "\n", 0, 1            );
141:                          out.flush();
142:                      }
143:                      socket.close();
144:                  }
145:                  catch( Exception e )
146:                  {   System.out.println(e.toString());
147:                  }
148:              }
149:
150:          public Socket_server.Client replicate()
151:          {   return new Connection_strategy();
152:          }
153:      };
154:      //------------------------------------------------------------
155:      public static void main( String[] args ) throws Exception
156:      {
157:
158:          Socket_server echo_server =
159:              new Socket_server
160:              (   9999,
161:                  10,
162:                  new Connection_strategy(),
163:                  new Socket_server.Death()
164:                  {   public void on_exit( Exception e )
165:                      {   System.out.println(
166:                              "goodbye world (" + e + ")");
167:                      }
168:                  }
169:              );
170:
171:          echo_server.start();
172:          connect("Hello\n");
173:          connect("World\n");
174:          echo_server.kill();
175:      }
176:      //------------------------------------------------------------
177:      private static void connect( String message ) throws Exception
178:      {
```

```
179:            Socket          client  = new Socket( "localhost", 9999 );
180:            BufferedReader  in      = new BufferedReader(
181:                                        new InputStreamReader(
182:                                          client.getInputStream() ));
183:            OutputStreamWriter out  = new OutputStreamWriter(
184:                                          client.getOutputStream());
185:
186:            // Write the argument string up to the echo server.
187:            out.write( message, 0, message.length() );
188:            out.flush();
189:
190:            // wait for it to be echoed back to us, then print it.
191:            System.out.println( in.readLine() );
192:
193:            client.close();
194:        }
195:    }
196: }
197:
```

The net result of all this work, then is an efficient reusable socket server to which you can assign any operation that you like to be performed when the clients connect. Though the example is complex, it does serve to illustrate why you might want to use thread pools in the real world.

Conclusion

So that's it for the current chapter. The Blocking_queue is an essential tool for inter-thread communication. In fact, the Blocking_queue can be the only object in the system that requires synchronization in many multi-threaded systems. (I'll look at these in Chapter 9.) The Thread_pool both demonstrates how to use the Blocking_queue effectively to solve an otherwise difficult problem—the overhead of thread creation—as is demonstrated in the generic Socket_server.

CHAPTER 9

Object-Oriented
Threading Architectures

THIS CHAPTER FINISHES UP the practical part of the book by talking about two more architectural solutions to threading problems that build on the previous chapter's notion of asynchronous messaging: A synchronous dispatcher (or "reactor") and an asynchronous dispatcher (or "Active Object"). These dispatchers can simplify the threading model considerably by letting you minimize—in some cases eliminate—the need for method-level synchronization, thereby making it much easier to write and debug multithreaded applications. Both of these design patterns leverage the object-oriented view of threading discussed in Chapter 8. I'll demonstrate the Active-Object architecture with an OutputStream derivative that allows two threads to simultaneously write to the console without getting the lines of text mixed together (a problem in UNIX systems).

Reactors and Active Objects

You'll remember from Chapter 8 that OO systems are designed in terms of synchronous and asynchronous messages, not in terms of threads of execution. (If you don't remember that, go back and read the chapter again.) The two strategies that I presented for implementing asynchronous messages (the one-thread-per-message and thread-pool techniques) work just fine in many applications, but in some ways present a worst-case threading scenario. If multiple asynchronous requests are simultaneously sent to a single object, then multiple threads will be spawned off as a result of the request, and all these threads will have simultaneous access to the same object (and its private fields). These fields would have to be guarded with mutexes, and the resulting code wouldn't be pretty.

For example, (remembering that atomic access to a long is not guaranteed by Java), the following code will have mysterious intermittent errors when multiple threads call modify() simultaneously:

```
class  Collision_1
{   long value;

    public modify( final long new_value )
    {   new Thread()
        {   public void run()
            {   value = new_value;
            }
        }
    }
}
```

Since multiple threads can modify value simultaneously, the value is undefined.

This chapter looks at two additional approaches that can all but eliminate the need for synchronization between messages. Both approaches leverage the fact that you typically don't care *when* an asynchronous request is handled, as long as it is handled eventually. The only requirement is that the method that initiates the asynchronous action returns immediately. There is no requirement that simultaneous requests actually be handled simultaneously. By serializing these requests—executing them one after another rather than in parallel—you can eliminate the contention for shared resources that causes difficulty in the one-thread-per-asynchronous-request technique.

This serialization is the natural behavior of properly synchronized systems in any event. Looking back at the example from a moment ago, you could fix the multiple-threads-accessing-a-single-resource problem with a roll-your-own lock as follows:

```
class Collision_2
{   long value;
    Object lock = new Object();

    public modify( final long new_value )
    {   new Thread()
        {   public void run()
            {   synchronized( lock ){ value = new_value; }
            }
        }
    }
}
```

Now we have effectively serialized the asynchronous-request handler threads because only one thread at a time can get into the monitor that guards the assignment operation. It's way too much overhead, however, to create potentially hundreds of threads when most of them are just going to block, waiting for permission to enter the monitor. Fortunately, there is a better way.

Synchronous Dispatching and Round-Robin Scheduling: Reactors and Proactors

A *synchronous dispatcher,* or round-robin scheduler, solves the synchronization problem by simulating multithreading within a single Java thread. Let's start out by considering two tasks that need to be executed in parallel:

Task 1, chunk 1	Task 2, chunk 1
Task 1, chunk 2	Task 2, chunk 2
Task 1, chunk 3	Task 2, chunk 3
Task 1, chunk 4	Task 2, chunk 4

Each of these tasks naturally divides into four chunks, and each could be executed on its own thread. Let's also imagine that the four chunks have to be atomic (they cannot tolerate interruption while they're executing), but it is not a problem if the task is preempted between chunks. The only way to get this atomicity in a normal preemptive multitasking environment is to synchronize the operations, with all the concomitant overhead and complexity.

To get from a single task divided into chunks to a synchronous dispatcher, imagine that we can break up the single task into four independent tasks, like this:

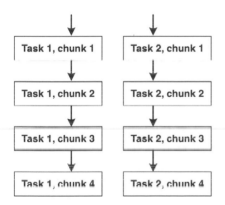

It is not too hard to imagine how we could implement the chunks—you could define each chunk as the run() method of a Runnable object, for example, put the objects into an array, and then write a simple scheduler that executes the objects one at a time with a sleep() or yield() between chunks:

```
Runnable[] first_task = new Runnable[]
{
    new Runnable(){ public void run(){  /* do chunk 1 here */ } },
    new Runnable(){ public void run(){  /* do chunk 2 here */ } },
    new Runnable(){ public void run(){  /* do chunk 3 here */ } },
    new Runnable(){ public void run(){  /* do chunk 4 here */ } },
};

for( int i = 0; i < first_task.length; ++i )
{   first_task[i].run();
    Thread.getCurrentThread().yield();
}
```

Doug Schmidt coined the term *reactor* for this design pattern. The Reactor pattern emerged from Schmidt's work on the ACE framework as a way to accumulate various operations that should occur when some event is triggered. The event handler then executes the `for` loop. The effect is essentially the same as several threads waiting on a single condition variable that is set true by the event. However, unlike a condition variable, you have control over both the sequence of execution and also of when you give up control.

Now let's imagine that I want to concurrently execute two complex tasks, each broken up into chunks. I can interleave the the two tasks like this:

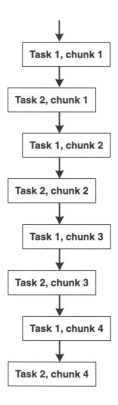

I can implement this strategy as follows:

```
Runnable[] first_task = new Runnable[]
{
    new Runnable(){ public void run(){  /* do task 1, chunk 1 here */ } },
    new Runnable(){ public void run(){  /* do task 1, chunk 2 here */ } },
    new Runnable(){ public void run(){  /* do task 1, chunk 3 here */ } },
    new Runnable(){ public void run(){  /* do task 1, chunk 4 here */ } },
};

Runnable[] second_task = new Runnable[]
{
    new Runnable(){ public void run(){  /* do task 2, chunk 1 here */ } },
    new Runnable(){ public void run(){  /* do task 2, chunk 2 here */ } },
    new Runnable(){ public void run(){  /* do task 2, chunk 3 here */ } },
    new Runnable(){ public void run(){  /* do task 2, chunk 4 here */ } },
};

for( int i = 0; i < first_task.length; ++i )
{   first_task[i].run();
    second_task[i].run();
    Thread.getCurrentThread().yield();
}
```

The foregoing isn't a particularly good general strategy because the loop has to know individually about each array, but I can also merge the two arrays into one large array before entering the loop:

```
Runnable[] both_tasks - new Runnable[]
{
    new Runnable(){ public void run(){  /* do task 1, chunk 1 here */ } },
    new Runnable(){ public void run(){  /* do task 2, chunk 1 here */ } },
    new Runnable(){ public void run(){  /* do task 1, chunk 2 here */ } },
    new Runnable(){ public void run(){  /* do task 2, chunk 2 here */ } },
    new Runnable(){ public void run(){  /* do task 1, chunk 3 here */ } },
    new Runnable(){ public void run(){  /* do task 2, chunk 3 here */ } },
    new Runnable(){ public void run(){  /* do task 1, chunk 4 here */ } },
    new Runnable(){ public void run(){  /* do task 2, chunk 4 here */ } },
};

for( int i = 0; i < first_task.length; ++i )
{   both_tasks[i].run();
    Thread.getCurrentThread().yield();
}
```

Note that I've interleaved the operations: Task 1, chunk 1 runs before Task 2, chunk 1; then Task 2, chunk 2 runs, and so forth. What's going on here, at least with respect to the two tasks, is a lot like what you'd see in a preemptive scheduler on a concurrent system (one CPU) in which each task was executing on its own thread. The big difference is that each chunk has control over when it gets "preempted."

You don't lose control until you return from the run() method that implements the chunk. In fact, this behavior is a lot like a multithreading cooperative system (in which you don't give up control until you explicitly yield to another thread). Because of the explicit yielding of control, you don't have to synchronize any of the fields used by either task, provided that you divide up the chunks carefully. You can always leave any referenced objects in a stable state when you give up control. Also, note that several threads can synchronously dispatch operations in parallel. This architecture is effectively the same as the Solaris mixed-green-thread-and-lightweight-process model. The synchronous dispatchers are effectively green threads, and the Java thread on which the dispatcher runs is effectively a lightweight process.

Synchronous dispatching is surprisingly useful, especially when speed is of the essence. All the chunks are executing on a single operating-system-level thread. There is no synchronization overhead at all and no expensive context swaps into the OS kernel. The main downside is that it is sometimes tricky to break up a single task into neat chunks.

I've solved the problem of implementing a synchronous dispatcher with the Synchronous_dispatcher class in Listing 9.1. You can use the dispatcher in two ways. First of all, tasks can be added independently and then executed. The following code prints the string "hello world" three times.

```
Synchronous_dispatcher dispatcher = new Synchronous_dispatcher();

dispatcher.add_handler( new Runnable()
                        {   public void run(){ System.out.print("hello "); }
                        }
                    );
dispatcher.add_handler( new Runnable()
                        {   public void run(){ System.out.print("world\n"); }
                        }
                    );

dispatcher.dispatch( 3 );
```

You can add a time delay between each chunk as follows:

```
dispatcher.metered_dispatch( 2, 1000 ); // one second delay between chunks
```

This call prints:

```
hello <pause> world <pause> hello <pause> world
```

A second version of add_handler() is provided to add an entire array of Runnable chunks to the dispatcher. The elements of the array are distributed as evenly as possible among the previously added chunks. For example, the following code prints "Hello (Bonjour) world (monde)."

```
Runnable[] first_task =
{   new Runnable(){ public void run(){ System.out.print("Hello"); }},
    new Runnable(){ public void run(){ System.out.print(" world");}}
};

Runnable[] second_task =
{   new Runnable(){ public void run(){ System.out.print(" (Bonjour)");}},
    new Runnable(){ public void run(){ System.out.print(" (monde)"  );}}
};

dispatcher = new Synchronous_dispatcher();
dispatcher.add_handler( first_task  );
dispatcher.add_handler( second_task );
dispatcher.dispatch( 1 );
```

The chunks of a task can share data, if necessary, through the instance variables of the class that contains the array definition. For example:

```
import com.holub.asynch.*;

class Sharing
{
    // Prints "hello world"

    private String text = null;

    private Runnable[] task =
    {   new Runnable(){ public void run(){ text  = "hello ";      }},
        new Runnable(){ public void run(){ text += "world";       }},
        new Runnable(){ public void run(){ System.out.println(text); }}
    };

    public Sharing()
    {   Synchronous_dispatcher dispatcher = new Synchronous_dispatcher();
        dispatcher.add_handler( task  );
        dispatcher.dispatch( 1 );
    }

    public static void main( String[] arguments )
    {   new Sharing();
    }
}
```

Of course, several dispatchers can each run on their own threads, in which case you have a situation much like Sun's green-thread model, where cooperative and preemptive threads both share the same process.

Looking at the implementation in Listing 9.1, the individual Runnable chunks are kept in the events LinkedList (Listing 9.1, line 8). The one-element version of add_handler(Runnable) (Listing 9.1, line 10) just tacks the new element onto the end of the list. The array version add_handler(Runnable[]) (Listing 9.1, line 14) is trickier to implement than you might expect because the incoming array could be larger than the existing list (in which case you want the existing list elements dispersed evenly between array elements), or the array could be smaller than the existing list (in which case you want the incoming array elements to be dispersed evenly through the existing list). I've chosen to make matters easier by first converting the list to an array so that I can work with two similar data structures. I then rebuild the linked list, first copying one or more elements from the larger array into the list, then copying one element from the smaller array, then one or more elements from the larger array, and so forth. An earlier version of this method did the same thing without first doing the list-to-array conversion, but it was both considerably more complex and slower than the current version.

The problem of dispatching is essentially the same problem that I discussed in the context of Observer notifications in Chapter 6. I don't want to synchronize dispatch(...) (Listing 9.1, line 57) because I don't want to disallow the addition of new operations while dispatching is in progress. Here, I've taken the easy way out and copied the list inside the synchronized statement (Listing 9.1, line 68). A multi-caster-based solution, as discussed in Chapter 6, could also work.

The metered_dispatch(...) (Listing 9.1, line 79) variant on dispatch just uses an Alarm (discussed in Chapter 5) to dispatch events at a fixed interval.

Listing 9.1: /src/com/holub/asynch/Synchronous_dispatcher.java

```
001: package com.holub.asynch;
002:
003: import java.util.*;
004: import com.holub.asynch.Alarm;
005:
      /*********************************************************************
```

A synchronous notification dispatcher, executes a sequence of operations sequentially. Allows two sets of linked operations to be interspersed and effectively executed in parallel, but without using multiple threads for this purpose.

This class is built on the JDK 1.2x LinkedList class, which must be present in the system.

@author *Allen I. Holub*
```
      */
```

```
006: public class Synchronous_dispatcher
007: {
008:     private LinkedList events = new LinkedList(); // Runnable objects
009:
```
/**
Add a new handler to the *end* of the current list of
subscribers.
*/
```
010:     public synchronized void add_handler( Runnable handler )
011:     {   events.add( handler );
012:     }
013:
```
/**
Add several listeners to the dispatcher, distributing them
as evenly as possible with respect to the current list.
*/
```
014:     public synchronized void add_handler( Runnable[] handlers )
015:     {
016:         if( events.size() == 0 )
017:         {   for( int i=0; i < handlers.length; )
018:                 events.add( handlers[i++] );
019:         }
020:         else
021:         {
022:             Object[] larger  = events.toArray();
023:             Object[] smaller = handlers;
024:
025:             if( larger.length < smaller.length )  // swap them
026:             {   Object[] swap = larger;
027:                 larger  = smaller;
028:                 smaller = swap;
029:             }
030:
031:             int distribution = larger.length / smaller.length;
032:
033:             LinkedList new_list = new LinkedList();
034:
035:             int large_source = 0;
036:             int small_source = 0;
037:
038:             // Could use the iterator's add() method instead of
039:             // building an array, but the current implementation
040:             // will work even for data structures whose iterators
041:             // don't support add().
042:
043:             while( small_source < smaller.length )
044:             {   for( int skip = 0; skip < distribution; ++skip )
045:                     new_list.add( larger[large_source++] );
046:                 new_list.add( smaller[small_source++] );
047:             }
048:
049:             events = new_list;
```

```
050:          }
051:      }
052:

          /***************************************************************
             Remove all handlers from the current dispatcher.
          */
053:      public synchronized void remove_all_handlers()
054:      {   events.clear();
055:      }
056:

       /**
          Dispatch the actions "iterations" times. Use -1 for
          "forever." This function is not synchronized so that the
          list of events can be modified while the dispatcher is run-
          ning. It makes a clone of the event list and then executes
          from the clone on each iteration through the list of subscr-
          bers. Events added to the list will be executed starting
          with the next iteration.
       */
057:      public void dispatch( int iterations )
058:      {
059:          // Dispatch operations. A simple copy-and-dispatch-from-copy
060:          // strategy is used, here. Eventually, I'll replace this code
061:          // with a <code>Multicaster</code>.
062:
063:
064:          if( events.size() > 0 )
065:              while( iterations==-1 || iterations-- > 0 )
066:              {
067:                  Object[] snapshot;
068:                  synchronized( this )
069:                  {   snapshot = events.toArray();
070:                  }
071:
072:                  for( int i = 0; i < snapshot.length; ++i )
073:                  {   ((Runnable)snapshot[i]).run();
074:                      Thread.currentThread().yield();
075:                  }
076:              }
077:      }
078:

       /**
          Dispatch actions iterations number of times, with an
          action dispatched every "interval" milliseconds. Note that
          the last action executed takes up the entire time slot, even
          if the run() function itself doesn't take interval milli-
          seconds to execute. Also note that the timing will be irreg-
          ular if any run() method executes in more than interval
          milliseconds. If you want a time interval between itera-
          tions but not between the operations performed in a single
          iteration, just insert a Runnable action that sleeps for a
          fixed number of milliseconds.
          @param iterations  number of times to loop through the
```

actions executing them. Use –1 to mean "forever."
#param *interval* An action is executed every "interval" milliseconds.
       */

```
079:    public void metered_dispatch( int iterations, int interval )
080:    {
081:        Alarm timer = new Alarm(interval, Alarm.MULTI_SHOT, false);
082:        timer.start();
083:
084:        while( iterations==-1 || --iterations >= 0 )
085:        {
086:            Object[] snapshot;
087:            synchronized( this )
088:            {   snapshot = events.toArray();
089:            }
090:
091:            for( int i = 0; i < snapshot.length; ++i )
092:            {   ((Runnable)snapshot[i]).run();
093:                timer.await();
094:                timer.start();
095:            }
096:        }
097:
098:        timer.stop();
099:    }
100:
101:    static public final class Test
102:    {
103:        // Execute the test with:
104:        //   java "com.holub.asynch.Synchronous_dispatcher\$Test"
105:        //
106:
107:        public static void main( String[] args )
108:        {
109:            Synchronous_dispatcher dispatcher =
110:                                    new Synchronous_dispatcher();
111:
112:            dispatcher.add_handler(
113:                new Runnable()
114:                {   public void run()
115:                    {   System.out.print("hello");
116:                    }
117:                }
118:            );
119:
120:            dispatcher.add_handler(
121:                new Runnable()
122:                {   public void run()
123:                    {   System.out.println(" world");
124:                    }
125:                }
126:            );
127:
128:            dispatcher.dispatch( 1 );
```

261

```
129:                dispatcher.metered_dispatch( 2, 1000 );
130:
131:                //-----------------------------------------------
132:                // Test two tasks, passed to the dispatcher as arrays
133:                // of chunks. Should print:
134:                //          Hello (Bonjour) world (monde)
135:
136:                Runnable[] first_task =
137:                {   new Runnable()
138:                        { public void run(){ System.out.print("Hello"); }},
139:                    new Runnable()
140:                        { public void run(){ System.out.print(" World");}}
141:                };
142:
143:                Runnable[] second_task =
144:                {   new Runnable()
145:                        { public void run(){ System.out.print(" Bonjour");}},
146:                    new Runnable()
147:                        { public void run(){ System.out.print(" Monde\n");}}
148:                };
149:
150:                dispatcher = new Synchronous_dispatcher();
151:                dispatcher.add_handler( first_task  );
152:                dispatcher.add_handler( second_task );
153:                dispatcher.dispatch( 1 );
154:        }
155:    }
156: }
```

Asynchronous Dispatching: Active Objects

The second architectural design pattern of interest in implementing asynchronous methods is "Active Object." Though we can thank Greg Lavender and Doug Schmidt for the name, the architecture has been around for a while—the first time I saw it (dinosaur that I am) was in Intel's RMX-80 operating system circa 1980. The Active-Object pattern is also built into the Ada programming language.

Though none of us will be programming for RMX-80, Intel's terminology is useful in describing the pattern: RMX-80 (the Real-time Multitasking eXecutive) was an OS for embedded systems—think of a multithreaded operating system that supports only a single process that remains resident in core. All threads share a single address space, and there is no virtual memory. Figure 9.1 shows the general architecture. RMX-80 looks at the world as a series of *tasks*, not threads. Each task has an input queue. And each task effectively runs on a single thread. You activate a task by sending it an asynchronous message. In RMX-80, you literally put a data structure onto the task's input queue. The task starts out idle, waiting for request to be queued. It wakes up when a message arrives, performs the requested operation, then goes back to sleep. If messages arrive while the task is busy, they remain in the queue until the current operation is complete, and then are dequeued and executed sequentially. Each message carries with it a return address—a message queue to which the task posts the original message data structure (perhaps modified by the task to contain a completion status or output data) when the task completes the requested operation.

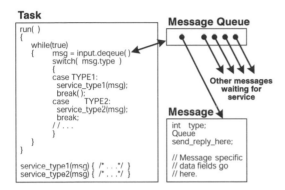

Figure 9.1. The RMX-80 System Architecture

You use this system by creating a task for every desired operation. For example, you might create a "File I/O" task whose job was to access a single file. You'd send data to that file by queueing up a write request on that task's input queue. The I/O task would perform the operation, then send the data structure representing the write-request to the task whose input queue was listed in the message as the return address. A special garbage-collector task was provided solely to provide a place to send these reply messages when the originating task wasn't interested in the reply. (The garbage collector simply freed any memory that arrived in its queue.) You'd read the file by posting an empty read-request message to the File I/O task's input queue. The File I/O task fills that message with data, and then posts the message back to the included return address.

The main advantage of the Active-Object architecture is that the individual operations do not have to be synchronized since they are executing sequentially on the task object's thread. In fact, the only synchronization necessary in the entire system is in the enqueue and dequeue operations.

Of course, from an OO-design perspective, a task is simply an object that can accept (nothing but) asynchronous messages. There is no requirement that asynchronous requests must execute in parallel. From the perspective of the object that sends the message, as long as the request returns immediately, it's okay for the receiving object to perform the operation whenever it gets around to it.

A General Solution

I've adapted the idea of the Active Object to my own ends with a general solution to the dispatch problem. Figure 9.2 shows how my implementation works. The main difference from RMX-80 is that, rather than queuing up passive data structures that contain an ID identifying the requested operation, I'm queuing up Runnable objects that actually do the operation (the Command pattern again.) This way, a given Active Object can handle many requests without actually knowing what those requests actually do.

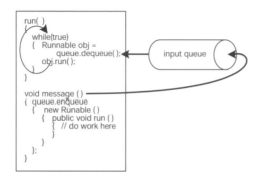

Figure 9.2. Active Objects in Java

The implementation of an Active-Object dispatcher (Listing 9.2) is not much more complicated than the picture. Create and start up a dispatcher like this:

```
Active_object dispatcher = new Active_object();
dispatcher.start();
```

Ask the Active Object to do something for you like this:

```
dispatcher.dispatch
(   new Runnable()
    {   public void run()
        {   System.out.println("hello world");
        }
    }
);
```

When you're done with the dispatcher, close it:

```
dispatcher.close();
```

Thereafter, any attempts to dispatch() a new request will be rejected with an exception toss, though the dispatcher does execute those requests that are waiting to be serviced when you send the close() message. As was the case with the thread pool, discussed in the previous chapter, you can use a Generic_command to execute a method with an arbitrary number of arguments:

```
private f( String first, String second )     // arbitrary method
{   System.out.println( first + " " + second );
}

dispatcher.dispatch
(   new Generic_command(this, "f", new Object[]{"hello", "world"}));
);
```

The Active_object class, like the Thread_pool, also defines an overload of dispatch() that takes a Command object and a single argument for the command:

```
dispatcher.dispatch
(   new Command()
    {   public void execute( Object argument )
        {   System.out.println( argument );
        }
    },
    "Hello world."  // Argument passed to Command object
);                  // when it's executed by the Active Object.
```

Looking at the implementation in Listing 9.2, the input queue [requests (Listing 9.2, line 8)] in Figure 9.2 is an instance of the Blocking_queue class, discussed in Chapter 8. The dispatch() (Listing 9.2, line 33) and close() (Listing 9.2, line 45) methods are just simple wrappers around the equivalent Blocking_queue methods. The enqueued "request" is just a Runnable object, whose run() method is executed on the Active-Object's thread.

Note how close() uses the Blocking_queue's enqueue_final_item() method to work elegantly without having to synchronize. Once a Blocking_queue is closed by calling enqueue_final_item() any further attempts to enqueue new items is rejected with an exception toss. Moreover, the queue is closed automatically when the final item is dequeued. I've enqueued null as a sentinel.

The only other method in the Active_object class is run() (Listing 9.2, line 13). (An Active_object class extends Thread, so it implements run() directly.) The run() method sits in a tight loop, dequeueing and executing requests as they come in, and most of the time, the run() will be blocked waiting to dequeue a request. The loop terminates when the null, enqueued by the close() method, is dequeued. In order to be a good citizen, I yield() after every request is executed to give other threads at my priority level a chance to run.

Notice that none of the methods of Active_object are synchronized. They don't need to be because, with the single exception of run(), all the methods of

`Active_object` are simple wrappers around calls to the `Blocking_queue`, which is synchronized. Moreover, the `Active_object` itself is the only thread that dequeues from the queue, so extra synchronization on the dequeue operation is also unnecessary.

Listing 9.2: /src/com/holub/asynch/Active_object.java

```
01: package com.holub.asynch;
02:
03: import   com.holub.asynch.Blocking_queue;
04: import   com.holub.tools.Command;
05:
    /******************************************************************
        A dispatcher for use in implementing Active Objects. Create and
        start up a dispatcher like this:

            Active_object dispatcher = new Active_object();
            dispatcher.start();

        Ask the Active Object to do something for you like this:
            dispatcher.dispatch
            (   new Runnable()
                {   public void run()
                    {   System.out.println("hello world");
                    }
                }
            );
        When you're done with the dispatcher, close it:

            dispatcher.close();

        Variations on these themes are also possible. See the main
        documentation for more details.

        ..........................................................................

                          © 2000, Allen I. Holub
        This code may not be distributed by yourself except in binary
        form, incorporated into a java .class file. You may use this code
         freely for personal purposes, but you may not incorporate it in
        to any commercial product without the express written per-
        mission of Allen I. Holub.

        ..........................................................................

        @author Allen I. Holub

    */
06: public class Active_object extends Thread
07: {
08:     private Blocking_queue requests = new Blocking_queue();
09:
```

```
        /****************************************************************
            Create an Active Object. The object is a Daemon thread that
            waits for dispatch() requests, then executes them in the
            order that they were enqueued. Since the thread is a daemon,
            it will not keep the process alive.
         */
10:     public Active_object()
11:     {   setDaemon( true );
12:     }
        /****************************************************************
            This fact that this method is public is an artifact of
            extending Thread. Do not call this method. The dis-
            patcher's event loop is found here.
         */
13:     public void run()
14:     {   try
15:         {   Runnable the_request;
16:             while((the_request = (Runnable)(requests.dequeue())) !=null)
17:             {   the_request.run();
18:                 the_request  = null;
19:                 yield();     // give other threads a chance to run
20:             }
21:         }
22:         catch( InterruptedException e )
23:         {   // Thread was interrupted while blocked on a dequeue,
24:             // Treat it as a close request and ignore it.
25:         }
26:     }
27:
```

```
        /****************************************************************
            Cause an operation to be performed on the current Active-
            Object's event-handler thread. Operations are executed serially
            in the order received.
            @param operation A Runnable "Command" object that encapsu-
            lates the operation to perform. If operation is null then the active
            object will shut itself down when that request is dequeued (in its
            turn). Any operations posted after a null request is dispatched
            are not executed.
            @throws Blocking_queue.Closed if you attempt to dispatch
            on a closed object.
            @see com.holub.tools.Generic_command
         **/
28:     public final void dispatch( Runnable operation )
29:     {   requests.enqueue( operation );
30:     }
31:
32:
```

```
        /****************************************************************
            Request that the Active Object execute the execute() method
            of the Command object. Otherwise works like  dispatch(Runnable).
         */
```

```
33:     public final synchronized void dispatch(
34:                                     final Command action,
35:                                     final Object  argument )
36:                                     throws Blocking_queue.Closed
37:     {   dispatch(    new Runnable()
38:                         {   public void run()
39:                                 {   action.execute( argument );
40:                                 }
41:                         }
42:                     );
43:     }
44:
```

```
        /**************************************************************
```

Close the `Active Object` (render it unwilling to accept new
"dispatch" requests.) All pending requests are executed,
but new ones are not accepted. This method returns immed-.
iately before the pending requests have been processed
`Active_object` shuts down. You can block until the pending
requests are handled by sending the `Active_object`
object a `join()` message:

```
    Active_object dispatcher = new Active_object();
    //...
    dispatcher.close(); // cause it to reject new requests
    dispatcher.join();  // wait for existing request to be processed
```

You can also cause the `Active_object` to terminate gracefully
(without blocking) by calling `dispatch(null)`. Any requests
that are "dispatched" after a `dispatch(null)` is issued are
silently ignored, however.

Attempts to close a closed queue are silently ignored.

```
        **/
```

```
45:     public final void close()
46:     {   requests.enqueue_final_item( null );
47:     }
48: }
```

Detangling Console Output

A more realistic example of using an `Active_object` is in the `Console` class in Listing
9.3. The main problem with console-based I/O in multithreaded applications is
that the strings that are being printed by different threads tend to get mixed up
with one another, particularly if these strings are being printed one piece at a time
rather than as single, monolithic units. The Active-Object pattern can be used to
solve this problem by creating a console task whose job is to write to the console.
Rather than calling `System.out.println()` (or equivalent) directly, you send the output to the console task. The task keeps buffers for every thread that is using it, and
flushes the buffer to the actual console when a newline is encountered. Because

the console task is single threaded, strings created by separate threads won't be mixed together.

My implementation of the console task is in Listing 9.3. The Console class is a Singleton, so you can't create one with new; use Console.out() to get a reference to the actual Console object. I've chosen to implement the Console as an extension of java.io.OutputStream. This way, you can wrap the single Console object in any of the standard *java.io* wrappers (such as DataOutputStream) to add functionality to it. For example, use:

```
DataOutputStream data_writer = new DataOutputStream( Console.out() );
```

or

```
PrintWriter writer = new PrintWriter( Console.out() );
```

Looking at the code, the object is created by out() (Listing 9.3, line 19) using the double-check locking strategy discussed in Chapter 7. I've also used the JDK_11_unloading_bug_fix class discussed in the same chapter. The interesting code—at least for this chapter—concerns the Active-Object dispatcher (Listing 9.3, line 11).

The only method that is doing real work is write(int) (Listing 9.3, line 40), which creates a Handler Command object and passes it to the dispatcher for execution. The run() method of the Handler class (Listing 9.3, line 56) is called by the dispatcher in its turn to handle a single-character write request.

If the character isn't a newline, the handler buffers it up in a Vector that is associated with the current thread (it's the value component of a Map that uses a reference to the thread that issued the request as a key). Note that I can't call Thread.currentThread() in the Handler's run() method because I'd get a reference to the Active-Object's thread, not the thread that is issuing the write request. The current-thread reference is determined on line 43 when I dispatch the request. (The write() method runs on the thread that requests the write operation; Handler.run() runs on the Active-Object's thread at some later time.)

If the character passed to run() through the Handler is a newline, the else clause on line 66 prints all the buffered characters to the console (along with the newline) and then destroys the buffer. That is, the users Map contains buffers only for those threads that are in the process of assembling a line. Once the line is flushed, the buffer is discarded.

I've also implemented the OutputStream's flush() (Listing 9.3, line 80) and close() (Listing 9.3, line 86) methods. Note that flush() flushes the partially assembled buffers for *all* threads to standard output.

The Test class (Listing 9.3, line 100) encapsulates a small test routine that creates two threads, each of which prints a message with random sleeps inserted between each character-write operation to make sure that the write requests will get jumbled up.

Finally, a couple of style notes: First, nothing at all is synchronized (and nothing needs to be), because all write requests are executed serially on a single thread (the Active-Object's event-loop thread). Second, whenever possible, I've written code in terms of the most abstract class or interface available. For example, even though the list of actively-writing threads is maintained in a HashMap, the actual reference (users [Listing 9.3, line 13]) is declared as a Map reference. This is just good OO-programming, but many Java programmers don't do it. By using the most abstract class possible, I can replace the HashMap with a different data structure (such as a TreeMap) at any time simply by changing the single new invocation on line 24. The rest of the code adapts automatically.

Listing 9.3: /src/com/holub/io/Console.java

```
001: package com.holub.io;
002:
003: import java.io.*;
004: import java.util.*;
005: import com.holub.asynch.Active_object;
006: import com.holub.asynch.Mutex;
007: import com.holub.asynch.JDK_11_unloading_bug_fix;
008:
     /********************************************************************
```

A console "task" that demonstrates how to use the Active_object class. The Console is an OutputStream that multiple threads can use to write to the console. Unlike a normal PrintStream, the current class guarantees that lines print intact. (Characters from one line will not be inserted into another line.)

....

....

@author *Allen I. Holub*

```
     */
009: public final class Console extends OutputStream
010: {
011:     private static  Active_object  dispatcher  = null;
012:     private static  Console        the_console = null;
013:     private static  Map            users       = null;
014:
     /********************************************************************
```

A private constructor makes it impossible to create a Console using new. Use System.out() to get a reference to the Console.

```
     */
```

```
015:     private Console()
016:     {   new JDK_11_unloading_bug_fix( Console.class );
017:     }
018:
```

/***
    The Console is a Singleton—only one is permitted to exist.
    The Console has a private constructor, so you cannot manu-
    facture one with new. Get a reference to the one-and-only
    instance of the Console by calling Console.out().
    @return *a* thread-safe OutputStream that you can wrap with
    any of the standard *java.io* decorators. This OutputStream
    buffers characters on a per-thread basis until a newline sent
    by that thread is encountered. The Console object then
    sends the entire line to the standard output as a single unit.
    */

```
019:     public static final Console out()
020:     {   if( the_console == null )
021:         {   synchronized( OutputStream.class )
022:             {   if( the_console == null )
023:                 {   the_console = new Console();
024:                     users       = new HashMap();
025:                     dispatcher  = new Active_object();
026:                     dispatcher.start();
027:                 }
028:             }
029:         }
030:         return the_console;
031:     }
032:
```

/***
    Shut down the Console in an orderly way. The Console uses
    a daemon thread to do its work, so it's not essential to shut
    it down explicitly, but you can call shut_down() to kill the
    thread in situations where you know that no more output
    is expected. Any characters that have been buffered, but
    not yet sent to the console, will be lost.

    You can actually call out() after shut_down(), but it's
    inefficient to do so.
    */

```
033:     public static void shut_down()
034:     {   dispatcher.close();
035:         dispatcher  = null;
036:         the_console = null;
037:         users       = null;
038:     }
039:
```

/***
    Overrides the OutputStream write(int) function. Use the
    inherited functions for all other OutputStream functionality.

For a given thread, no output at all is flushed until a newline is encountered. (This behavior is accomplished using
a hash table, indexed by a Thread object, that contains a
buffer of accumulated characters.) The entire line is
flushed as a unit when the newline is encountered.

Once the Console is closed, (see close), any requests to
write characters are silently ignored.

```
        */
040:    public void write(final int character) throws IOException
041:    {   if( character != 0 )
042:            dispatcher.dispatch(
043:                    new Handler(character, Thread.currentThread()) );
044:    }
045:

        /****************************************************************
        The request object that's sent to the Active_object. All
        the real work is done here.
        */
046:    private final class Handler implements Runnable
047:    {
048:        private int      character;
049:        private Object   key;
050:
051:        Handler( int character, Object key )
052:        {   this.character = character;
053:            this.key       = key;
054:        }
055:
056:        public void run()
057:        {   List buffer = (List)( users.get(key) );
058:
059:            if( character != '\n' )
060:            {   if( buffer == null ) // 1st time this thread requested
061:                {   buffer = new Vector();
062:                    users.put( key, buffer );
063:                }
064:                buffer.add( new int[]{ character } );
065:            }
066:            else
067:            {   if( buffer != null )
068:                {   for( Iterator i= ((List)buffer).iterator();
069:                                                    i.hasNext(); )
070:                    {   int c = ( (int[])( i.next() ) )[0];
071:                        System.out.print( (char)c );
072:                    }
073:                    users.remove( key );
074:                }
075:                System.out.print( '\n' );
076:            }
077:        }
078:    }
```

```
079:
          /****************************************************************
              Overrides the OutputStream flush() method. All partially-
              buffered lines are printed. A newline is added automatically
              to the end of each text string. This method does not block.
           **/
080:      public void flush() throws IOException
081:      {   Set keys = users.keySet();
082:          for( Iterator i = keys.iterator(); i.hasNext(); )
083:              dispatcher.dispatch( new Handler('\n', i.next()) );
084:      }
085:
          /****************************************************************
              Overrides the OutputStream close() method. Output is flushed
              (see flush). Subsequent output requests are silently ignored.
           **/
086:      public void close() throws IOException
087:      {   flush();
088:          dispatcher.close();      // blocks until everything stops.
089:      }
090:
          /****************************************************************
              Convenience method, this method provides a simple way to
              print a string without having to wrap the Console.out() stream
              in a DataOutputStream.
           **/
091:      public void println( final String s )
092:      {   try
093:          {   for( int i = 0; i < s.length(); ++i )
094:                  write( s.charAt(i) );
095:              write( '\n' );
096:          }
097:          catch( IOException e ){ /*ignore it*/ }
098:      }
099:
          /****************************************************************
              A test class that prints two messages in parallel on two
              threads, with random sleeps between each character.
           */
100:      static public final class Test extends Thread
101:      {
102:          private String message;
103:          private DataOutputStream data =
104:                                  new DataOutputStream( Console.out() );
105:
106:          public Test( String message )
107:          {   this.message = message;
108:          }
109:
110:          public void run()
111:          {   try
```

```
112:                    {   Random indeterminate_time = new Random();
113:                        for(int count = 2; --count >= 0 ;)
114:                        {   for( int i = 0; i < message.length(); ++i )
115:                            {   Console.out().write( message.charAt(i) );
116:                                sleep(
117:                                    Math.abs(indeterminate_time.nextInt())%20);
118:                            }
119:
120:                            Console.out().println( "(" + count + ")" );
121:                            sleep( Math.abs(indeterminate_time.nextInt()) % 20);
122:
123:                            data.writeChars( "[" + count + "]" );
124:                            sleep( Math.abs(indeterminate_time.nextInt()) % 20);
125:
126:                            Console.out().write('\n');
127:                        }
128:                    }
129:                    catch( Exception e )
130:                    {   Console.out().println( e.toString() );
131:                    }
132:                }
133:
134:            static public void main( String[] args ) throws Exception
135:            {
136:                Thread one = new Test( "THIS MESSAGE IS FROM THREAD ONE" );
137:                Thread two = new Test( "this message is from thread two" );
138:
139:                one.start();
140:                two.start();
141:
142:                one.join(); // Wait for everything to get enqueued
143:                two.join();
144:
145:                Console.out().close();  // wait for everything to be printed
146:            }
147:        }
148: }
```

That's It

So, that is it for threads. The first nine chapters in this book, when taken together, give you a pretty good introduction to *real* Java threading (as compared to the simplified version found in most books). I've covered everything from thread architectures, to common problems in multithreaded system, to atomic-level synchronization classes, to the architectural approach to threading discussed in the current chapter. The tools I've developed along the way provide a good foundation to a multithreaded toolbox that can make your life as a Java-thread programmer much easier.

The only question that remains is, given all my griping about Java's threading model, how would I fix things? That's the subject of Chapter 10.

If I Were King: Fixing Java's Threading Problems

IN A WAY, THE PREVIOUS CHAPTERS are a litany of everything wrong with the Java threading model and a set of Band-Aid solutions to those problems. I call the classes Band-Aids because the problems addressed by the classes should really be part of the syntax of the Java language. Using syntactic methods rather than libraries can give you better code in the long run since the compiler and JVM working together can perform optimizations that would be difficult or impossible with a library approach.

In this chapter, I want to approach the threading problem in a more positive light by suggesting a few changes to Java that would provide solutions to those problems. These proposals are very tentative—they are just one person's thoughts on the matter, and they would need a lot of work and peer review before being viable. But they're a start. The proposals are also rather bold. Several people have suggested subtle, and minimal, changes to the Java-Language Specification (JLS) to fix currently ambiguous JVM behavior, but I want more sweeping improvement.

On a practical note, many of my proposals involve the introduction of new keywords to the language. Though the usual requirement that you don't want to break existing code is certainly valid, if the language is not to stagnate and thus become obsolete, it must be possible to introduce keywords. In order to introduce keywords that won't conflict with existing identifiers, I've deliberately used a character ($) which is illegal in an identifier. (For example, $task rather than task). A compiler command-line switch could perhaps enable variants on these keywords that would omit the dollar sign.

The Task

The fundamental problem with Java's threading model is the fact that it is not in the least bit object oriented. A thread is effectively nothing but a procedure [run()] which calls other procedures. Notions of objects, asynchronous versus synchronous messages, and the like, are simply not addressed.

One solution to this problem is the `Active_object` class presented in Chapter 9, but a better solution would be to modify the language itself to support asynchronous messaging directly. The asynchronous messages running on an Active Object are effectively synchronous with respect to each other. Consequently, you can eliminate much of the synchronization hassles required to program in a more procedural model by using an Active Object.

My first proposal, then, is to incorporate Active Objects into the language itself by incorporating the notion of a *task* into Java. A task has a built-in Active-Object dispatcher, and takes care of all the mechanics of handling asynchronous messages automatically. You would define a task exactly as you would a class, except that the `asynchronous` modifier could be applied to methods of the task to indicate that those methods should execute in the background on the Active-Object dispatcher. To see the parallels with the class-based approach discussed in Chapter 9, consider the following file I/O class, which uses my `Active_object` to implement an asynchronous write operation:

```
Interface Exception_handler
{   void handle_exception( Throwable e );
}

class File_io_task
{   Active_object dispatcher = new Active_object();

    final OutputStream      file;
    final Exception_handler handler;

    File_io_task( String file_name, Exception_handler handler )
                                            throws IOException
    {   file = new FileOutputStream( file_name );
        this.handler = handler;
    }

    public void write( final byte[] bytes )
    {
        dispatcher.dispatch
        (   new Runnable()
            {   public void run()
                {
                    try
                    {   byte[] copy new byte[ bytes.length ];
                        System.arrayCopy(   bytes,  0,
                                            copy,   0,
                                            bytes.length );
                        file.write( copy );
                    }
                    catch( Throwable problem )
                    {   handler.handle_exception( problem );
                    }
                }
        }
```

```
        }
    );
  }
}
```

All write requests are queued up on the Active-Object's input queue with a dispatch() call. Any exceptions that occur while processing the asynchronous message in the background are handled by the Exception_handler object that's passed into the File_io_task's constructor. You would write to the file like this:

```
File_io_task io =   new File_io_task
                    ( "foo.txt"
                        new Exception_handler
                        {   public void handle( Throwable e )
                            {    e.printStackTrace();
                            }
                        }
                    );
//...
io.write( some_bytes );
```

Introducing the $task and $asynchronous keywords to the language lets you rewrite the previous code as follows:

```
$task File_io $error{ $.printStackTrace(); }
{
    OutputStream file;

    File_io( String file_name ) throws IOException
    {   file = new FileOutputStream( file_name );
    }

    asynchronous public write( byte[] bytes )
    {   file.write( copy );
    }
}
```

Note that asynchronous methods don't specify return values because the handler returns immediately, long before the requested operation completes. Consequently, there is no reasonable value that could be returned. The $task keyword should work exactly like class with respect to the derivation model: A $task could implement interfaces and extend classes and other tasks. Methods marked with the asynchronous keyword are handled by the $task in the background. Other methods would work synchronously, just as they do in classes.

The $task keyword can be modified with an optional $error clause (as shown), which specifies a default handler for any exceptions that are not caught by the asynchronous methods themselves. I've used $ to represent the thrown exception object. If no $error clause is specified, then a reasonable error message (and probably stack trace) is printed.

Note that the arguments to the asynchronous method must be immutable to be thread safe. The run-time system should take care of any semantics required to guarantee this immutability. (A simple copy is often not sufficient.) All task objects would have to support a few pseudo-messages as well:

`some_task.close()`   Any asynchronous messages sent after this call is issued would throw a `TaskClosedException`. Messages waiting on the Active-Object queue will be serviced, however.

`some_task.join()`   The caller blocks until the task is closed and all pending requests are processed.

In addition to the usual modifiers (such as `public`), the `task` keyword would accept the `$pooled(n)` modifier, which would cause the `task` to use a thread pool rather than a single thread to run the asynchronous requests. The n specifies the desired pool size; the pool can grow if necessary, but should deflate to the original size when the additional threads aren't required. The server-side socket handler that I used as an example of thread-pool usage in Chapter 8 could be rewritten in the proposed syntax as follows:

```
abstract $pooled(10) $task Socket_server
{
    public asynchronous listen(ServerSocket server, Client_handler client)
    {   while(true)
        {   client.handle( server.accept() );
        }
    }

    interface Client_handler
    {   asynchronous void handle( Socket s );
    }
}

//...

Socket_server listener = new Socket_server();

listener.listen (   new ServerSocket(some_port),
                    new Socket_server.Client_handler()
                    { public asynchronous void handle( Socket s )
                      { // client-handling code goes here.
                      }
                    }
                );
```

The arguments to `listen()` can just as easily be constructor arguments, of course.

Improvements to `synchronized`

Though a `$task` eliminates the need for synchronization in many situations, all multithreaded systems cannot be implemented solely in terms of tasks. Consequently, the existing threading model needs to be updated as well. The `synchronized` keyword has several flaws:

1. You cannot specify a timeout value.

2. You cannot interrupt a thread that is waiting to acquire a lock.

3. You cannot safely acquire multiple locks. (Multiple locks should always be acquired in the same order.)

You can solve these problems by extending the syntax of `synchronized` both to support a list of multiple arguments and to accept a timeout specification (specified in brackets, next): Here's the syntax that I'd like:

`synchronized(x && y && z)`	Acquire the locks on the x, y, and z objects.
`synchronized(x || y || z)`	Acquire the locks on the x, y, or z objects.
`synchronized( (x && y ) || z)`	Obvious extension of the previous code.
`synchronized (. . .) [1000]`	Acquire designated locks with a one-second timeout.
`synchronized [1000] f() {. . .}`	Acquire the lock for this, but with a one-second timeout.

A timeout is necessary, but not sufficient, for making the code robust. You also need to be able to terminate the wait to acquire the lock externally. Consequently, the `interrupt()` method, when sent to a thread that is waiting to acquire a lock, should break the waiting thread out of the acquisition block by tossing a `SynchronizationException` object. This exception should be a `RuntimeException` derivative so that the it would not have to be handled explicitly.

The main problem with these proposed modifications to the `synchronized` syntax is that they would require changes at the byte-code level, which currently implements `synchronized` using enter-monitor and exit-monitor instructions. These instructions take no arguments, so the byte-code definition would have to be extended to support the acquisition of multiple locks. This change is no more serious than the changes added to the JVM in Java 2, however, and would be backward compatible with existing Java code.

Improvements to `wait()` and `notify()`

The `wait()`/`notify()` system also has problems:

1. There is no way to detect whether `wait()` has returned normally or because of a timeout.

2. There is no way to implement a traditional condition variable that remains in a "signaled" state.

3. Nested-monitor lockout can happen too easily

The timeout-detection problem is easily solved by redefining `wait()` to return a `boolean` (rather than `void`). A `true` return value would indicate a normal return, `false` would indicate a timeout.

The notion of a state-based condition variable is an important one: The variable can be set to a `false` state in which waiting threads will block until the variable entered a `true` state, and any thread that waits on a `true` condition variable is released immediately. [The `wait()` call won't block in this case.] You can support this functionality by extending the syntax of `notify()` as follows:

`notify();`	Waiting threads without changing the state of the underlying condition variable.
`notify(true);`	Set the condition variable's state to `true` and release any waiting threads. Subsequent calls to `wait()` won't block.
`notify(false);`	Set the condition variable's state to `false` (subsequent calls to `wait()` or `wait(true)` will block.

The nested-monitor-lockout problem is thornier, and I don't have an easy solution. One possible solution is for `wait()` to release *all* the locks that the current thread has acquired in the opposite order of acquisition and then reacquire them in the original acquisition order when when the wait is satisfied. I can imagine that code that leveraged this behavior would be almost impossible for a human being to figure out, however, so I don't think that this is really a viable solution. If anybody has any ideas, send me email (*aih@holub.com*).

I'd also like to be able to wait for complex conditions to become true. For example:

```
[a && [b || c]].wait();
```

where a, b, and c are any `Object`. I've used brackets rather than parentheses to make it easier for the compiler to distinguish this sort of expression from an arithmetic expression, but I can think of alternative syntaxes that would serve the same purpose.

Fixing the **Thread** Class

The ability to support both preemptive and cooperative threads is essential in some server applications, especially if you intend to squeeze maximum performance out of the system. I suggest that Java has gone too far in simplifying the threading model, and that the Posix/Solaris notion of a "green thread" and a "lightweight process" that I discussed in Chapter 1 should be supported by Java. This means, of course, that some JVM implementations (such as NT implementations) would have to simulate cooperative threads internally, and other JVMs would have to simulate preemptive threading, but adding these extensions to the JVM is reasonably easy to do.

A Java thread, then, should always be preemptive. That is, a Java thread should work much like a Solaris lightweight process. The Runnable interface can be used to define a a Solaris-like green thread that must explicitly yield control to other green threads running on the same lightweight process. For example, the current syntax of:

```
class My_thread implements Runnable
{    public void run(){ /*...*/ }
}

new Thread( new My_thread );
```

would effectively create a green thread for the Runnable object and bind that green thread to the lightweight process represented by the Thread object. This change in implementation is transparent to existing code since the effective behavior is the same as at present.

By thinking of Runnable objects as green threads, you can expand Java's existing syntax to support multiple green threads bound to a single lightweight processes simply by passing several Runnable objects to the Thread constructor. (The green threads would be cooperative with respect to each other, but could be preempted by other green threads [Runnable objects] running on other lightweight processes [Thread objects]). For example, the following code would create a green thread for each of the Runnable objects, and these green threads would share the lightweight process represented by the Thread object.

```
new Thread( new My_runnable_object(), new My_other_runnable_object() );
```

The existing idiom of overriding Thread and implementing run() should still work, but it should map to a single green thread bound to a lightweight process. (The default run() method in the Thread class would effectively create a second Runnable object internally.)

Inter-Thread Coordination

More facilities should be added to the language to support inter-thread communication. Right now, the `PipedInputStream` and `PipedOutputStream` classes can be used for this purpose, but they are much too inefficient for most applications. I propose the following additions to the `Thread` class:

1. Add a `wait_for_start()` method that blocks until a thread's `run()` method starts up. (It would be okay if the waiting thread was released just before `run()` was called.) This way one thread could create one or more auxiliary threads, and then be assured that the auxiliary threads were running before the creating thread continued with some operation.

2. Add (to the `Object` class) `$send(Object o)` and `Object=$receive()` methods that would use an internal blocking queue to pass objects between threads. The blocking queue would be created automatically as a side effect of the first `$send()` call. The `$send()` call would enqueue the object; the `$receive()` call would block until an object was enqueued, and then return that object. Variants on these methods would support timeouts on both the enqueue and dequeue operations: `$send(Object o, long timeout)` and `$receive(long timeout)`.

Internal Support for Reader/Writer Locks

The notion of a reader/writer lock should be built into Java. To remind you, a reader-writer lock enforces the rule that multiple threads can simultaneously access an object, but only one thread at a time can modify the object, and modifications cannot go on while accesses are in progress. The syntax for a reader/writer lock can be borrowed from that of the `synchronized` keyword:

```
static Object global_resource;

//...

public void f()
{
    $reading( global_resource )
    {   // While in this block, other threads requesting read
        // access to global_resource will get it, but threads
        // requesting write access will block.
    }
}
```

```
public void g()
{
    $writing( global_resource )
    {   // Blocks until all ongoing read or write operations on
        // global_resource are complete. No read or write
        // operation or global_resource can be initiated while
        // within this block.
    }
}

public $reading void f()
{   // just like $reading(this)...
}

public $writing void g()
{   // just like $writing(this)...
}
```

Access to Partially Constructed Objects Should Be Illegal

The JLS currently permits access to a partially created object. For example, a thread created within a constructor can access the object being constructed, even though that object might not be fully constructed. The behavior of the following code is undefined:

```
class Broken
{   private long x;

    Broken()
    {   new Thread()
        {   public void run()
            {   x = -1;
            }
        }.start();

        x = 0;
    }
}
```

The thread that sets x to –1 can run in parallel to the thread that sets x to 0. Consequently, the value of x is unpredictable.

One possible solution to this problem is to require that the run() methods of threads started from within a constructor not execute until that constructor returns, even if the thread created by the constructor is of higher priority than the one that called new. That is, the start() request must be deferred until the constructor returns.

Alternatively, Java could permit the synchronization of constructors. In other words, the following code (which is currently illegal) would work as expected:

```
class Illegal
{   private long x;

    synchronized Broken()
    {   new Thread()
        {   public void run()
            {   synchronized( Illegal.this )
                {
                    x = -1;
                }
            }
        }.start();

        x = 0;
    }
}
```

I think that the first approach is cleaner than the second one, but it is admittedly harder to implement.

Volatile Should Always Work as Expected

The compiler and JVM are both permitted to shuffle around your code, provided that the semantics of the code doesn't change. For example, in the following source code the assignment to first might be made *after* the assignment to second, in which case the g() method, which uses a test on first to decide what to pass to some_method() won't work correctly. The value false might be passed to some_method().

```
class Broken
{
    volatile boolean first  = false;;
    volatile boolean second = false;;

    public void f()
    {   first  = true;
        second = true;
    }

    public void g()
    {   if( second )
            Some_class.some_method( first );
    }
}
```

This code movement is desirable because some optimizations (such as loop-invariant code motion) require it. Nonetheless, it makes the non-synchronized use of volatile rather risky. One possible solution is to require that if a method accesses several volatile fields in sequence, that the fields always be accessed in declaration order. This is a really tough one to implement, but would probably be worth the trouble.

Access Issues

The lack of good access control makes threading more difficult than necessary. Often, methods don't have to be thread safe if you can guarantee that they be called only from synchronized subsystems. I'd tighten up Java's notion of access privilege as follows:

1. Require explicit use of the package keyword to specify package access. I think that the very existence of a default behavior is a flaw in any computer language, and I am mystified that a default access privilege even exists (and am even more mystified that the default is "package" rather than "private"). Java doesn't use defaults anywhere else. Even though the requirement for an explicit package specifier would break existing code, it would make that code a lot easier to read and could eliminate whole classes of potential bugs (if the the access privilege had been omitted in error rather than deliberately, for example).

2. Reintroduce private protected, which works just like protected does now, but does not permit package access.

3. Permit the syntax private private to specify "implementation access:" private to all outside objects, even objects of the same class as the current object. The only reference permitted to the left of the (implicit or explicit) dot is this.

4. Extend the syntax of public to grant access to specific classes. For example, the following code would permit objects of class Fred to call some_method(), but the method would be private with respect to all other classes of objects.

    ```
    public(Fred) void some_method()
    {
    }
    ```

    This proposal is different from the C++ "friend" mechanism, which grants a class full access to *all* private parts of another class. Here, I'm suggesting a tightly controlled access to a limited set of methods. This way one class could define an interface to another class that would be invisible to the rest of the system.

5. Require all field definitions to be private unless they reference truly immutable objects or define static final primitive types. Directly accessing the fields of a class violates two basic principles of OO design: abstraction and encapsulation. From the threading perspective, allowing direct access to

fields just makes it easier to inadvertently have non-synchronized access to a field.

6. Add the $property keyword: Objects tagged in this way are accessible to a "bean box" application that is using the introspection APIs defined in the Class class, but otherwise works identically to private private. The $property attribute should be applicable to both fields and methods so that existing JavaBean getter/setter methods could be easily defined as properties.

Immutability

The notion of immutability (an object whose value cannot change once it's created) is invaluable in multithreaded situations since read-only access to immutable objects doesn't have to be synchronized. Java's implementation of immutability isn't tight enough for two reasons:

1. It is possible for an immutable object be accessed before its fully created, and this access might yield an incorrect value for some field.

2. The definition of immutable (a class, all of whose fields are final) is too loose: Objects addressed by final references can indeed change state, even though the reference itself cannot change state.

The first problem is related to the access-to-partially-constructed-objects problem discussed above.

The second problem can be solved by requiring that final references point to immutable objects. That is, an object is really immutable only if all of its fields are final and all of the fields of any referenced objects are final as well. In order not to break existing code, this definition could be enforced by the compiler only when a class is explicitly tagged as immutable as follows:

```
$immutable public class Fred
{
    // all fields in this class must be final, and if the
    // field is a reference, all fields in the referenced
    // class must be final as well (recursively).

    static int x constant = 0;  // use of `final` is optional when $immutable
                                // is present.
}
```

Given the $immutable tag, the use of final in the field definitions could be optional.

Finally, a bug in the Java compiler makes it impossible to reliably create immutable objects when inner classes are on the scene. When a class has nontrivial inner classes (as most of mine do), the compiler often incorrectly prints the error message: "Blank final variable '*name*' may not have been initialized. It must be assigned a value in an initializer, or in every constructor," even though the blank final is indeed initialized in every constructor. This bug has been in the compiler since inner classes were first introduced in version 1.1, and at this writing (three years later—May 2000) the bug is still there. It's about time that this bug was fixed.

Instance-Level Access of Class-Level Fields

In addition to access privileges, there is also the problem that both class-level (static) methods and instance (non-static) methods can directly access class-level (static) fields. This access is dangerous because synchronizing the instance method doesn't grab the class-level lock, so a synchronized static method can access the class field at the same time as a synchronized instance method. The obvious solution to this problem is to require that non-immutable static fields be accessed from instance methods via static accessor methods. This requirement would mandate both compile and run-time checks, of course. Under these guidelines, the following code would be illegal:

```
class Broken
{
    static long x;

    synchronized static void f()
    {   x = 0;
    }

    synchronized void g()
    {   x = -1;
    }
};
```

because f() and g() can run in parallel and modify x simultaneously (with undefined results). Remember, there are two locks here: the static method acquires the lock associated with the Class object and the non-static method acquires the lock associated with the instance. The compiler should either require the following structure when accessing non-immutable static fields from instance methods:

```
class Broken
{
    static long x;

    synchronized private static accessor( long value )
    {   x = value;
    }
```

```
                    synchronized static void f()
                    {   x = 0;
                    }

                    synchronized void g()
                    {   accessor( -1 );
                    }
              }
```

or the compiler should require the use of a reader/writer lock:

```
          class Broken
          {
              static long x;

              synchronized static void f()
              {   $writing(x){ x = 0 };
              }

              synchronized void g()
              {   $writing(x){ x = -1 };
              }
          }
```

Alternatively—and this is the ideal solution—the compiler should *automatically* synchronize access to non-immutable `static` fields with a reader/writer lock so that the programmer wouldn't have to worry about it.

Singleton Destruction

The singleton-destruction problem discussed in Chapter 7 is a serious one. The best solution is to introduce the `$singleton` tag to the class definition. The Singleton creation would then be handled automatically by the system. For example, if you defined a class as follows:

```
          $singleton class Fred
          {   //...
          }
```

then *all* calls to `new Fred()` would return a reference to the *same* object, and that object would not be created until the first call to `new Fred()`. Moreover, the language should guarantee that the finalizer method of a `$singleton` object will always be called as part of the JVM shut-down process.

Abrupt Shut Down of Daemon Threads

Daemon threads are shut down abruptly when all the non-daemon threads terminate. This is a problem when the daemon has created some sort of global resource (such as a database connection or a temporary file), but hasn't closed or destroyed that resource when it is terminated.

I'd solve that problem by making the rule that the JVM will not shut down the application if any:

1. non-daemon threads are running, or

2. daemon threads are executing a synchronized method or synchronized block of code.

The daemon thread would be subject to abrupt termination as soon as it left the synchronized block or synchronized method.

Bring Back the **stop()**, **suspend()**, and **resume()** Methods

This one may not be possible for practical reasons, but I'd like stop() not to be deprecated [in both Thread and ThreadGroup]. I would change the semantics so that calling stop() wouldn't break your code, however: The problem with stop(), you'll remember, is that stop() gives up any locks when the thread terminates, thereby potentially leaving the objects that the thread is working on in an unstable (partially modified) state. These objects can nonetheless be accessed since the stopped thread has released its lock on the object. This problem can be solved by redefining the behavior of stop() such that the thread would terminate immediately only if it is holding no locks. If it is holding locks, I'd like the thread to be terminated immediately after releasing the last one. You could implement this behavior with a mechanism similar to an exception toss. The stopped thread would set a flag that would be tested immediately after exiting all synchronized blocks. If the flag was set, an implicit exception would be thrown, but the exception would not be catchable and would not cause any output to be generated when the thread terminated. Note that Microsoft's NT operating system doesn't handle an abrupt externally implied stop very well. (It doesn't notify dynamic-link libraries of the stop, so systemwide resource leaks can develop.) That's why I'm recommending an exception-like approach that simply causes run() to return.

The practical problem with this exception-style approach is that you'd have insert code to test the "stopped" flag at the end of every synchronized block, and this extra code would both slow down the program and make it larger. Another approach that comes to mind is to make stop() implement a "lazy" stop in which the thread terminates the next time it calls wait() or yield(). I'd also add isStopped() and stopped() methods to Thread [which would work much like isInterrupted()

and `interrupted()`, but would detect the "stop-requested" state.] This solution isn't as universal as the first, but is probably workable and wouldn't have the overhead.

The `suspend()` and `resume()` methods should just be put back into Java. They're useful, and I don't like being treated like a kindergartener: Removing them simply because they are potentially dangerous—a thread can be holding a lock when suspended—is insulting. Let me decide whether or not I want to use them. Sun could always make it a run-time exception for `suspend()` to be called if the receiving thread is holding any locks, or better yet, defer the actual suspension until the thread gives up its locks.

Blocking I/O Should Work Correctly

You should be able to interrupt any blocking operation, not just just `wait()` and `sleep()`. I discussed this issue in the context of sockets in Chapter 2, but right now, the only way to interrupt a blocking I/O operation on a socket is to close the socket, and there's no way to interrupt a blocking I/O operation on a file. Once you initiate a read request, for example, the thread is blocked until it actually reads something. Even closing the file handle does not break you out of the read operation.

Moreover, your program must be able to time out of a blocking I/O operation. All objects on which blocking operations can occur (such as `InputStream` objects) should support a method like this:

```
InputStream s = ...;
s.set_timeout( 1000 );
```

(this is the equivalent to the `Socket` class's `setSoTimeout(time)` method. Similarly, you should be able to pass a timeout into the blocking call as an argument.

The `ThreadGroup` Class

`ThreadGroup` should implement all the methods of `Thread` that can change a thread's state. I particularly want it to implement `join()` so that I can wait for all threads in the group to terminate.

Wrapping Up

So that's my list. As I said in the title of this chapter: if I were king... (sigh). I'm hoping that some of these changes (or their equivalent) will eventually migrate into the language. I really think that Java is a great programming language; but I also think that Java's threading model simply wasn't thought out well enough, and that's a pity. Java is evolving, however, so there is a path to follow to improve the situation.

This section also wraps up the book. Programming threads properly is difficult but rewarding, simultaneously frustrating and fun. I hope that the code I've offered here will take some of the frustration out of the process. As I said in the Preface, the code is not in the public domain, but I'm happy to grant permission to anyone to use it in exchange for a mention (of both my name and URL) in your "about box," your "startup" screen, or if you don't have either in your program, your documentation. I'm also *really* interested in any bugs you find (please send me email at *bugs@holub.com*). The most recent version of the code is available on my Web site *http://www.holub.com*.

Have fun.

Index

Symbols

A

B

C